East Sus

Within Living

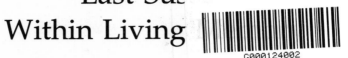

G000124002

WITHIN LIVING MEMORY SERIES

Other Counties in this series include:

Bedfordshire

Buckinghamshire

Cheshire

Cumbria

Devon

Essex

Hampshire

Herefordshire

Hertfordshire

Isle of Wight

East Kent

West Kent

Leicestershire & Rutland

Lincolnshire

Norfolk

Northamptonshire

Nottinghamshire

Oxfordshire

Shropshire

Somerset

Staffordshire

Suffolk

Surrey

West Sussex

Warwickshire

Wiltshire

Worcestershire

North Yorkshire

East Sussex Within Living Memory

Compiled by the East Sussex Federation
of Women's Institutes from notes sent by
Institutes in the County

Published jointly by
Countryside Books, Newbury
and
ESFWI, Lewes

First Published 1995
© East Sussex Federation of Women's Institutes 1995

COUNTRYSIDE BOOKS
3 Catherine Road
Newbury, Berkshire

ISBN 1 85306 365 7

The cover photograph shows Patcham village, 1922.

Designed by Mon Mohan
Produced through MRM Associates Ltd, Reading
Typeset by Acorn Bookwork, Salisbury
Printed by J. W. Arrowsmith, Bristol

Contents

Foreword

Our East Sussex *Within Living Memory* is a splendid collection of members' contributions of recollections of bygone years. Our way of life has changed so much during this century and our members have listened to and written down the memories of older relations and friends that we might all share in this heritage.

We are blessed with a rich mixture in our County – tiny villages set in the heart of the countryside, with tales of farming, village schools and their busy communities, and not far away the coastal towns from Hove to Rye with their stories of the seaside landlady, the beaches and the summer season and in earlier times – the smugglers. Our County Town of Lewes, a delightful old market town, is steeped in history and where we are fortunate enough to have our County Headquarters.

Special thanks to Anne Whitehead who has cheerfully co-ordinated all the material for this project and to Barbara Cornwell for helping in the later stages. We do thank them for their enthusiasm. Now we are sure you will enjoy the fruits of their labours.

Donna Barker
County Chairman

Acknowledgements

The story of the creation of our book, *East Sussex Within Living Memory*, would – if told – be full of fun and humour – of meeting and talking to many of our members – and, above all, of memories! After all, that is what our book is all about and so many of you have responded generously to my pleas for words and photographs. It all started very slowly – was I going to have to write it all myself? No, you said, oh ye of little faith, all will be well. And it was!

Thank you to Di Harwood for her typing skills, to Barbara Cornwell for her map and to Jean White for her drawings. Thanks also to all contributors for their words, photos, ideas, interest and support.

It has been great fun!

Anne Whitehead
Co-ordinator

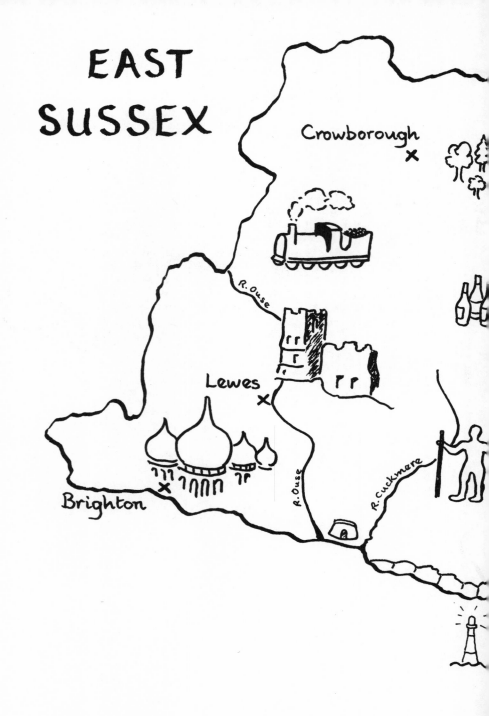

Mayfield

R. Rother

R. Rother

Battle

Rye

Hastings

English

Channel

Eastbourne

Beachy Head

TOWN & COUNTRY LIFE

The smock mill at Chailey Heritage

SOME TOWNS AND VILLAGES REMEMBERED

There have been so many changes in town and village life since the days when the ring of the blacksmith's hammer was an every-day sound and market day brought in the world and his wife – and their animals! The lamplighter on his rounds and horse-drawn delivery vans are still within living memory. Here are just a few snapshots of life as it used to be in East Sussex.

LITTLE COMMON AND COODEN

'My memories of East Sussex go back to 1927 when, as a child of six, I came with my mother and stepfather to live in Cooden. In those days Cooden consisted only of a few houses, the Metropolitan Men's Convalescent Home, the Coastguard cottages and the golf club. The station was just a couple of platforms reached by steps, with a shelter; this was only made into a smart station when the De la Warr Pavilion was built and opened in 1935 by the then Duke and Duchess of York (now the Queen Mother). There was a bathing station at Cooden Beach and a few little shops, one a photographer's, where the Cooden Beach Hotel now stands.

On the other side, and there to this day, was Jumbo's, then run by the Hollins family, which sold cakes and sweets. There was a great local character, Mrs de Winton, who used to drive her horse and car-riage down to the sea with her dalmatian trotting underneath. As they got near Jumbo's he would make a dash and grab anything he could off the counter, so if they heard him coming they would rush to shut the door. Mrs de Winton always dressed as a man, with a beret on her head, and a cigarette in her mouth, never wore a skirt. The story goes that at a Pony Club dance in the Sackville someone said to her, "I bet you've got your trousers on under that dress." "Yes," she said, and threw up her skirt to show everyone.

Little Common was our local village, with all the shops one could need, and, if one wanted, the butcher's and grocer's in Bexhill would send out a man on a bicycle to take orders, and bring the required foodstuffs back in time for lunch; no refrigerators nor deep freezers then. There was a post office with lending library, a newsagent's cum barber's, garage, forge, two grocers, a butcher, cobbler, stationer and confectioner, which sold beautiful Christmas cards for one penny, as well as an electrical shop, greengrocer, dairy, dress shop and wool shop, also a fire station. What more could one want? The blacksmith was a giant of an old man called Crocker, with piercing blue eyes, who wore a black suit and cap. A set of shoes for a horse cost four shillings and three shillings for a pony. There were, of course, several more forges in Bexhill and Sidley.

Buses ran every half hour into Bexhill, and trams, later trolley buses, from Cooden Beach along Cooden Drive. The fare was sixpence return. The only public house was the Wheatsheaf in Little Common, with the Denbigh the next nearest almost into Bexhill, but I don't know much about them. It wasn't the thing to do! When we had expectant mothers from London at the beginning of the war they gathered there at every opportunity with their curlers and "fags", much to the disgust of the villagers.

The local policeman was a very tall man with red hair who rode a bike with his fishing rod strapped to the cross-bar and his terrier in a box on the back.

Our house had been built for an officer from Cooden Camp in the First World War and then added on to at both ends. It was lovely in summer, but perishing cold in winter and all the pipes being on the north side froze regularly, but there were splendid general builders in the village.

I remember Sir Alan Cobham's "Flying Circus" coming to Little Common recreation ground, and giving trips at ten shillings a time. I was not allowed to go up! There was a wonderful pantomime which came every year to the South Coast towns, and we always went to the Devonshire Park Theatre in Eastbourne to see it. It was run by an old man called Murray King who was the Dame, dressed in black with a pair of pink corsets. It was always the same cast with a celebrity such as Pat Kirkwood as Principal Boy, and a marvellous transformation scene, which must have cost a packet. Murray King appeared at the end in full evening dress, cape, opera hat and cane, accompanied by his little white dog.

The Bonfire Society used to process round the village and the schools in Collington Lane and finish up with an enormous bonfire and fireworks on Cooden Mount, and this started again after the war.'

BATTLE

'Around 1920 when my sister in law and I were living in Battle as children, it was a very small market town, dominated by the abbey and the ancient black and white building of the Pilgrims' Rest, and all the history of the Norman Conquest attached to them. There was a much smaller population, few, if any, cars and a private bus operated by a Mr Sheather which ran once a week between Battle and Hastings.

My parents lived on a farm called Saxon Hill, opposite Battle hospital which was then the local workhouse and providing shelter to the tramps who wandered in and out of the town from time to time. My parents' only means of transport was a pony and trap. Saxon Hill has since been divided into flats.

There have been many changes in Battle since those days. A cattle market was held once a week to serve the local farming community. It was supervised by the auctioneer and estate agent, Mr James Woodhams – a well known local character. Opposite the market place was the elegant Towers Hotel, now replaced by the fire station.

Many social events were held in the nearby Drill Hall, including the annual Farmers Ball, and regular Saturday night dances for the many troops stationed in the vicinity during the Second World War. This hall has since been replaced by the telephone exchange. One soldier who has since become quite famous was Desmond Lewellyn, "Q" of James Bond fame. The young army officer used to spend his leaves in Battle and often read the lessons in Battle church.

Many activities have centred upon the abbey down the ages. For many years it has been a girls' school, and from time to time plays performed by the senior girls were open to the general public, along with performances by visiting celebrities, often famous musicians, as part of the girls' education. The abbey provided the magnificent background for the wedding of Mrs Harboard, one of the daughters of Sir Augustus Webster, whose ancestors purchased the abbey and its vast estates in 1719. Later the immediate grounds of the abbey were the setting for Gwen Lally's famous pageant tracing the history of Battle from 1066. English Heritage now uses the abbey for staging events.

In the autumn two regular events took place in Battle. First there were the noisy celebrations for 5th November with a torchlight procession through the town, culminating in the lighting of a huge bonfire on the green, usually by a local doctor whose birthday fell on that day. The local band of Bonfire Boys spent many months each year planning the celebrations and making their own fireworks illicitly in their kitchens. These giant sized squibs or "Battle Rousers" struck terror into the onlookers as they shot noisily in all directions up and down the High Street, bringing memories of the days when Battle had a thriving gunpowder industry in Powder Mill Lane. Although the bonfire celebrations still go on, several nasty accidents put paid to the making of "Battle Rousers".

14

On 22nd November, the town fair was held on the green, which really was of green grass, bringing a host of sideshows, sweet stalls, hot chestnuts, toffee apples, and home-made lollipops, with the traditional colourful roundabouts with galloping horses and cheerful music, as a focal point.

Along with the powder mills, several other industries which once provided employment in the town gradually ceased to exist. Amongst these was the tannery on Tanyard Hill, above the station. The closing down of this industry caused little regret because of the unpleasant stench it made in that part of the town. The "Battle Jack" in Lower Lake, owned by Jack Bailey, gave employment to many women making gloves and fine leather goods. Newberys jam factory, in the centre of the town, produced excellent jam, distributed all over the country.

The two private schools, Battle Abbey for girls and Glengorse Preparatory School for boys, provided an excellent education for the children of the rich, who liked the idea of their offspring being educated in such an historic place, but for the ordinary inhabitants who could not afford the fees of these establishments, there was only the Battle and Langton church school in Marley Lane, in its ancient stark Victorian premises, or a small private school ran by an Australian lady called Miss Coles, who was also the Guide mistress. In the Guide hut this excellent lady provided a first rate education to a small group of pupils of all ages up to nine or ten years of age, after which they had to go to senior schools in Hastings, Bexhill or Rye. In Miss Coles' small establishment there were even specialist teachers for dancing, French and music. French lessons were given by Mrs Allwork, the delightful Swiss wife of Walter Allwork who owned the high class grocery business in the town, now Oakshott's supermarket. Mrs Allwork's father was the chef at Battle Abbey school. On his retirement Walter Allwork built all the houses in Saxonwood Road, and himself lived in the one at the end which is now a nursing and retirement home.'

'Essentially Battle was a town of small businesses, some of which still remain under their original owners. The attractive old pharmacy halfway up the High Street has been in the Emeleus family for several generations. The original Finnish owner was a great character in Battle, with his small beard and broken English.

Since there was no easy transport in those times, inhabitants had to purchase most of their clothes in the town. Winsborrows, draper's and ladies and gents outfitter's, provided very comprehensively for everyone's needs and carried a huge stock on its several floors, added to which they were always happy to order anything special which they did not usually stock, and it was always service with a smile.

The town was also served by Tills the ironmonger's, two excellent butchers in the High Street, a good fishmonger and two greengrocers. On one corner of Mount Street was an excellent bakery and below this Pallets toy and sweet shop, known as Penny Pallets. A penny went a long way in the 1920s, and represented probably the whole of a child's weekly pocket money.

On the other side of the High Street was Quaifes, corn merchants. On the opposite corner the George Hotel has been in existence for centuries, originally as a coaching inn. At the top of the High Street was the beautiful Old Guild Hall, the home of one of the town's solicitors. There are still Fovargues in the old established solicitors of Raper and Fovargue.

In those days the High Street was a colourful place with the glow of the furnace as the blacksmith shoed horses on another corner of Mount Street, and the huntsmen in their red coats paraded down the High Street with their pack of eager hounds on Boxing Day to meet on the village green, and to drink the stirrup cup from the ancient Starr Inn, now the 1066.

There was a comfortable cinema in Lower Lake where Burstow and Hewett's auction rooms now stand, but very little other entertainment. For children there was Sunday school and the Church Fellowship and as we grew older, tennis, horse riding, cycling and walking. There was the Women's Institute and Mothers' Union for women, Freemasons and a bowling club for men.

All the while there was a background of gentility and class consciousness, evidenced in such families as Lady Brassey, Lady Catherine Ashburnham, the Egertons and the Websters. The only existing bank, the Westminster, numbered some very wealthy people amongst its customers. In this solid edifice my brother and I were born and from the upstairs windows of the bank premises viewed some amusing sights, such as the time when a cow strayed into a small gift shop opposite the bank, knocked over a few ornaments and then went out to rejoin the herd in the High Street. In those far off days cattle were driven into the town for the regular cattle markets.

Most people in Battle knew one another and amongst the interesting characters we remember were the sweep who always seemed to be covered in soot, the lamplighter, and the milkman who brought the milk in churns in his little cart and ladled it out into jugs for his customers.'

16

'Five Ashes is a village which has, in its own way and with the interest and support of a number of old families – some of whom have lived and worked in the area over many years – grown to have a considerable life of its own apart from its larger immediate neighbour Mayfield.

The original road from Mayfield through the village was part of the Roman road from Tonbridge to the coast. The present busy A267 was the first concrete road to be built in East Sussex by the East Sussex County Council in the early 1930s.

The story goes that the village was called Five Ashes because there once stood adjoining the green a large ash tree; this was cut down but from it five further ash trees grew. The Hon Lothian Nicholson, who lived in the manor house at Skippers Hill, gave five ash trees to be planted on the green in memory of the fallen in the First World War. There is also a silver birch tree on a corner of Spring Lane which commemorates King George V's Silver Jubilee.

Overlooking the green are the Five Ashes public house and an antiques shop; the latter used to be the general store and post office for the village. This shop sold everything for man, his family and his animals, including coal, cattle food and seeds, and those who remember it recall the pots and pans and other hardware which used to hang from the ceiling. Early in the present century a terrace of houses was built further down the road, together with a village shop and this later became the present post office.

The school, which is just above the green, was originally built in 1872 with two classrooms and a third was added in 1904. The classes were divided between the infants, the seven to elevens and the twelve to 14s, but later the older group of children were taken by bus to Mayfield. Those who were pupils there remember that it became possible for them to attend larger schools for their further education, for example to the Skinners School in Tunbridge Wells for the boys and to Lewes for the girls.

In the early years of this century there was no playing field but football was played on a field in Leeds Lane; quoits was played on that part of the green belonging to the public house and known as the Quoits Bed.

With the increased use of coal being mined in the north of England for the iron industry, and the fact that the production of charcoal was destroying the forests in the Weald, the production of iron in the area ceased. With the clearing of the woods, land became available for the growth of crops; hops were much grown around Five Ashes as is

Alfriston High Street in the 1930s. Ye Olde Tea Shoppe provided both teas and petrol.

evidenced by the number of oast houses to be found but many are now converted into living accommodation.

Following the First World War a piece of land in Leeds Lane was given to provide a reading room and working men's club and this, at a later date, was given to the WI. At the end of the Second World War the village agreed to raise a fund to provide a Memorial Playing Field; this was raised by weekly dances, which achieved the sum of £500 that bought the field. Some 20 years later with further tremendous collective efforts which included the sale of the old WI hall and site, the village finally acquired its own village hall.'

SEAFORD

'Seaford in the 1920s and 1930s was a thriving town; a homely town where almost everyone knew everyone else, and the shopkeepers gave you a name and a smile. Come for a stroll round the town and meet some of them.

As today, the main shopping area was in Broad Street. To meet your needs in furnishing and bedding was Bravery and Son, presided over by Charles Joseph Bravery and ably assisted by sons Fred and Wilfred and Fred's wife Bett. Their weekly instalment scheme of payment for goods was very popular, and people today may still be using furniture bought at a shilling a week. Across Broad Street at Gable End – originally the principal farmhouse in the town – was the book and music shop owned by Lewis Leroy. Here he started up his travel business which became well known as Leroy Travel with its headquarters in Tunbridge Wells.

18

Opposite Gable End was C. J. Barber, the men's outfitters, where the men of the town took their time selecting jackets, trousers and the latest in ties, and just below was the Misses Gale's Lower Embroidery Shop, where a quiet charm prevailed whenever one entered these delightful premises.

Seaford post office was at this time situated in Broad Street, and here the residents met for a chat while they waited to be served by the staff, who loved to show each other their holiday snaps – a regular occurrence in those days.

There were two jewellers and watchmakers in Broad Street – Bruce and Hart and Harry Hawke. Harry Hawke was a formidable character, but was in fact a kindly man and an attentive shopkeeper. His family lived over the shop and his three daughters, Gladys, Muriel and Hilda were well known in the town. Hilda taught the piano, and there must still be people around in whom she instilled a love of music and who will remember the family dog, Nigger, who used to "sing along" during the music lessons.

Those of us in need of medical attention probably called on Dr Gervis at Hurdis House, where mostly he dispensed his own pills and potions. For other medical supplies and toiletries there was Cameron's, which is still in evidence today though under different management.

Opposite The Old Tree public house, where the town's pillory used to stand, was Lea and Son the butcher's, where Leslie and his son Bobby presided and had their own slaughterhouse at the back of the premises.

From Lea's one could look up High Street to the Albert Hall, where my mother was playing the piano when news came of Queen Victoria's death in 1901. She used, jokingly, to tell people she had played the piano at the Albert Hall, to their amazement! Opposite the Albert Hall was a very popular sweetshop run by Miss Howell, where such delights as sherbet fountains and liquorice sticks could be bought four for a penny.

The Old House, at the bottom of High Street, goes back to the days of Cromwell, and in 1712 was the residence of Thomas Tufton, "Bailiff of the Town and Cinque Port of Seaford". The Old House is one of Seaford's most picturesque buildings, and a reminder of the town's historic and varied past. For many years, and still today, one could purchase antique furniture, old plate, porcelain, silver and glass in a unique setting. Next to the Old House stood Sayers, the baker's, where Miss Edith James waited while customers chose their cakes from the many delights on display. The clock still stands above the shop.

Now round into Church Street, where the 11th century church of St Leonard dominates the scene. Just below the church was the ice cream parlour run by an Italian family, the Valentis, a great favourite of children and adults, and where the General Post Office now stands was Kent's the newsagent's, where *Home Chat*, *Peg's Paper* and *Home Notes* were readily purchased. This again was a family business.

At the top of Church Street and on the corner of Clinton Place was Woolgar's, a veritable treasure house of an ironmonger's, where Mr Baker and his sons held sway, and across the road was Headley's, another treasure trove of haberdashery and clothing where Lily Richardson and her colleagues ran the shop with great efficiency.

And that takes us round the shopping streets of Seaford in the 1920s and 1930s. One can only look back with a sense of nostalgia for the old days and ways.'

OVINGDEAN

'My father farmed for 54 years for Farmer Henry Cowley, son William Cowley and then Percy Filkins, all resident at The Grange, so I grew up on the farm. Thrashing was done by a steam engine, hide and seek was played in the stooks and planks were used in the barn for see-saws. Sheep were dipped in the horse trough and they nibbled at the bracken on the Downs thus keeping it under control.

Children were still mischievous, setting off rockets in the pipe laid down to drain water from the Downs at Bonfire Night time. A finger caught in the granary turned septic, so this resulted in walking over the Downs to what is now the Royal Sussex County Hospital and a five week stay. School attendance required a long walk up the Ainsworth track, passing two poultry farms, and over the Downs in all weathers. As wellingtons had not been invented, the long leather boots worn were saturated in wet weather. A caring mother cooked potatoes in the kitchen range, wrapped them in scarves and so hands were kept warm. Skylarks and partridges were frequently seen on the Downs.

Sunday school was insisted upon and parties were held on the land belonging to the old rectory – sports, sandwiches, jellies and cakes were the order of the day. Autumn saw a horse and cart travelling over the Downs to Kemp Town to collect a ton of coal for the winter for one cottage. There was a village cricket team and villagers were able to go to "away" matches by paying to travel in the carrier's waggon – his name being Taylor. Mothers' Union meetings were held in the church room.

Village roads were swept every other day and were safe enough for children to play there. Lilac trees surrounded the "clomp" (green) and Longhill Road was a sight to be seen in the spring with cherry blossom and lilac trees lining the pathway. Pampas grass made a handsome frontage to The Grange. Milk and butter was sold at The Grange and a pony and trap used for delivering milk from there. "Teas" were available from various cottages and The Grange.

The pond was useful for cleaning the muddy feet of the farm-workers and horses. Ducks added a picturesque touch to this village area. Village girls helped on the farm or went into service. Some went to London to work but not all liked the completely different life.

A village store opened about 1924 in an army hut on the site of the present building. Otherwise, and in earlier years, Cruse, Meads and the Co-op came round for orders and then delivered the goods. Journeys into Brighton were done on foot with a spare pair of shoes if the weather was wet.

There was a girls' stoolball club, the game being played on the field opposite the pond. A school photograph with the girls in flour-starched white pinafores taken on Armistice Day is recalled.

Woodland Grange (Ovingdean Close) owned by the Van der Elst family, gave refuge to Haile Selassie for a while during the Second World War. Ovingdean Hall was occupied by a squadron of Canadian tanks. There are signs of breaks in the flint wall near Ainsworth Avenue behind which they hid ready to advance on invading forces. Bombs were dropped on surrounding fields and at least one farm-worker was killed.

Ian Fraser House, St Dunstan's, was taken over by the Navy as was Roedean school, the latter as an instructor's base. Much amusement was caused by a notice: "If you wish a mistress in the night, press the bell." Ack-ack guns and barbed wire were visible along the cliffs. Farmer Filkins, Colonel TA, was in charge of the Home Guard. There was a firing range near the pond pointing up the farm path. Colonel Filkins invited the London Territorial Army to camp in the field bordering Greenways for several summers.

The Ovingdean population grew after the First World War when retired people bought plots of land and left-over army huts and railway carriages.'

ASHURST WOOD PEOPLE

'When we came to the village of Ashurst Wood from London 39 years ago, it was a very different place. None of the new houses down Woods Hill Lane had been built. There were a few Victorian houses and cottages at the top and bottom of the lane, but the road was not made up – just a sandy track with a large outcropping of rock at the top of the hill, a ski-run for toboganning in the winter when there was snow about.

There were some outstanding characters in the village in those days. One was known as "Spring-heel Jack" on account of his unusual walk. He was very tall with long thin legs. I used to watch him every morning about 7.30 am from my bedroom window, as he bounced along Maypole Road up the hill to the top and round the corner and down Wall Hill to Forest Row, where he worked for a firm of builders. Then back again at 5.30 pm in the opposite direction – after a nine hour working day!

Then there was Annie Jenner, a stalwart character, who had been one of the original land girls during the First World War. She told me that if you lay down and put your ear to the rocks in Woods Hill Lane, you could hear the guns in France, and when you think of the seam of rocks which runs through the village, I think it was probably true.

Finally Alf Cook, a builder, whose wife ran the grocer's store opposite the village hall. When we first came to the village he orga- nised a grand bonfire night in the playing fields on 5th November. A procession of villagers with torches, some in fancy dress, marched up Maypole Road, accompanied by a village band, round the corner into Hammerwood Road and into the playing field, where a high bonfire had been laid ready. This was lit and the fireworks let off. "Cookie" as he was affectionately known, did many good works in the village, including retiling the village hall, and climbing St Dunstan's church steeple to mend it when it had been struck by lightning. He charged ridiculously small amounts for doing these jobs, looking on it as his contribution towards the community – but the steeple still stands as a memorial to him.'

BURWASH WEALD

'My first memories of Burwash Weald go back 60 years. I was living in Burwash at that time and as a special treat my mother and I would walk to Burwash Weald to buy sweets at Tollgate Cottage, opposite the Wheel Inn. The shop was owned by Mrs Fuller, who would dig the sticky humbugs out of a tall glass jar onto brass scales, then transfer them into a home-made paper cone. They cost one penny an ounce. Mr Fuller, her husband, travelled to local fairgrounds with swings and a roundabout, which he turned by hand.

In the 1920s there were two grocery shops. Mr Harmer kept one, a very small shop with an oil lamp hanging from the ceiling and scrubbing brushes, boot laces and many other articles on hooks. The small brown drawers behind the counter always fascinated me, with their glass knobs and gold letters announcing that they contained rice or sugar or matches. At an earlier date the back of the shop had been used as a poor house, where young men were given food and religious instruction. The second shop, now known as Honeychurch House, had a shed built to one side, where during the Second World War soldiers stopped for tea and toast when passing through the village.

Many of the cottages in the village were very old, and at one time all had a well in the garden from which water was drawn up in an iron bucket on a rope. I remember seeing a lady with a long black dress and a white apron leaning on the garden gate after filling her bucket.

Burwash Common is about two miles west of Burwash Weald and this is where St Philip's church and school are to be found. They were both built by the three Misses Trower. On 1st May the children remember the three ladies by placing flowers on their grave. When the school was in use the children would then march to the school for prizegiving, followed by maypole dancing. A bun and an orange were given to each child to take home.

At one time double decker buses ran from Hawkhurst to Brighton every hour, stopping at the villages. The Red Car went to Tunbridge Wells and back four times a day, and so many people used the bus that by the time it got to the end of its journey it was standing room only.

I remember Mr Coombs, the sexton at St Philip's, with his squeaky boots. He pumped the organ for the organist, Miss Jarvis, who was the daughter of the local butcher. The shop (now the nursing home) had large sides of beef and sausages hooked on rails near the ceiling, and a chopping block in the centre of the floor where the meat was cut into joints using knives, choppers and saws. On the shelf stood large enamel bowls full of fat-covered brawn. Mr Coombs would deliver meat to your home on foot or driving a pony and trap, with a high-stepping piebald pony called Jack Sprat.'

NUTLEY

'The village was a place busy and alive with interchange of birth, marriage and death in families who, for the most part, were related in some way. There were three grocery shops that sold everything from a mousetrap to a bag of coal, the post office, a fish shop, Freelands the butcher's, and a newsagent. A coalman served the village, selling coal at two shillings and fourpence a hundredweight – a measure that would now cost nearer £10.

There were the buses, the fetes on the green and a sixpenny hop on certain evenings. Servants at the larger houses had to be in by 9 pm or 10 pm on their days off, and some of the maids would be brought home riding on the crossbars of the footmen's bicycles.

The local aristocracy, and others who lived in the big local houses, took quite an active interest in the village and its children, even if that interest was sometimes unsought and unwanted.

Lady Kent would position herself outside the school on Empire Day in readiness for the children's exit at home time. As each child came out they were instructed to recite the chant: "I vow to thee my country.." If they could do so all through and correctly, Lady Kent would pin a medal on their chests.'

HASTINGS

'The Old Town of Hastings is a village of very close knit families with everybody knowing virtually everybody else, and many families related through marriage.

Most families in the 1930s were involved in the fishing industry in one capacity or another and times then were extremely hard with the work mainly manual and very arduous. My grandfather and father, great uncles and uncles were sea-going fishermen, having grown up into that occupation, and it seemed to me as a child that the house was always full of nets, either being made or repaired, or full of wet clothing being dried for the following day's sea trips.

The Old Town houses were mostly very small with very limited facilities, no bathrooms, outside toilets, coal stored beneath the stairs – which in itself caused quite a problem whenever coal was delivered as the coalman had to carry it in bags from the front door, through the "best room", into the kitchen or living room before tipping the coal. This resulted in either a large cloud of dust or sploshes of wet coal dust all over the house, depending on the weather at the time.

Mothers worked extremely hard at keeping the houses and contents clean with very little in the way of labour-saving devices. Front steps were scrubbed and whitened with a substance known as "pipe

Hastings at the turn of the century.

clay". This was a very light grey clay collected from below the cliffs at Rock-a-Nore. In fact one man subsidised his income by selling this door to door to those unable to collect their own. He was always known as "Billy Pipe Clay".

In the houses we occupied there was no hot water and laundry facilities were a shared washhouse at the top of a row of six cottages, each cottage having a day in the washhouse. There was a coal fired boiler and cold water in this washhouse, which was actually situated beneath the footpath. Washing was all done by hand and heavily soiled articles were scrubbed by stiff brush and a board, rinsed and then put through a large mangle before being hung to dry on a long line stretched the length of the yard at the front of the houses. When we youngsters became strong enough to assist we were co-opted to turn the mangle handle, which not only helped but kept us out of youthful mischief.

Summers seemed to last for ever and play for children consisted mainly of games such as hopscotch, hoops, whip and top, and other such games. We also had stone throwing competitions on the beach with a floating object being thrown into the sea and then stones thrown at it to see who could get most direct hits.

Both of our families have strong Hastings lifeboat connections and have been involved in the rescue and saving of a considerable number of lives from the sea. My father was a crew member for

25

some 15 years, ten of which were as coxswain. Two of my uncles were crew members and one of these, being discharged from the Royal Navy through a disability, became the coxswain of the lifeboat and on his first and only service launch rescued the crew of the minesweeper *Caulunia* in an extremely hazardous operation in Rye Bay for which he was awarded a Gold Medal of the RNLI. Unfortunately posthumously, as he was shortly afterwards killed at sea when the fishing boat *Boy Billy* was blown up by a mine caught in their nets, during April 1942.'

FAIRLIGHT

'I came to Fairlight, adjacent to the Firehills, as a newly-wed in 1925. In those days the gorse on the Firehills was absolutely lovely. Unfortunately someone's bonfire caught the gorse alight. We had a pond in our garden at Fairlight Cottage and the firemen had to use this as Fairlight's water supply was inadequate, but they were still unable to control the fire and my husband and others assisted by beating out the flames. The Firehills have never recovered their original beauty – paths were put in afterwards as firebreaks.

Soon after, in 1927, the then Prince of Wales came to officially open the Firehills as an "open space", as it had been donated to the people of Hastings. He arrived on 6th April at 3 pm and left at 3.25 pm. From his general expression he did not appear to be enjoying the experience at all!

In those days the local doctor, Dr McGower, used to hold a surgery three times a week in a shed in the garden of the farmhouse in Waites Lane. If he gave you a prescription you had to go to Ore, about three miles away, to have it dispensed.

There were three shops in the village, one in Lower Wites Lane at the junction with the Avenue, the Circle shop which sold everything, and another little shop in Shepherds Way called the Woolpack, now a private house.

We used to swim quite a lot from Fairlight Cove as before the land was eroded there was a large meadow where you could park your car and then walk down to the sea. When they built Channel Way they put in a Jacob's ladder which enabled you to get down to the beach opposite the "Harbour", but this has long since been washed away.'

WESTFIELD

'Westfield was a lovely little village as I remember it at the beginning of the century. Looking round now one can hardly realise it is the same place. The nearest town was five miles away and the villagers generally walked there, often pushing a baby or two in a pram. For threepence one could ride in the carrier's cart, but by the time his numerous parcels were delivered and others collected to take back, it was really quicker to walk. My earliest recollection of all is as a baby in a three-wheeled pram waiting with my mother at a farm gate for two great oxen and a plough to cross the road. The little carter boy who drove the oxen was told by the head carter *not* to address the oxen as he did 'osses!

The public houses were open all day. The waggoner and his boy could get a penny glass of beer and a pennyworth of bread and cheese for their dinner. If they could afford it, a ha'porth of pickles could be bought.

Newspapers were unknown to the villagers, only the big houses had them and they were brought in either by the milkman returning from early morning delivery in the town or the postman. Later papers for the villagers were brought in every Friday evening by a returning laundry van and were left at the village shop. If not called for by their customers they were delivered with the groceries some-time on Saturday. We had a Sunday post in those days of very few letters. The mail was carried from the postal town five miles away in an open two-wheeled high cart in *all* weathers.

The village shops sold everything, even to oil of cloves or tar for toothaches, Zox powders for headaches and sweet nitre and

The last ox team to work the Downs at Exceat. The oxen were Lamb and Leader, Lark and Linnet, and Quick and Nimble, and they were driven by Curly Page and Ray Kemp.

asafoetida – though what ailments they were used for I do not know. Boots hung from the ceiling and there were boxes of artificial flowers – lilac, roses, pansies, marguerites, poppies, cornflowers etc – for the very pretty hats worn then.

It was a friendly community. Everyone was poor (except the tradesmen), but they were wise in their generation. Most of the men had nicknames given them by their mates, such as Bumper, Grinny, Swaller, Porky, Buff, Monkey Tom and a host of others. People would probably be annoyed if they were thus nicknamed now.

A relieving officer visited the village once a week and each old person was given a half a crown and a stone of flour. This charity was called the "Dole". The poor old people worked as long as they were able to keep themselves from the workhouse.

Periodically Cheap Jacks would visit the village and the women would buy their crockery. Along came Tinker Jimmy too, who sat by the roadside and mended leaky kettles, cans and pots, and recaned chairs or mended the door mats. Cheerful old Tinker Jimmy was an Irishman and was always laughing. Then there were the stone tappers. Large flints were deposited in a byway (a gap by the side of the road) and the tapper would break them down quite small, to be used for road mending. A good tapper would earn three shillings a day. The carter once thought he'd try his hand at stone tapping, but at the end of the day he had earned only a shilling so he went back to his job as a carter!

Tramps and gypsies were always passing through the village. How often did my mother fill the tramp's tea can with boiling water after adding a pinch of tea, and cut him a couple of thick slices of bread and butter. The gypsies did not beg but generally had pegs or lace to sell.'

EASTBOURNE

'When I was a child in Eastbourne we loved the "flicks", as we called it. We sat in the ninepennies and as the programme was continuous you could see the whole thing round twice. The only cinema banned to us was the Tivoli, which was known as the "flea pit". There was a good rep company at the Hippodrome and we went weekly up into the "gods" for about one shilling and sixpence.

Wireless was fun too. We sat round with headphones on and they were all run by enormous batteries that had to be recharged.

In the summer it was the beach. There was a tent holdall at the Wish Tower in which you kept your tent (paying a rent) and it was put up each day for changing in. We bathed every day and had a picnic lunchtime.

Travelling was buses or train, but mostly walking. The Downs were a great joy. We lived in Willingdon Road and in order to get on the Downs we went down Eldon Road and then up through the council estate known as "The Hutments". As we walked past the houses small boys would shout at us and pelt us with stones. My father would say, "Take no notice, just walk on"! In the winter we had a great time tobogganning on the Downs.

Cycling was another way of getting around and my schoolfriend and I used to go miles with picnics enjoying the countryside. I had an uncle at Mayfield and we frequently cycled up there, 20 miles and thought nothing of it.

Tea dances at the Winter Garden with Harry Loveday's Band were very popular. There would be a host and hostess to find you partners or dance with you.

Prawning at Birling Gap was a yearly event. We walked over the Downs from East Dean Road, taking with us a frying pan, spoons, nets and gins. And plenty of fish bait! We would arrive on a tide about 6 am and work the bait in. It was a big family party and the mothers would organise the children to collect driftwood, then light a fire and have bacon, sausage and egg sizzling away when the older children and the men came back with their catch in wicker baskets hung over their shoulders. Then home and for supper, prawns – delicious.

If you put out a large card marked with a "W", the Walls ice cream man, riding his stop-me-and-buy-one bicycle with a large ice box on wheels beside, would call. He rang his bell all the time as he cycled down the streets. All the tradesmen called – the butcher twice a day, the fishmonger once a week, the poulterer and egg man once a week, and the grocer once a week. They took your order and then delivered the goods.

There was a certain snobbery about life in Eastbourne. It never did to be seen in the town with a basket on your arm after noon!'

HERSTMONCEUX FIRE BRIGADE

'Herstmonceux Fire Brigade was formed in 1893, and my own memories of the brigade go back a long way. I met my husband when I was 16 and he was 22. He had been a fireman then for five years, and he remained in the fire service until he retired as Sub Officer John Haris of Herstmonceux Fire Brigade.

All firemen had to be dedicated to the job, as money was only paid after the insurance had been collected, often six months later, and there was no retainer fee.

29

The ladies of Herstmonceux Women's Institute in 1924. A hat was essential outdoor wear for both men and women.

I remember during the war the engine was housed behind the Brewers Arms and the crew slept where "Nat West" Bank is now situated. It then moved to the Nissen hut built on Higham Hill.

I was a firewoman at Herstmonceux, and it was an unusual post. There were, I think, no more than three women at that time in East Sussex retained sub stations. My job was to keep the log book, recording the times the house bells were sounded direct from Lewes headquarters to firemen's homes, also the names and times of when the crew arrived, and when the engine left the station.

The old open engine held nine or ten men seated each side and didn't carry water. The newer covered engine had a water container and carried five or six men. When the officer in charge reached a fire he assessed the job and if necessary called Lewes for help. If he needed two more engines he would say "make pumps three".

One fire call was to the Old Brewery, West End owned by Mr Curteis, who built the village cinema. It was always packed with young and old and I remember sitting there with my two young sons at a Saturday matinee, and being amused to see a row of young French children sharing an ice cream, licking and passing along the line. Sometimes we went to the New Zealand Transport Cafe for an ice cream, a wooden building at the bottom of Rectory Hill.

It is never easy to get country men to talk of a job that was often life or death, but we had our lighter moments in the station and remembered the days gone by like Stan Taylor talking about the fire at Cowbeech when the windmill was struck by lightning in 1911. The sweeps caught fire and began turning like a huge catherine wheel. Talking about fireworks, faces were red at the station when one bonfire night the engine wouldn't start and revellers had to push it down the slope that led to the new fire station that opened in 1958.'

THE RYE HARBOUR LIFEBOAT DISASTER

'It was November 1928 when the Rye Harbour lifeboat was lost with all its crew. My parents were then living in Brighton. Although closely associated with most of the drowned men they were not near enough to be notified by the police or receive an immediate telegram from shocked relatives. Telephones, the usual means of quick communication nowadays, were rare. Radio was in its infancy and television non-existent. In this era a radio bulletin covering such a disaster would have been on the air in a very short time.

So how did my parents learn of a disaster which affected them closely? My father as usual bought a newspaper on the way to work and seeing the headlines stopped to read the story. He immediately returned home to tell his wife. Together they studied the dreadful news.

Father had lost a brother in law (Coxswain Herbert Head) and two nephews, mother several cousins. In addition, having been born and brought up in Rye Harbour she knew everyone in the crew.'

'I remember the *Mary Stanford* lifeboat disaster that devastated the little village of Rye Harbour in 1928. I was eight years old at the time. I remember the dark and stormy day, and my mother being very silent and sad, and later our teacher asking us to bring toys to the village school. We had all the toddlers there as it was the day of the burial. I remember climbing onto a school desk wondering what was going on; I then saw something that has always remained in my memory. It was the sight of a long line of coffins seeming to me at that age to go on for ever. I'll never forget it.

At eight years old I didn't realise, I suppose, what a disaster of this size meant to our little village, but as I grew older I knew that it tore it apart, hardly a household was left that had not lost a husband or a son. Seventeen brave men died on that fateful day.

I was a lucky child. My dad was one of the launchers.'

THE 1945 WHIRLWIND

'The day started off as normal, just another working day for the staff at Allwoods Brothers, Wivelsfield. It was 30th October 1945, and promised to be warm, but suddenly the sky became dark and the rain came lashing down. The roaring sound filled the air and looking up we saw a spiral shape hurtling towards us. To escape we flung ourselves flat on the ground. We were used to doing this during the war! Now above the sound of torrential rain came the crash of broken glass and within minutes it was all over.

Some 25 members of staff had been at work in the area. We surveyed the damage. The roof of one large greenhouse had been lifted off and had crashed on to the one next to it. The iron uprights of the wrecked greenhouse were twisted and wrenched out of the ground. Oak trees had been stripped of their branches. There were a number of minor casualties, but only one girl was removed to hospital where she received eight stitches in an arm and a leg. In spite of the damage to the greenhouses, the carnation plants we had been tending were undamaged.'

BRIGHTON AND HOVE

Just a few memories of old Brighton and Hove, from the 'boys in blue' at the hospital to the stalwart members of the fire brigade.

BRIGHTON IN MY YOUTH

'My aunt is now 82 and has lived in Brighton all her life. She lived in St Helens Road, the youngest child of five, three others having died of diphtheria. The house did not have a bathroom and everyone bathed once a week in a zinc bath in front of the kitchen fire. All cooking was done on a coal range oven. The Christmas cake was mixed and sent to be cooked at a baker's shop in Elm Grove.

She remembers going to Hassocks once a year with St Wilfrid's Sunday school outing. This cost elevenpence, though the fairground was free. Sing-song around the piano at home and family gatherings in the small front room were always enjoyed.

She started work at 14 years of age at Restings store, working through every department. She met her husband to be on the tram. He waited a year before even speaking to her!

Among her memories from between the wars are "Shylock" the

street singer, who played a concertina and sold oranges on Christmas morning. If he didn't sell them all he tipped them down Hartington Road! There were also winkle sellers, brandy ball sellers and herrings at a penny each. The rag and bone man would shout around the streets, and the lamplighter came to light the gas street lights each evening. The *Argus* was called loudly a penny a copy.

Ivy's sister was a VAD nurse during the First World War. Wounded soldiers in the Brighton General Hospital – previously the workhouse – all wore blue and were known in the town as "the boys in blue".

Times were hard and on Brighton race days before the Second World War men used to line up and hang over the wall of the workhouse in Elm Grove begging with their caps for money. Thousands of people walked up Elm Grove to go to the races.'

'In the 1920s, when I was a small child in Brighton, we lived in a terraced house on the east side of the Old Steine. When we walked down the steps from our home we looked right up the valley towards the Royal Pavilion, straight ahead to the Steine Gardens with its tall central fountain, or left towards the Front. Though there was a lot to be seen, and to ask questions about, in any direction, the most intriguing and satisfying from a five year old's point of view was definitely the Front.

Once we had negotiated the traffic, including the trams on their slippery rails, and arrived at the entrance to the Palace Pier there were more decisions to be taken: westwards along the promenade towards the West Pier or eastwards between the Madeira Drive and the shingle-strewn pavement almost on the beach? Either choice had its attractions, especially in summer when the town was crowded with visitors and the lower level of Madeira Drive was a resting place for weary charabancs. Going east also meant watching – or as a treat riding on – the Volks Electric Railway to Black Rock. In our parents' childhood the tracks of Magnus Volk's unique railway had been laid on the shore as far as Black Rock and then across the water below the cliffs on a "Daddy Longlegs" carriage to Rottingdean and back. I can remember a very short stretch of the ride being actually above the waves just before the end of the trip at Black Rock but all that was left of the more exciting route was a jumble of rusty girders exposed at low tide. Nevertheless it was still a popular ride.

From Black Rock one could take a breezy walk along the cliff-top, where the ground rose and fell in smooth green folds ending in the sudden drop of chalk cliffs to the sea. The handsome bulk of Roedean School marked about the halfway point and then Rottingdean windmill stood out black against the eastern skyline. When we arrived in the village with its one narrow High Street we could picnic on the cliff, or have tea in a tea-shop, or we could, on payment of one penny, pass through a small shop, cross its back garden and emerge through the garden gate on to the cliffs again heading for Saltdean over the next brow. I cannot remember if we had to pay another penny on the return trip.

If you had wanted to make the journey along the beach below the cliffs you would have had to be very sure of the state of the tide as there was no Undercliff Walk constructed until I was in my teens and the Channel can be very ferocious when roused.

Jolting along on the return trip on the railway we would pass the gay canvas awning of the Concert Party's stage. Striped deckchairs were arranged for the audience who paid a small sum in order to relax and enjoy the song-and-dance routines. Often, when just roaming aimlessly in that area we children would slip our feet onto the bars of the iron railings bordering the enclosure and admire the performance for free. An added attraction in that part of the Front was an ice cream kiosk where one could obtain a cone for a half-penny!

Back at the Palace Pier again there were many attractions. The pier itself, of course, was fascinating, although "What the Butler Saw" on the penny-in-the-slot machines hardly interested my sister and me. Looking back through the railings to the crowded beaches, or down between the wooden slats which formed the decking to see the tide ebbing or flowing and dragging the shingle to and fro gave us just as much amusement. I cannot recall that we visited the pier very often although its strings of coloured lights, its throngs of trippers in "Kiss-me-Quick" hats, its anglers and the summer visits of the steamer which took fortunate, and affluent, holidaymakers along the coast to Worthing or even to the Isle of Wight were familiar features of our childhood.

Surveying the busy sea-front was enjoyable, but actually "going down on the beach" was an exciting expedition. Buckets and spades were essential, although it always galled me that my brother, as a young boy, was allowed to have a real metal spade which could actually move the heavy shingle on Brighton beach, whereas I, as a mere girl, was only allowed to have a wooden spade – an enlarged wooden spoon – which was worse than useless! As a toddler on the beach I was bundled into a mackintosh garment called "waders". It was elasticated round the waist and legs with a bib and brace top, and all my normal clothes were tucked into it. A cotton sun-bonnet protected my head and neck and I had canvas sand-shoes to

Friends on Brighton beach in 1930.

complete the outfit. My brother ran free in an all-in-one cotton bathing costume with short sleeves, and his feet were left bare to squelch up any wet, sandy patches between his toes. It was a repeat of the sex discrimination shown in the choice of hoops, metal for him, wooden for me, which I also found so puzzling and frustrating.

Nevertheless an afternoon on the beach, particularly if the tide were low and had left rippled sandy stretches and intriguing little pools with rocks and sea-weed, home to shrimps perhaps, but more often resting places for vicious sand-flies, was a very happy event. Some sandwiches and a bottle of "pop" guarded by the accompanying adult, together with our gaudy, striped beach towels, completed the simple outing. In those early years I was not encouraged to do more than paddle in the ripples; swimming came later.

Immediately west of the Palace Pier is the Banjo Groyne – so named for its shape – which was constructed with fringe walls about four feet high so that one could walk along it safely and even relax on a sunny day on wooden benches along its sides. This was another favourite spot for anglers, and idle loungers could also share the excitement of the catch.

That part of the Front had a strong fishy smell as the Brighton Fish Market was still located there most weekday mornings. After being at sea all night the fishing smacks were winched up the shingle to the flat apron at the top and the fishermen stowed their gear in cabins under the Promenade, known as the Arches. I remember my brother coming home before breakfast one summer morning carrying a bag of fresh shrimps from the market.

Another feature of that area was, and still is although somewhat updated, the Aquarium. We were taken as children to see the tanks of tropical fish, but in those days there were no dolphins displaying their agility and it was not a treat to which we begged to be taken repeatedly. The building itself, however, was a permanent feature of our environment and it was necessary to pass across its entrance, with its long flight of steps down to the darkened halls containing the fish tanks, to reach the lower Madeira Drive where my sister and I learned to ride our fairy cycles. Under cover and shielded from traffic by thick evergreen hedges it was an ideal place for such an activity. Balance and road-sense once mastered, the freedom gained from cycling was a permanent feature of our youth. Acting almost as a third leg, our bikes and ourselves were seldom separated.

Proceeding westward from the Palace Pier the Promenade was raised above the beach, forming a roof over the Arches, and one could view at one glance several stretches of beach between the flint groynes. In addition to the steamers whose visits were infrequent, there was often a speedboat trailing a long frothy wake across the water between the two piers. If the sea was choppy it seemed to bounce as it rushed along and we could imagine the excitement of its passengers. The West Pier, although shorter than the Palace, was a handsome construction. At the shore end there was a bumper-car arena which passers-by could watch and on the far, seaward end we could see the girdled tower of a helter-skelter which we longed to ride.

Below the Promenade towards Hove there was a series of sunken gardens, very attractive in summer sunshine, and a paddling pool for small children. At some time in our childhood there was a man who sold donkey rides along that lower walk. We loved to watch, and to be allowed to stroke the donkey's nose.

Ending on the Hove border "our" Front was marked by the tall statue of Peace, which was erected after the First World War, and from there on the well-manicured Lawns seemed to accentuate the subtle difference between being a sedate resident of Hove or, like us, a breezy Brightonian.'

'Many years ago, having just moved to Brighton with my parents, my first job was in a solicitor's office in Castle Square.

It was summer and it seemed some of my colleagues were in the habit of going to the beach each lunch time to swim. This was known as the Fishmarket Beach, west of the Palace Pier, and I was invited to join them. There were always many other office workers there, a very jolly and mischievous crowd. We would swim out to an anchored fishing boat known as *The Peace and Plenty*, and hang on to the side to the annoyance of the old fisherman, who would grab an oar and threaten to push us off, so what did we do but swim to the other side where he would again appear with his oar. Round and round we would go, so you can imagine his frustration running from side to side. Of course, eventually we took pity on him and swam back to the beach, ate our sandwiches and returned to work.

It was naughty fun but I think in some ways he enjoyed the game and just pretended to be mad.'

SUMMER LODGERS

'My parents lived in a two-storey terraced house in Kemp Town and I was the youngest of seven children. Living conditions were very cramped. As in many of the houses in Kemp Town, my mother took in summer lodgers. The lodgers had the first floor front bedroom and the downstairs front parlour. They paid for bed and breakfast and bought their own food for other meals which my mother cooked for them. During the school holidays I had to wait on them, a job I really hated.'

THE BRIGHTON FIRE BRIGADE

'I loved to visit my grandfather and my aunt for weekends and short holidays. My grandfather, to me, was always an elderly gentleman, with his white curly hair and neat Van Dyke beard, but as a past member of the Brighton Fire Brigade he had a wealth of stories to tell.

There was a particular delight, as a nine year old, in polishing his brass helmet until I could see my face reflected quite grotesquely in the shiny curved surface, almost as good as the "magic mirrors" on the pier. Some of the stories my grandfather entertained me with were associated with his father, who had been a founder member of the Brighton Voluntary Fire Brigade.

Great grandfather had helped with the hand-pulled engine from the base in Duke Street. I remember hearing of the pride my grandfather had felt when his father had been made "Captain" James A. Mills. In 1888 when the voluntary service was disbanded, he then became the first captain of the official Brighton Fire Brigade based in Preston Circus.

Another memory for me as a child was to stay up until midnight on New Year's Eve, and hear my grandfather herald in the new year, in the street, by crowing like a cockerel. His voice echoed over Brighton, in competition with the hooting of the boats and the trains.'

'I was born in Brighton in the 1920s. We lived near Preston Circus because my father was a fireman. At that time there was no accommodation at the station so each fireman had a fire-bell fixed inside their homes. Ours was on the staircase, near to my parents' bedroom.

When my father was on call his trousers were put hanging over the end of the bed, with his jack boots underneath, so he could jump straight into them. I'll always remember him running down the road, putting his jacket on as he ran.

There was no canteen in the station at that time either, and it was my job to take his dinner to the station for him. It was dished up on a plate, with another one over the top, and they were wrapped up in a clean teacloth. My instructions were to go straight there, and as quickly as possible, without spilling the gravy. You couldn't do it quickly today, not with all that traffic around Preston Circus.

We also got a lot of pleasure in going to the station yard to watch the men practise fire drills in the tower. One of the men would dress up in his wife's nightdress and be up at the top of the tower, calling for help. The long turn-table ladder would then go up and he would be "rescued", and brought down over a fireman's shoulder.'

THE LAST OF THE TRAMS

'A treat in the 1920s was to be taken to the theatre in Brighton, and then come home on the tram, hoping it would be the one with all the lights around the top. It was not so good if it rained, of course, and the only seats were on the top. Some trams, though, if you were in luck, had mackintosh covers attached to the seat in front, that you could pull over your knees.'

'As a child in the 1930s I lived opposite St Peter's church in Brighton and remember each week cattle and sheep being driven down Lewes Road, from outlying farms, round the south end of the church, up Trafalgar Street to a slaughterhouse next to a butcher's. Our doctor lived next door but one to us, and was the only person in our road with a car. Us kids would stand around and admire his bull-nosed Morris, as this was still the time of the horse.

The Brighton trams finished in 1939 and workmen lifted the old tram lines which were set in wood blocks, the size of house bricks and covered in tar. These were piled on the sides of the road for anyone who wanted them. People came with sacks and filled them up to take home to burn on their fire instead of coal. In the summer the old trams had coloured lights all round the top which used to light up my bedroom ceiling as the trams clanked by. Trolley buses replaced the trams and the day they started free rides were given, starting at the south end of the Level on a circular tour up Lewes Road, along Union Road and down Ditchling Road.

CHARACTERS OF HOVE

'My father, now aged 93, has lived in Hove all his life. He has seen the town grow from a sparsely populated area to the busy town it is today. One of his memories is of the "lost" village of West Blatchington, now incorporated into the town of Hove. He knew the village well, because as a young man he delivered bread to the villagers.

He described some of the vendors and characters that could be seen on the streets of Hove in the early years of the century. There were, for instance, bird catchers, who carried long poles and nets on their backs and used bird lime to trap the birds. Organ grinders pulled their musical machines round the streets on a barrow, playing them by turning a handle, while a monkey on a long lead went in and out of the crowd begging for money. German bands could be seen playing on street corners.

The milkman delivered using barrows with brass churns on them. I should think each churn held about 20 gallons. From the framework hung pint and half pint measuring cans. Ice cream sellers had a street cry like "Hoki hoki" and travelled with a barrow with a tub of ice cream packed in ice. Watercress was sold from wicker baskets, the men calling "Watercress" as they walked along the roads tying the cress in bunches with strands of long reeded grass. You could always buy winkles, whelks and shrimps on a Sunday. Their wares were carried in baskets and measured out in a half pint mug.

Fish could be bought from a flat barrow which was pushed around the streets. The fish was cheap then, with herring at 24 for a shilling and mackerel the same. There were no fridges in those days either. Most of the fish men also sold rabbit, freshly skinned in the street. Ice merchants would supply ice in large blocks which they broke up outside a shop with a pricker. They supplied ice to fishmongers and butchers. They got the ice from the works in Holland Road and transported it on horse-drawn carts. Knife grinders travelled around sharpening the knives of the local butchers and fishmongers. Using a sandstone wheel fitted to a barrow, they sharpened the knives by working a foot pedal which turned the wheel.

There would be chestnut and hot potato vendors selling their wares from barrows containing coke fires. Coffee was also sold from two-wheeled barrows. These men had pitches in Eaton Road (outside the church), Holland Road, Old Shoreham Road, the top of Sackville Road, the top of Langdale Gardens, by the clock tower and at Brighton station. The stalls were heated by paraffin, and you could buy hot tea and cake. The men came out at seven o'clock and stayed out all night.

There were many men out of work in those days and in 1912 you could hear them singing in the street: "I'm out of work, I'm out of work, So give us a job instead of a bob, I'm out of work today." Often men who were unemployed or unfit for work would walk the streets with a card tied round their neck by a piece of string, with a message such as "Eight children to support" written on it. They sold matches, a penny a box. Other men would sell wild mushrooms or blackberries to local shops to raise money for their families, or draw wonderful chalk pictures on the pavement in the hope that people would give something. There was a soup kitchen in Coleridge Street corporation yard, where soup was sold for a halfpenny a gallon – it was very nice, too.'

CHURCH AND CHAPEL

Church and chapel were central to our lives, and Sundays were kept as a day of rest in many families. Most of us attended Sunday school as children, as well as services on Sunday, and looked forward with delighted anticipation to the annual treat, perhaps the only outing some of us got through the year.

THE SABBATH DAY

'At Westfield there were two chapels and a church and in my young days at the turn of the century all three were practically full on Sundays. One chapel even had a little orchestra, but oh! didn't they preach "hellfire" and put the fear of God into us!

We were really taught to respect the Sabbath Day. Children walked sedately to Sunday school with the collect for the day learned by heart. This was from 9.30 am to 10.30 am. Then they went in to the church service until noon. It was back to Sunday school again in the afternoon from 2.30 pm to 3.30 pm, when a hymn and a verse or two from the Bible were learnt together with the commandments and catechism. Finally we all went to the evening service at 6.30 pm. We were not allowed to play or whistle on Sundays, and for entertainment we either went for a walk or read a book.'

WE ALL WENT TO SUNDAY SCHOOL

'Sunday school was something you "did" on Sunday afternoons. While Mother cooked the roast for exactly 12.30, Father cleaned the pram. At precisely 2.20 you set off to walk to Wadhurst church for the three o'clock service looking resplendent in your Sunday best.

It did help, if you didn't have much spare money, for your mother to be good with her needle. I well remember being dressed up in a mustard coloured hat and coat made from an old pair of my father's cricketing trousers, and always a velvet collar, probably made with a remnant from one of the "lady" clients she made dresses for. There was a sort of pecking order where you sat in church. We sat three rows from the front in the back half, with the pram at the end of the pew.

Maggie Manktelow was our Sunday school teacher in the 1940s, always dressed in a dark suit with a black pork pie hat, and a funny lace bit across her bosom in cream.

The highlight of the year was the Sunday school outing, usually to Hastings. We arrived at Wadhurst station early in the morning to board "Maggie's Special". A whole train of excited children, for some the only outing of the year. One year I remember was not so happy, when after ten minutes sitting on the beach my brother came out of the sea with a very bloody hole in his knee. We spent the rest of our day in Hastings Hospital, but it was nevertheless a great adventure.'

'Living in Eastbourne in the 1920s, I attended Upperton Congregational church services every Sunday with my parents, brother and sister. Halfway through the service the young children would go out to the children's church, where the lectern and altar were scaled down to size.

After Sunday roast dinner we children walked back to Sunday school where we had Bible stories and made models to place in sand trays. The highlight of the year was the Sunday school outing. We boarded a single decker open air charabanc and went off singing and shouting to a farm in Mayfield, Lower Gardens. There we played games and sports and there were always cherries for sale.

The Sunday school party was fun too. We played games like "Here we go round the mulberry bush", "Oranges and lemons", "Poor Mary sits a-weeping", "In and out of the windows", "I sent a letter to my love" and musical chairs.'

THE TREAT

'Before the First World War we always wore "pinnies" (pinafores) to school and usually laced boots, but mostly I had button boots on Sundays. Without exception, all Rye children went to one or other Sunday school and each place of worship provided a treat in the summer for the children, as well as a party in the winter. These "treats" for a number of years consisted of the children marching in a long file to a field outside the town, where races were held and there was a coconut shy and tea was provided. Later on, the treats became outings to Hastings or Dymchurch for the afternoon. Now, sadly, all the Sunday schools are poorly attended.'

'The annual outing for village families at Rotherfield was the Sunday school treat. We went by train to Eastbourne – prams in the guard's van – and the steam train filled up with water before it left the station. Lunch was sandwiches on the beach, then at 4 pm we would meet and form a crocodile to walk to a church hall for tea, with more sandwiches, sticky buns, jelly and orange squash. At Christmas we would have the Sunday school party in the Memorial Institute (the village hall). We always had to wear a hat to church.'

'We were up very early on the morning of the Sunday school treat. After a scanty breakfast – too excited to eat – my younger brother and I were away across the fields to the village. The team was ready when we got there, the waggons newly painted blue and the horses with gleaming brasses in their harness and coloured braid plaited in their manes and tails. Boxes of food and soft drink were loaded into the waggon and planks laid across to serve as seats. We climbed aboard, the carter cracked his whip, spoke to his horses and we were away. A small gathering of relatives and friends waved us goodbye. Were they envious or thankful to be free of us for the day?
    It was not a rapid journey. The two heavy shire horses plodded steadily up the village street, along the foot of the Downs, through Litlington village and on to the winding river through the Cuckmere Valley. We crossed the river at Exceat and turned off the road by what is now the Golden Galleon Tea Rooms. There were shouts of glee as we reached Cuckmere Haven and clambered down from the

waggons. We swam – those of us that could, we paddled, dug in the sand and looked for winkles in the pools, or limpets on the rocks. We soon learnt the trick of a sharp blow to dislodge these creatures. A second knock was useless, they were prepared and hung tight, hence the saying "stick like a limpet". We made little fires and cooked the limpets upside down in their shells.

After a picnic tea there were races, games and prize-giving, until weary but happy we climbed back into the waggon and started for home. The little ones fell asleep in their mothers' arms but we sang all the songs we knew and told jokes and stories. It was a lovely day.'

GETTING ABOUT

How times have changed since we relied on horses for transportation – and we walked miles and thought nothing of it. Gradually the carrier was replaced by the country bus services, and the steam trains were always a favourite, while the pony and trap gave way to the motor car. What a difference it made to the roads!

THE CARRIER

'The main form of transport before the car was the horse and cart, although Northiam was lucky to have a railway. The trains ran three times a day from Headcorn through to Robertsbridge where you could catch a train to London. Another means of travel was the bicycle; people used to cycle to the Harrow and leave their cycles there while they caught a tram in to Hastings to do their shopping. If they had parcels to bring home they would use the carrier service. This was widely used – the carrier called at the shop for you and collected your parcels and brought them home for you by horse and cart, for a small sum.'

'Transport was very limited from Laughton in the 1920s. Isteds the carrier from Herstmonceux would take passengers on his way to Brighton, and later Southdown buses provided an hourly service – one shilling and twopence return to Lewes and two shillings and sixpence return to Brighton.'

FROM HORSES TO MOTORS

'Our family came to Mark Cross about 200 years ago and built the Tower windmill and mill house, established a brickworks, a bakery business, grew hops which were dried in the oast houses and ran several farms.

I was born in 1903 and my brother, two sisters and myself were taught at home by our aunt when we were very young, but at about the age of seven years we used to go by train from Rotherfield and Mark Cross station to school in Tunbridge Wells. To get to the station we went by governess cart when we were small – then by horse and trap and later we cycled. The porter used to call out the names of all the stations as far as Eastbourne and we knew them by heart – he always said Rotherfield twice: "Rotherfield, Rotherfield and Mark Cross!" We were teased by our friends who said that was because Rotherfield was twice as important.

My father was a keen cyclist and he would take us four children on our bikes down to Eastbourne where we learnt to swim in the sea. My mother would travel on the train, with the picnic basket, and any one of us who was very tired would be allowed to travel part of the way home by train.

At the outbreak of the war in 1914 all our working farm horses were taken, and there was a great fuss, as it was impossible to run a farm without them (this was the time before tractors). They were all returned to us so the work could continue.

I remember the excitement of the first car coming through the village, we all ran out to see. My brother taught me to drive in his Austin car in 1926. I would walk to meet him as he drove home from Tunbridge Wells each evening and he would let me drive the rest of the way home, but before being allowed to drive he first taught me all about the workings of the engine. I didn't have to take a driving test but just bought a licence. Of course, travel was much slower then.'

'In Kingston, privately owned motor cars were rare until the late 1920s. Most people walked or used a pony and trap and travelled by rail further afield. Buses became available towards the late 1920s too, but they were few and far between and none came in to the centre of the village.

Occasionally my father took an afternoon off from the milking and we would have a day out visiting my grandmother, a journey of 40 miles there and back. Our horse Molly was harnessed to the trap and with my parents facing forwards and me at the back, off we would go. Molly could be frisky and often shied at strange objects so the journey was usually eventful. When we arrived she was unharnessed and rested for our return home.

In the late 1920s my parents acquired an old car, one of the first in the village. Every Tuesday, for many years, my father would transport any spare produce from the farm and from several neighbours who had smallholdings, in the car to the Lewes WI produce market. They also marketed the wild mushrooms which seasonally grew in profusion in our fields – encouraged, no doubt, by the cow pats!'

'On schooldays in 1922, it was a delight to see a horse and van coming down the road on the way to Battle. The driver would take anything that way and also collect laundry, because anyone in lodgings would give him their washing to bring home to us at Dallington for mum to wash. Later on his return it was exciting to meet him and have a ride!

Medicines were carried in the same way, but later on, of course, it was by car. The driver would collect the packet from the chemist, and the story goes that he would shake the parcel – if there were pills in it he would charge an extra sixpence.

Bus tickets from the Eastbourne area

When driving in a trap to Battle, after getting to the top of Creep Hill the horse would start to trot along the road when suddenly the sound would change and the road sounded hollow. People said there was an underground passage from Hastings caves, as far out as Rushlake Green.

The roads were kept in good condition, and the verges were cut by hand and the grass cleared up. Roadmen had to walk their "beat", or cycle and there was no waterproof clothing then, so if they got wet that was that.

On holidays I used to go with my Dad in a horse and trap to market at Heathfield or Battle, a six mile drive either way. There were three shops in Dallington at that time, as well as two butchers and the post office. There was also a blacksmith and wheelwright at Woods Corner, who would cut the hair of the local lads for sixpence.

Horses with timber tugs used to pull out trees from the woods, and they kept falling, poor things; it was a sight I wish I'd never seen and I cannot forget.

By the 1940s buses were running every two hours to Hastings and Tunbridge Wells, and it was possible to go to the cinema in Battle in the evening as the last bus got into the village at 10.45 pm.'

'Every Saturday in the 1930s we used to be taken to Camber Sands with a ride on the train which ran from Rye. There were only two houses in Camber then.

My father worked at Rye railway station, in the office. The station delivered all the parcels with a horse and trailer, the man sitting high up with long reins.'

'The carrier's waggonette ran from Tenterden to Rye, and on entering Rye a horn was sounded, which attracted all the children. There were also other carriers from the villages to and from Rye, delivering parcels etc. The Rye and Camber tram, of which my father was a driver, operated every day, including Sundays, when it was most patronised by members of the Rye golf club who played on the links at Camber.'

A PART OF OUR LIVES

'When I was a child there were very few cars and no motor buses passing through the village where I lived. If we wanted to go to Rye, we had either to walk, cycle or go on the horse-bus which ran from Tenterden to Rye three times a week. When I was allowed to go on this bus I contrived to sit by the driver while my mother sat inside. I believe there were seats for six passengers inside and occasionally people would ride on the roof. The vehicle was drawn by two horses.

It was a red-letter day when the coach owners, Bennetts of Tenterden, replaced the horse-bus with a twelve-seater motor bus which ran more than one journey every weekday. Mr Bert, the old horse-bus driver, became conductor and Len Godden, who had recently come out of the RAF, was the driver of the new "Times" bus. Mr Bert smoked cheap cigars most of the time. Occasionally he offered one to Len who said they tasted of cabbage leaves.

At first the motor bus carried more parcels than passengers. Quite often there was a parcel for my father's shop. Len would get out of the driver's seat and walk across the small village green, stopping for a chat in the shop before continuing.

The early buses were not very reliable. Punctures were frequent. Once, not having a spare wheel and not being near a telephone, Len had the bright idea of stuffing grass into the tyre to get the bus moving. He drove off but after a short distance the grass got lumpy. It was a very bumpy ride into Rye that day. Another time, Len had to be towed back to the Tenterden depot by a steam-engine – "and didn't I get black!" he said.

Other, more reliable, Times buses followed and as time went on they had competition from other bus companies. I remember they would leave Rye at the same time and race to be the first one up Rye Hill and reach the passengers along the way. Eventually the Times bus was taken over by Maidstone & District Motor Company. Len Godden was not happy working the unsociable hours the new company demanded, so when he heard that Mr Dengate of Beckley was planning to shut his garage repair business to concentrate on his bus company, Len did not hesitate. He took over the garage with the petrol pumps on one side of the road and the repair shop on the other. When 1939 came supplies of petrol and spare parts stopped and business fell off. So Len turned to agricultural contracting which later on, after the war, was combined with bus driving on a part-time basis.

When I married in 1945, I renewed my acquaintance with Len. I came to live in the house next door to his bungalow and the bus depot. In the 1950s a bus journey could still be an experience, even if it wasn't the same as the early years when passengers might get out and push an overloaded bus up Rye Hill. A generation of school-children remember buses that broke down and the driver making roadside repairs, because at that time of day there was no one in the depot to bring out a spare bus.

Dengate's bus drivers had no great regard for bus stops. They would put down passengers anywhere they requested and, before the war, would often wait for regular passengers to fetch in their washing or finish some other chore before boarding the bus. Their routes covered Hastings, Hawkhurst and Northiam as well as Rye. To the end of their existence, there always seemed to be problems with the engines. My daughter always held her breath halfway up Brede Hill in case the bus didn't make it to the top on the way home from Hastings. Once in dreadful weather a bus got stuck on that hill and had to stay there all night – and the driver with it.

Looking back it was an adventure riding on the old buses. In post-war years Dengate's buses were a familiar sight in the area. You could tell the time by them despite the breakdowns. They were a regular part of our lives and I wasn't surprised when one of my daughter's first words was "bus".'

WAITING AT THE STOP

'It is a sunny afternoon in spring and I am waiting on the corner of Old Steine and Castle Square in Brighton. I am six years old and wearing my green school tunic, cream blouse, green blazer with the school badge on the pocket and a cream panama hat with a green and cream ribbon round the crown. Passers-by do not appear to notice me and I am full of my own thoughts as I hook my right arm round a fire hydrant which is part of the street furniture and, leaning outwards, swing happily round and round.

An open-topped tram comes clanging along the tram-lines from its terminus opposite the Royal Albion Hotel and stops in the middle of the road opposite me. Some people walk out to it and get aboard. Two men climb the outside stairs to sit on the top deck in the sun-shine. The tram bears a large medallion on either side of the top deck showing a capital "N". This means that it will swing along past the war memorial and the Valley Gardens, past St Peter's church, along London Road and up New England Hill to Seven Dials and Dyke Road. The "N" stands for North. A tram marked "S" only goes as far as North Road and Queen's Road to the station where the driver will use a long hooked pole to detach the overhead trolley arm, walk it round 180° and connect it up again. He will then mount the tram at the opposite end, clang the bell, and come swinging down the hills again, along the far side of the gardens to the terminus. The sound of these trams, and the hope of a ride "up top" sometime, make me feel very happy.

The bus which brought me back from the Brighton and Hove High School and left me on this corner is not half as glamorous in my eyes, although it too was open-topped and great fun on a windy day.

The charabancs which share the busy terminus during the summer and deposit their loads of Londoners on day-trips to our pebbly beach are not Brightonians. They will not be passing our door after the summer holidays, nor will they share the buffeting of autumn gales and winter rains when "our" buses and trams have black waterproof seat covers to cower under on the top deck and you have to anchor your school hat down with its chin elastic.

From my corner I look across the Old Steine to my home in one of the terraced houses on the eastern side of the valley. The tall central fountain is playing in the sunshine and if I could stand at the right spot on the surrounding gravel as the sea breeze was blowing I could catch a cooling shower-bath straight from the dolphin's mouth.

This particular afternoon I am getting a bit tired of waiting and am looking forward to my tea (a piece of bread and butter and *then* a piece of bread and butter and jam). I look across the gardens yet again and am happy to see a familiar figure on his way to collect me. It is my father's office boy, the only non-family person with whom I will leave my waiting position. No one, of course, has paid me much attention during my ten minute wait; after all I am only one small child following my parents' instructions and no one else need be concerned about me.'

TROLLEY BUSES IN BRIGHTON

'I remember very well the trolley buses that ran in Brighton during the 1930s and 1940s. Everybody used to queue in a very orderly fashion at The Duke of York cinema bus stop, where I waited for the trolley every morning.

While waiting, I would be wondering whether I would be able to get on the inside, because if you were unlucky enough to have to go upstairs to the top deck the air would be so thick with cigarette smoke you could almost cut it with a knife.

It was always worse in the winter, as then all the windows would be closed tight, so my eyes would run from the effects of all that smoke.

I hated getting up on cold winter mornings, as the only heating in the house was a small coal fire, which everyone tried to get close to. Consequently I was often cutting the time very fine for getting to work. I don't know why, but on those days it seemed that more often than not the arm of the trolley bus came off the wires. Passengers sat waiting for the conductor to get the long pole from somewhere under the bus, to enable him to reconnect the arm to the wires so that we could continue our journey.'

BUSES WERE ALWAYS FULL

'For those children who lived on the route, a bus could be taken from the William IV public house at one end of Nutley to the school at the other end of the village – it saved the long walk. The journey cost a penny and was only to be undertaken when there was a real downpour. Pennies were short.

Buses ran frequently to Uckfield, at five miles the nearest town. The buses were always full, and the fare was fivepence to the northern tip of the town and sixpence to the bus depot at the other end.

So popular and well used were the buses at a time when cars were hardly known in the villages, that it was necessary to board a bus going away from the required destination and travel as far as Chelwood Gate in the opposite direction in order to make sure of a seat on the journey back into Uckfield. People were lucky to get on the last homeward bus from the town, and there was a relief vehicle only on Bank Holidays. The railway was in operation then, but was not much used by the young people. The buses also ran to Eastbourne and Brighton and that was enough – if you could get on them!'

THE RAILWAY THROUGH ROTHERFIELD

'The railway line that ran through Rotherfield was part of the South East Coast Railway but to the people of Rotherfield it was always known as the Cuckoo Line. The first cuckoos in spring were thought to have followed the river Cuckmere to Heathfield, known as "Heffle", two stations down the line from Rotherfield.

Rotherfield station had a very busy coalyard which is still there today. All the farmers and smallholders from the surrounding area used to send their chickens, ducks and eggs to the weekly market at Heathfield. At certain times of the year racing pigeons were sent down from the North of England to the local stations including Rotherfield and the porters were asked to release them to fly back to their homes.

The station was a busy place with good connections to London and Brighton. I remember going to Eastbourne every year for our Sunday school treat. It was a thrill never to be forgotten. I attended Rotherfield school in the late 1920s and early 1930s and the senior girls were sent to Heathfield by train once a week for cookery lessons at the Goward Hall and we also went to Hartfield by train for stoolball matches. We really enjoyed these outings because children rarely left their villages. I remember a dog called Prince – he belonged to the Eridge stationmaster and loved riding on the trains. He also went into the cab with the engine drivers who made a great fuss of him.

50

He used to go down to Eastbourne where he went into the engine sheds, staying there until he caught the train back at night. He always crossed over by the footbridge at Eridge, never on the railway line. He was a little black and white collie. In 1952 BBC TV followed up a report in the local paper, the *Courier*, and made a film about this little dog.

The porters were always very helpful to their passengers and if in the winter the trains were late or held up they would telephone the wives of some of the businessmen to let them know. This helped people as they came from quite a long way to catch the trains at Rotherfield.

During the war troops and war materials passed through the station, especially when they were preparing for D-Day. I also saw some of our own prisoners of war coming through, dropping messages to their people before going on to the hospitals.

Evacuees came down from London by train, they stayed in various houses and went to the local school – some settled in Rotherfield and are still here today. Hop pickers also travelled down by train as there were hopfields all around Rotherfield, Eridge, Groombridge and through into Kent.

Sadly the day came when the line had to close as part of Dr Beeching's branch line cuts. It was on 12th June 1965. On this day the last train drew out of Rotherfield station – banners and flags flew from the windows of houses along the track, fireworks were let off and many people watched and waved goodbye with so many different memories. My husband worked on the Cuckoo Line for 22 years and misses both the trains and the comrades he worked with 30 years ago.'

THE A27 – THEN AND NOW

'As you speed along the new, revamped, somewhat terrifying A27 between Falmer and Kingston, think for a moment what it is like for those of us who live and work beside this road, where vehicle speeds are hardly ever less than 70 mph.

You may like to know how the A27 was in the past. Perhaps we should think back to the times between 1940 and 1945, part of my childhood. The traffic, such as it was then because of the war and petrol rationing, and also the fact that there were far less cars about anyway, went sedately along this road at about 35 to 40 mph. The coal lorry perhaps, the local grocer, the milkman, the baker and the laundry van for example, all mixed up with the Austin Sevens, Morris Eights, Rileys and Standards of that time, and maybe the odd

Jaguar – no foreign cars in those days. The postman came out from Lewes on his bicycle to deliver to the local farms and houses, and PC Baker from the village would frequently pass by on his bicycle heading for Lewes to report to his superiors at the police station there. He was even passing by one night in 1944 when a Mosquito fighter plane which had been shot down crashed on the roadside.

The newspapers arrived by Southdown bus and were thrown over the garden wall by the conductor, whilst the bus driver waited for him to do this service each day on their way to Brighton, and the bus would *always* wait for a second passenger to come running out if he or she had misjudged the time of the bus to school!

In those days the road was fairly narrow and of course single car-riageway only, meandering through the centre of Falmer down to Kingston by a series of bends, now long since ironed out, but which did cause some bad accidents even in those days. The road was kept tidy and clean by Mr Watson and his mate who took pride in clear-ing the gutters of leaves, paper and sometimes a bottle or two, all of which went into their pushcart to be emptied at the end of the day. As they wandered down the road they were never too busy to stop for a chat and a joke, and they always knew what was happening up and down the roadside. They could tell the time by the passing buses, as every one of us who lived beside the road could, every twelve minutes either to Lewes or Brighton, and one shilling and sixpence for the return journey. You could go almost anywhere from Lewes on the buses which passed along the A27, Ringmer, East-bourne, Tunbridge Wells and many more of the local villages.

The road was so quiet that I can remember being allowed to drive a horse and cart along it with the cart loaded with potatoes. That at the age of about twelve years old – who would venture anywhere near this road now with a horse, leave alone a cart? At one time there was an old woman tramp called "Mothball Molly" who used to walk the road pushing a pram with all her worldly possessions in it, and selling "mothballs" to anyone who would buy them. Sadly one evening at dusk an army gun carrier knocked her down and she was killed. During this time one did see the army convoys passing, and as D-Day approached in 1944 the tanks would rumble by and the soldiers give you a wave which was quite exciting for a youngster, but mostly this was a quiet road to live beside.

As I write this in the summer sunshine in my garden, there is as always the noise of the traffic rushing by, and I remember with nos-talgia the quiet days of "then" when only the occasional car went slowly by practically unnoticed as opposed to the huge volume of traffic "now".'

HOUSE & HOME

At home in East Sussex

LOOKING BACK

Our lives were very different at the beginning of the century, as these memories show. The first was written in 1956 by a lady who was looking back to her own childhood 70 years before, taking us back into Victorian days.

MEMORIES OF MY VILLAGE

'Life was hard for the agricultural labourer. Fifteen shillings was the average, yet people seemed happy, very healthy and brought up large families – a lesson in thrift and industry for us today.

Rents varied for the cottages in Westfield from one shilling and sixpence to three shillings a week and were seldom more for a cottage of two to three bedrooms. Each had a faggot stack, a chopping block and a "sawing horse". Not much coal was burned, even at one shilling and fourpence a hundredweight, which was more than half a day's pay. Some of the cheaper cottages had no cooking range for baking but either "brand-irons" or a "duck's nest" fireplace. A large oval iron boiler was hooked on to a chain which was attached to a large nail up the chimney. Everything was cooked in the boiler in string bags – cabbage in one, root vegetables in another, and perhaps a beef pudding or a piece of bacon was also put in the boiler, whilst gravy was made from the water in which the vegetables, pudding or meat was cooked thus retaining all the necessary vitamins. The chain could be raised or lowered for boiling or simmering by a pulley.

Most of the very old cottages had a brick or bread oven (their only means of baking). When the bread was baked and the oven reheated (with wood only) joints of meat, cakes, pies, flead cakes and buns could be cooked to a turn. Those which took longest to cook were put at the back, and the smaller things in the front of the oven. All were placed on a long-handled flat iron shovel to be put in position in the oven. Bread cooked this way was delicious.

Tea was made from dried privet leaves or the used tea leaves from the big house. On high days and holidays only was real tea used.

Kettle broth consisted of boiling water poured over broken-up bread in a bowl, pepper and salt with a piece of butter or dripping added with a few marigold petals sprinkled on the top, This was for the man's tea after a hard day's work. Meat could only be eaten once a week unless a rabbit was found. Bread, butter, cheese were all good and there were always the Sunday substantial beef puddings with a four inch crust, rabbit pies and the lovely pumpkin pies and well puddings (never served with cream!).

To make matrimony tarts we lined a plate with short pastry, sprinkled with sugar, then a good layer of currants (washed but not too well dried), sprinkled again with sugar and spice. Put on the top crust and bake. Why they were called matrimony tarts I do not know.

Most of the peasants kept a pig and a few chickens, and the men had good allotments which were always occupied. All farmers sent their milk into Hastings twice a day, and cottagers could get milk only from the "little man" who kept one or two cows, but one could buy a small tin of condensed skimmed milk for two and a half pence.

The public houses were open all day. The waggoner and his boy could get a penny glass of beer and a pennyworth of bread and cheese for their dinners. If they could afford it a ha'porth of pickles could be bought.

Going back about 85 years, my father left school when he was eight years of age and started work with his father. His breakfast consisted of bread and turnip, and he washed his little face and hands in the dew as he trudged behind his Dad. Wages were a shilling a week for him and ten shillings for Dad!

The village women had hard lives. All water had to be drawn from wells or springs and the amount of clothes worn made a lot of washing. Wood had to be chopped to use for fuel to light the copper for boiling. The copper was generally a low red brick affair. Not many people had mangles, and irons were heated on the open fires. There was much patching and cutting down of worn garments to fit smaller children. When stockings could not be darned any more in the foot, they were "fottled" ie the best parts of the old pair were used for this, cut to the shape of the old foot and neatly stitched round.

Women worked in the hay fields, the hop gardens (tying and picking the hops), hoeing, cutting turnip tops, fruit picking and laundry work. We had six or seven hand laundries in the village. The wife of the carter told me she worked right up to the day before her first child was born for a shilling a day. She is now 85 years of age!

District nurses did not exist, but a village woman generally acted as midwife. I often accompanied my mother to help a neighbour in her confinement. Clean hands and a clean apron were all the equipment that was thought necessary! If the confinement appeared difficult the husband had to walk five miles for the doctor who came by dog-cart. There were no telephones, and bicycles were not for the peasants till much later. What a good kind man was Dr Kendall! How many, many times did he "forget" to send his bill in to the poor man; one of God's good men. Dear Dr Kendall – you are still remembered with love and gratitude.

The school was excellent, and children from two and a half years of age were taken. I was among the lucky(?) ones who went at this age. I don't remember what was taught but well recollect the kind teacher, who, when little heads began to nod, picked us up and carried us to a classroom where we were placed on little mattresses and covered with patchwork quilts. This school was good, perhaps because we had a headmaster and mistress who did not "spare the rod". Our very first slates had no frames. We used our own slate pencils and slate rags. Woe betide the scholars caught cleaning slates with pinafore or coat sleeve! Just before slate cleaning time the teacher would say "Show slate rags!"

If late for school we had to forfeit playtime and write "late" 100 times on the slate. Incorrect spelling was also treated in this way. It was no use telling parents we had had the cane or had been kept in. Another hiding might have been the result of misbehaving!

Children were really bundles of clothes in those days. For girls winter wear consisted of a thick vest made of "sailors' flannel" a calico chemise, stays of several thicknesses of flannelette shaped under the arms and tied with three bows of tape, drawers which buttoned on to the stays (three buttonholes in the front band and two in the back band). Then on top of all this were two flannel or flannelette petticoats, a frock with high neck and long sleeves and finally a pinafore without which no girl was ever seen (except when she went to church). Legs were enclosed in thick woollen stockings and there were always boots on the feet.

Funerals in my village were a most impressive sight. No matter what hour of the day or early evening a death occurred, the passing bell would toll. Coffins were made in the village and the "bearers" would be eight village men dressed in white smocks. Four would carry the coffin on their shoulders for so far, and then they were relieved by the other four. These bearers were dressed in white and the line of mourners in deep black and carrying wreaths or crosses. These made a never to be forgotten sight. The following Sunday all went to church – bearers and mourners. I remember one old chap in the village who was very clever in making white flowers for wreaths out of the pith of rushes. What patience!

For funerals a black velvet pall with a white fringe could be hired for five shillings from the local choirmaster.

There were two chapels and a church in my village and in my

56

young days all three were practically full on Sundays. One chapel even had a little orchestra, but oh! didn't they preach "hell-fire" and put the fear of God into us. The vicar's lady was very good to the poor.

Westfield was a lovely village. Wild flowers grew everywhere. The roads were narrow (and dusty) and the hedges were high, festooned with wild roses and honeysuckle in the summer, and blackberries and nuts in the autumn.

We gathered herbs such as agrimony and the pink flowered centaury. We grew our own horehound, pennyroyal and rue to be dried and in the winter to be used for all sorts of aches and pains. The petals of the white cottage lily were gathered, put into a clean jar and covered with brandy. A festering finger soon healed after a lily petal or two had been applied.

So many trees have been cut down that no rooks fly lazily "home from school". Now no flitter mice are to be seen in the twilight, no swifts or "swallows twittering from the straw-built shed". Hedges are chopped down to the lowest level and where are our wild flowers gone?'

MEMORIES BEFORE 1914

'Were they the good old days, or does distance lend enchantment? Certainly there was much class distinction. Being poor then, was to be really poor. If one fell on hard times, parish relief was granted, after a lot of fuss. For a family without a breadwinner, it was seven shillings and sixpence per week for a month, then five shillings checked out carefully. Doctors were called only in real trouble, as each visit was charged for. The doctor here at Five Ashes came on horseback, when a member of the family was sent out to hold the horse's head, a great honour. The midwife, not qualified, also acted as a layer-out of the dead. A parish bag was loaned, for one shilling per confinement, which contained essentials for a new babe, then everything was carefully washed and returned for use by another poor mum. The ladies' Dorcas sewing classes made these as part of their good works. The mother did not go out to visit until she had been churched, a thanksgiving service for a new life, a safe delivery. This was usually private.

How much the children in the family knew is open to question, but one old lady, the only girl in a family of boys, begged for a sister, not another blooming boy, but didn't get her wish. Instead of being the pampered sister, she was expected to always help Mum. She told me her best Christmas present was a flannel petticoat, made of

57

samples, herringbone stitched; she called it Joseph, of course. One wonders how such lovely work was done by lamp and candlelight. On a beam in this cottage is a hook, very strong, from which the lamp, trimmed, filled and polished, hung.

Most girls sewed for their bottom drawer, and when a wedding took place the paper report listed every wedding present, so you didn't dare give a tea strainer!

Lots of people with large gardens, or able to "hive out", kept bees. Honey sold at three shillings and sixpence per lb. Mead was made (powerful stuff this, not allowed to children) and all sorts of other wine too, plus jam, pickles, preserves. Wild rabbits made a good pie or stew. Mushrooms were plentiful. Bee wine made from a culture sat in the window; nothing to do with bees, but the warmth made the movement, up and down, like a bee. Did all this powerful stuff help the birthrate? Bread was made in the oven, heated first with wood, then the ashes raked out, cakes too. The temperature was judged by placing a piece of brown paper in, if it scorched it was too hot! A cake made like a big scone, with raisins, was called a plum heavy. Milk, unless you had a house cow, was skimmed; full milk and cream went to the gentry. Some days a beef pudding in a cloth was made. The grown ups ate the meat, the children the suet crust and gravy.

The fare from Mayfield to London was five shillings return. Two small private bus companies carried passengers to Tunbridge Wells and vied for custom, waited and put you down at the door!

Little boys stayed in petticoats until about three years old. Getting all the washing done and dried must have been a problem. Wood was collected to heat the copper, in which boiling was done, also the bath water – for a tin tub in the scullery. Christmas puds too, were always boiled in wash boilers.

A big family bible was a treasure, with a brass clasp. The happenings of all were recorded on the flyleaf and, if you "brought trouble", eradicated. Grandma or Grandpa always had a corner in a son's or daughter's home.

Harvest suppers in the farmer's barn meant beery songs until late in the evening: *Sussex by the Sea*, or *The Farmer's Boy*, about the orphan lad taken in, who made good and married the farmer's daughter – tears would fall in this one.

Winters were harsh, life was hard, and those who have survived till this time learned the secret of being content with the good things. Water was drawn from the well and the little house was up the garden, dark and cobwebby, smelly too, but you could read the newspaper on the nail! One old lady told me that when she went on a visit to some friends, she was given a lantern to find the way. She stood it on the seat, as she thought, but it disappeared. She didn't know there were two holes, one for children. Then she couldn't find the way back down the path.

One could write reams on old church services. Say a verse of a hymn and then sing it. Sermons at least an hour, hell and heaven, fire and brimstone. Chapel, too, was very strict. Most girls were in service; the master and mistress went in the morning, the servants in the evening. My mother played the organ which was "aired" by a lever working the pump manually. Once my father went to sleep, so not a sound came from the keyboard. Meals were taken that week in stony silence. I have a postcard, posted in the morning and delivered in the afternoon to where my mother was a companion. "Dear Ellen, I am not coming tonight, it's cold and wet and I don't want to." What a love letter, but he must have wanted to, as they did marry.'

CHILDHOOD AT NEWHAVEN FROM 1915

'Lower is an old Newhaven name and I am one of them. I liked my young life there. It was, and still is, a working class town. The men worked mainly on the railway or at the harbour. My father was a spare driver on the old London, Brighton and South Coast Railway. People were poor, nobody had much or expected much. I was one of the lucky ones, living in a decent house and my father in regular employment.

My mother's father was master of the old dredger *Meeching*, called after old Newhaven. My father's father was a fisherman and in his young days was a member of the lifeboat crew – this was in the days of the oars. My earliest recollection of church was going to the Seamen's Mission and the old "salts" calling out the names of their favourite hymns to be sung. *Pull for the shore sailor, Eternal Father*, etc. My grandmother Lower told me in her young days her father took the family to sea on a sailing vessel. One night, sitting at supper, she haughtily asked the cabin boy to fetch her a glass of water to which her father retorted, "If you want a glass of water, you fetch it yourself my girl!" Eventually she married the cabin boy – my grandfather!

In my mother's days, most of the girls went into service – some at Seaford which was supposed to be healthy and was full of boarding schools and convalescent homes.

We had a piano in the front room and lessons were sixpence. Practice in the front room on a winter's day was purgatory. The fire was only lit on a Sunday and I can see my brother holding up a newspaper in front of it to make it draw! Sunday we always had a lovely roast dinner, but Monday was not so nice with poor Mother struggling with the washing. Washing Dad's dirty dungarees was no easy job, so dinner was cold meat and bubble and squeak, usually followed by rice pudding and prunes! We had lots of suet puddings in those days which I loved – meat pudding, jam roly poly, treacle pudding, apple pudding etc. Doughnuts were seven for sixpence at Funnels the baker's. He used to bake the weekend cakes for people in his oven on a Saturday afternoon for a penny halfpenny per cake. You stuck your name on a piece of greaseproof paper on the top.

We had a gramophone, and I remember the record *Valencia* belting out, and later on a wireless set with an aerial and pole in the garden. If your pole was higher than your neighbour's, you got a better reception!

Sometimes my mother would take me to Brighton. They had "SPO" shops there – ie sausage, potato and onions cooking in the window. Very nice. One shilling.

Saturday night was bath night with the bath in front of the kitchen fire. Hair also had to be washed followed by a dose of syrup of figs or liquorice powder dissolved in a little water – horrible! Clean nightie and clothes ready for Sunday. It was usual to have three of everything – one on, one in the wash, and one in the drawer. Bedrooms were cold with linoleum on the floor. We went to bed by candlelight.

We had a workhouse at Newhaven and there were quite a lot of tramps around. I believe for a night's lodging they had to dig the allotment there next morning. I am told that before asking for a night's lodging some of them used to bury their cash in the allotment and retrieve it the next day so that in fact they had no money and could claim a free night's lodging. The workhouse master was a Mr Sanders. The area round Northway by the river was a slum area and known as "Cock's Sparrow". One of my playmates lived there – it was a large family, and they eventually went to the workhouse to live.

I remember going to Lewes on Bonfire Nights, and one Sunday being taken up Seaford Head where people were shaking hands with Sir Alan Cobham who had landed his aeroplane there.'

THE HOUSES WE LIVED IN

They could be picturesque with roses round the door but our homes were generally small and often overcrowded in the past. Perhaps they had a character, though, which means we look back with some nostalgia.

HOME HAD FOUR ROOMS

'Home at Rye was a four-roomed house, with a scullery across a back garden. This was roomy, since it included a large shallow sink, a bricked-in copper, an extra fireplace and the toilet, as well as all garden tools and coal cupboard. Our cooking was done by a good stove, similar to a kitchen range. This was kept black and polished. The hearth was always whitened and the fender and fire-irons were steel. The lamp was at first an oil lamp suspended from the ceiling, in addition to an ordinary one in the sitting room. Gas came later and then we just had a ring to supplement the stove.

When we had bloaters for tea they were cooked in a special utensil of heavy wire, which opened to lay the fish in and closed for cooking and this had hooks to hang on the top bar of the stove so that the fish cooked in part of the bars and the bottom of this was made boat-shaped to catch all the fat. All cooking was, of course, done at home, except for the Christmas cakes when, for years, we all sent them on special days to the baker's to be baked. When I was small this was quite a worry, as I was afraid we would get the wrong ones home! But they did have a slip of paper with our name on it.

We had the baker call daily, the milkman twice daily, when we had a pennyworth in the morning and a halfpennyworth at tea time, measured out by the milkman into our jug which stood on the windowsill. Occasionally we had a "fish lady" call, as did the others, at the back door. The boy, ringing his bell, came down the street with hot rolls in the morning. At certain times a cart without sides, like a flat tray, came loaded with bananas, I believe at twopence a pound. Once a week we had one of Gran's home-made loaves. Dad grew all our vegetables and mended all our shoes, at least mine, till I was old enough to work and pay for them to be done elsewhere. He also made and mended the nets he and his father used for eeling, which meant for both of them long walks after a long day's work. Mother made a good proportion of my clothes, except for a few "best" dresses. She was a wonderfully good cook as well.

The water tap was outside by the back door, so all water for washing had to be carried to the scullery. Later we had a tap put over the sink. The three front door steps were cleaned each week (not whitened) and the back paving stones by the back door were scrubbed with a bass broom each Saturday morning.'

LITTLE NORTONS

'Little Nortons at Kent Street was our home for six years in the 1920s. It was usually referred to as "The Cottage", though it was not my idea of one, being actually a wooden bungalow with a tiled roof. The boards were painted a buff colour and pointed downwards to keep off the rain. The house could be seen from the Hastings to Sedlescombe road.

A gravel path led from the gate along the front of the house and round to the back. A path led to the vegetable garden, tilled by Dad. This was the only garden Dad ever tried to look after. "Farmers make bad gardeners", as the saying goes. Apart from the side of our house which was flanked by the lane, the other three sides were completely surrounded by the wood and a path led from our back door through the wood to a stile and then on through the fields to Nortons Farm.

What was the cottage like inside? Suppose you walked up the front steps one sunny morning and knocked at the door (no bell, but a good loud iron knocker). A passage, light and fairly wide, led to the back of the house with two doors opening on each side, on the right to the dining room and the family bedroom and on the left to the guest bedroom and the kitchen.

Let's look at the kitchen first. The floor would strike you at once – bright red brick. On the left wall as you came in from the passage was the kitchen range, and opposite it, under the window, was the sink. You would no doubt wonder at the presence of three large galvanised buckets full of water. Dad filled them from the well outside every morning before he went off to the farm to work. The kitchen was also the bathroom. Somewhere, standing on its side, was a large shallow circular bath, white enamel inside and reddish-brown outside, which could be put in the centre of the room on bath nights. There was also a wooden table that had to be scrubbed and a wringer for the laundry.

In the dining room the fireplace was opposite the window and had a built-in cupboard or sideboard on the right. There was a square table in the centre of the room with chairs round it and scattered about were two armchairs and a sofa. From the centre of the ceiling hung an oil lamp. On dark winter afternoons I always looked forward to lamp-lighting time. You of the electric age can hardly have a notion how dark the winter used to be. Candles and oil lamps only light up a small circle in their immediate vicinity and even that light is dim and flickering. The corners and the passages remain dark and eerie and outside it could be pitch black.

The family bedroom had a brass-knobbed bed for Mum and Dad, while I slept in a small camp bed and my brother Rob in a cot. There was a big wardrobe in that room with a night-light on top, but I think that total darkness might have been better as the unsteady flame made moving shadows. The front bedroom was much nicer. Here the carpet was not worn as in the other rooms but still had fresh, bright colours.

There was no inside toilet. A little house across the backyard, without drainage, served this purpose. I was told that Dad took away the night soil to a place in the wood.'

TORONTO TERRACE

'My father worked at the Phoenix Iron Works in Lewes, known as Every's. I was born in 1922 and lived in Toronto Terrace for the first 16 years of my life. The rent was eleven shillings and fourpence per week. There were two rooms and a scullery downstairs and two bedrooms and an attic upstairs, later converted into a bedroom for my brother. Cooking was mostly on the kitchen range which had to be blackleaded each day, and the flues cleaned out once a week. There was also a small gas cooker in the scullery. Lighting was by gas, the mantles so delicate that one touch and they disintegrated. We took candles up to bed. No bathroom, of course, so on Fridays nights the large tin bath was brought in from the yard where it hung on a nail, and we bathed in front of the kitchen fire. Water was heated in saucepans and kettles on the kitchener. Daily washing was done at the kitchen sink.

The front room was only used on special occasions like Christmas, and had two uncomfortable armchairs, so rough to our bare legs.

On washing days, always a Monday, the fire was lit under the stone copper very early in the morning by my father, and by breakfast time the water was boiling. Sheets, pillowcases and all whites were washed first in the sink using Rinso and yellow carbolic soap, then boiled in the copper. After rinsing and the blue bag being added to the last water, the large mangle was brought into action. Coloureds were washed afterwards. Buttons had to be removed or the roller would crush them. All was then dried in the garden. One of my earliest recollections before I started school is of sitting on the backdoor mat on a wet Monday under an umbrella, because the door had to remain open because of the steam. We always had cold meat on Mondays, no time for cooking, followed by a suet roly poly of some sort.

We had a wireless set, put together by my Dad, and each week I had to go to the cycle shop to change the accumulator which ran the wireless. It cost fourpence, I believe.

We did have an inside toilet, off the scullery, but no proper toilet paper, so we cut up newspaper, the pieces threaded onto a string and hung inside the door.

On Sunday morning Dad's job was to clean knives with a special powder and chop the mint or horseradish for the sauce to accompany the joint. Saturday was baking day, when cakes and pastry were made and stored for the coming week. One thing I hated was to be sent to the Fruiterers Arms for a pint of "old and mild" from the bottle and jug department.

Meals revolved around the hooter which sounded at Every's five minutes before knocking off time. As it took my Dad five minutes to walk home, the food was on the table as he walked in. It sounded again five minutes before work was due to recommence.'

AUNT NELL'S KITCHEN

'If only the smell could be printed here! I have the picture in my mind, but how can I convey that special odour of ... brick floor, paraffin stove, bread, cabbage water, milk, smoky beams and a hint of farmer's boot?

I cannot remember that the door, which opened into a wide, brick floored back hallway, was ever closed. Just inside on the floor was a glazed earthenware crock with a wooden board on the top. This held the water for drinking, which Uncle Tom drew from the well, which was one of the deepest and most constant in the neighbourhood.

The dresser, against the same wall, held assorted china, and to me a fascinating collection of egg cups. Eggs were rationed at home, but at Aunt Nell's, when the hens were in lay, there were eggs aplenty, and the men had two each at tea time. With the tea service there was a capacious slop basin – a large bowl which was part of every tea service before the advent of tea bags. It needed to be large, for it accommodated not only the remaining tea leaves from each cup before the next one was poured, but Aunt Nell warmed the cups with hot water before pouring the first cup, and this half filled it at the very beginning of the meal.

The window overlooked one of the widest views in this part o. Sussex, a clean sweep to the sea – which was out of bounds to us during the war. There were only sunny days seen through this window it seemed. I suppose we did not even bother to look out on wet days, so for me the window always framed that lovely view.

Under the window, a brick sink. Not just the pillars which supported it, but the whole sink was made of paving bricks from which any mortar joints had long since been washed away. Washing up was done in a bowl, with the plates being left to drain on its spacious surface. A tap through the wall drew water from the high green painted rainwater tank outside, and a rough lead pipe took the water away I know not where. The scrape of enamel bowl and galvanized buckets on the sink's uneven surface would set the teeth on edge.

Near the other wall was an oil range. A "modern" contrivance with several burners in a pale green framework, and to me the greatest mystery (until I started science lessons at school), an inverted bottle of paraffin to feed it. On baking days a tin box of an oven was placed over the burners, which imparted a distinctive flavour to Aunt Nell's cooking.

The big coal range which stood in the chimney recess was never alight that I can recall, and served as a repository for all sorts of odds and ends, mainly belonging to Uncle Tom, including a bowl to take scraps to the chickens and a kilner jar. This jar was filled with cream which Aunt Nell had skimmed from the big flat pans in the dairy, and Uncle Tom would sit in his chair and thump the jar rhythmically on his knee until, if he stopped to let me see, the little tiny blobs of butter grew and congealed into a soft mass in the buttermilk which was surprisingly cream coloured, not blue like the skimmed milk I had seen left in the pan. A mystery I did *not* find an answer to in science lessons.

The scrubbed table, so fashionable again now, took the centre of the room and above it the sticky fly paper, spiralling up from its little cardboard drum to the pin in the beam above. It was always black with flies, but although I watched for what seemed hours, I never saw a fly actually set foot on the thing.'

ROSES ROUND THE DOOR

'Things were so different when I was young. I was born in a house on a farm at Guestling. It was along a track from the village. The farmhouse was thatched and had roses round the door. My father had a large kitchen garden and orchard. The house was very warm in the winter and cool in the summer.

In the kitchen stood a large black range, where all the cooking was done. The range was bricked in and along the side my mother would keep her lighting wood to dry. It was always handy to light the fire in the morning for an early cup of tea. Sometimes baby pigs or small chicks would be put in a box to warm by the fire. The range would have to be blackened each week, and Mother would sweep the flues of soot each day. There was always a risk of fire. Across the large chimney was a beam where in time gone by people would hang their bacon on the large hooks in the chimney to dry. During the war we also used this method and bacon kept very well. In the wall beside the range was a brick oven. My mother once tried to heat it by lighting a wood faggot, only to our dismay the kitchen filled with smoke, so after this we would store green tomatoes in it as they soon ripened in the dark.

Washday was a very busy time. On the Saturday all the wood for the boiler would have to be collected and put in the washhouse and the copper filled. This had to be finished on Saturday. In the corner of the washhouse was a large boiler, and on the top of the chimney was a cowl, which had to be turned to make sure the wind did not blow into it as the fire would not burn.

My father would come in to the house after milking for his breakfast. If my mother was short of bread she would hurriedly make some soda scones. They were lovely hot from the oven. We never bought jam as it was always home-made. We had lots of bottled fruit and tomatoes.

Once the house needed thatching and my father took the horse and cart to the reedbeds on the estate and brought back a load of reeds. Next day Mr Beeching the estate thatcher came to thatch it.

The lighting in the house was by oil lamp and candles. Later we had an Aladdin oil lamp. This gave a better light but if there was a draught the mantle would blacken with soot. We would have to sprinkle salt on it to clear or the mantle would collapse. It was always up to bed with a candle. If I was out late dancing or to a meeting my mother would put a candle in the window so I would have a light home. We had to be very careful in case there was a fire. A thatched roof would burn very quickly. In the wartime we were afraid the incendiary bombs would catch the house or corn stacks alight, so we always had buckets of water handy.'

VILLAGE WOMEN

'Nearly all the village women at Bishopstone in the 1930s cooked on a coal fired kitchen range. They made everything from bread to wine. Bowls of milk, left overnight covered with muslin, had the cream removed next morning to make butter. There were large larders with plenty of storage space for bottled fruit, pickles and jam. All the surplus eggs from the chickens that everybody kept, were put down in a crock full of waterglass to preserve them for the winter. All this came from the well kept gardens. Back gardens had fruit bushes and trees and plentiful supplies of vegetables.

Kitchen doors in those days were never locked. A roundsman called once a week with groceries. He let himself in, put the box on the kitchen table, picked up the money and next week's order and left. There were deliveries twice a week by the butcher's boy on his bicycle and the baker if needed. The village shop sold everything from elastic, sweets and cheese to paraffin and candles.'

MEMORIES OF HOME

'When I married in 1958 we rented a two-bed semi at Rotherfield for five years. There was a small kitchen, toilet, dining room, larder (for food), sitting room and two bedrooms. There was no bathroom or airing cupboard or central heating. I didn't have a washing machine, fridge, freezer, hoover, television, telephone or car but we were happy.

I had a copper to boil the "whites" which then went through the mangle, were rinsed by hand and mangled again. *Everything* was ironed to aid airing which was achieved on a wooden clothes-horse in front of the open fire. We filled a tin bath for the weekly bath in front of the fire. A broom, dustpan and brush for cleaning – from the inner corner towards the door, as taught at Brownies and Guides, after emptying the ashes and lighting the fire. To begin with I used firelighters (paraffin soaked pads) and wood but later we invested in a gas poker.

We only had carpet in the sitting room (a square surrounded by stained floor boards) and narrow carpet down the centre of the stairs. Elsewhere there was linoleum and rugs which we had made during our engagement. There could be ice on the inside of windows – no double glazing!

I shopped in the village. We all used to knit a lot in those days and would be knitting on buses and trains, going to school and work, and up the rec etc in any spare moment. One would need help to wind the wool from the skeins or use a chair as makeshift. My only leisure was Young Wives Group meetings once a month until the Rotherfield Evening WI was formed in 1965.

Unfortunately my children had to leave the village because of the cost of housing. Village life will never be the same again because villages always consisted of generations of the same families. They all got involved in the local activities and helped one another. We were able to go to the shop and leave the doors unlocked, windows open and baby in the pram in the front garden.'

TIED COTTAGE

'We got married in October 1947 and our first home was a tied cottage at Lions Green, near Horam.

We had a kitchen which had a black kitchen range and a shallow sink. The only furniture we had in it was a deal top table and two chairs, which cost ten shillings. We had a pantry which also had a brick floor and three shelves along one wall.

In the living room we had a brick floor and a tile fireplace. We were given a settee and paid 30 shillings for an oak table with four chairs and a wooden tea trolley, and we saved for nine months to buy a wireless which cost ten shillings.

We had three bedrooms, two which we didn't furnish because we could not afford it. In our bedroom we had lino on the floor, a mahogany bed which we bought in Bracketts sale rooms in Tunbridge Wells for £25, and a dressing table and a chest of drawers from friends of my mother for £4 10s.

We only had cold water to the sink in the kitchen. We had a washhouse outside with cold water and an old copper; three families used this on the first three days of the week. Our toilet was a bucket at the top of the garden.

We had no car and if we wanted to catch a bus we had to walk to Waldron or Horam.'

KEY MONEY

'I first came to East Sussex the year I married, in 1949. My husband and I paid "key money" for our flat. Although partly furnished, this was a recognised thing to do in those days.

As you walked in the huge front door you were greeted with brown wallpaper and brown lino, which led to an equally dark and dismal dining room. The kitchen was a hideous green, and there was a black cooker. The first thing you saw as you went up the creaking staircase was the brass rods which held the stair lino in place. At the

The Co-op provided many of our everyday needs, including furnishings – and there was the 'divi' to look forward to.

top of the stairs was a huge bathroom, with the most frightening geyser above the bath. When you lit it, it seemed to almost blow you out of the bathroom. Further along from the bathroom and up three more stairs lay two big bedrooms, which were surprisingly pleasant and nicely furnished.

Our flat was on the boundary of Hove and Portslade. If you lived on the Hove side of the road, you always said that it was Boundary Road. The other side of the road however was called Station Road, and still is to this day.

This was, and still is a very busy road, with every shop available. In those days there was Greenfields the greengrocer's, World Stores, Liptons, Sainsbury's and Dewhurst the butcher's.

Rationing was still in force at that time, but you could buy cracked eggs, broken biscuits, tit-bits from the butchers and all for a few pence. This not only helped your menu, but also your budget. Wages were very low, but we lived accordingly. On pay day, you would put away the milk money, insurance money, gas and electric, along with the rent money. Each would be in its own jam jar, and no one dared touch it.'

LIGHT AND WATER

The lack of basic 'mod cons' is what we remember most vividly about home life in the past – only oil or gas lamps or candles for lighting, the kitchen range or the fire for cooking, the well or the pump for water, and the 'little house' at the bottom of the garden. Getting the water was a particular chore each day – especially on washday!

GATE COURT

'The origins of Gate Court, Northiam can be traced back as far as 1235. This house is said to be the only house in Northiam to be used continuously as a farmhouse since these early times. In 1919 Capt A. R. J. Cyster, later to become my husband, bought the farm. The farmhouse had nine bedrooms and numerous attics along with four oast houses and several outbuildings.

I went to live at Gate Court as a young bride. In those days there were no taps for running water. We had two hand pumps, one for cold water and one for pumping the water upstairs. We also had a rain butt in the scullery and I used to heat the water from this butt every morning for my husband to shave with. Also in the scullery was a copper which had to be filled with water and heated by placing lighted faggots under it.

Washing was done by hand in an outside shed where there were two coppers. One was used for boiling the washing, the other was used for cooking the pig food. The charlady came for three hours a day and she was paid threepence a day and fourpence on Mondays, which was washday.

Cooking was done on an oil stove which had three burners. The oven was a separate item and it had handles fitted on both sides so that you could lift it on and off the stove. The oven was placed on two of the burners, leaving just one burner for the saucepans.

The only means of lighting was by oil lamps and candles, and my first baby was born by candlelight. In the summer of 1934 electricity was brought to the oast houses where it was used to dry the hops. In October 1934 electricity was laid on to the farmhouse. Luxury!'

A NIGHTMARE

'Our semi-detached house at Eastbourne had three floors and a cellar. Tradesmen always came round the back. There was a painted front door and always a canvas striped curtain over it in summer to prevent the paint blistering. Our lighting, heating and cooking was all by gas. Lights were nerve racking. You had to hold the match to the mantle and then the gas gave a pop. If you poked the match through the mantle you were in trouble as they were not cheap to replace, but oh so flimsy. Heating the bath water was a nightmare. There was a large copper geyser above one end of the bath and a kind of tray swung out which contained several gas jets. So you lit your match or better still a taper, switched on and whoosh! bang! she went. Then you swung the tray back and waited a bit for the water to heat.

Our very long, cold passages were also very dark. We had the gas fire on during meals in the dining room only and a coal fire in the evening to sit by. There was no heat in the bedrooms but hot water bottles every night. We slept in bedsocks and had a special vest under our nighties too in the winter.

Curtains were always changed to white in the summer and then back to velvet or whatever in the winter.'

GETTING A TAN!

'Our home had no electricity, gas, mains drainage nor mains water. That was during my childhood in Chiddingly, in the 1920s and 1930s.

We had paraffin lamps for lighting. Some were single ones with a glass mantle and a brass plate behind to reflect the light. In the sitting room we had Tilley lamps that had to be pumped up to make them shine brightly and, best of all, there was a ceiling lamp having four lights with a yellow silk "skirt" around them. Occasionally we used candles and often night-lights in the bedroom. What a lovely flickering light all these gave.

We had a coke boiler in the corner of the kitchen to give us hot water. Coal and/or log fires in the rooms were always welcoming and made me look forward to winter evenings, singing round the piano, playing board games, sewing, knitting, painting, playing with my dolls and dolls' house, using Plasticine and Glitter Wax, reading and talking. Looking back, I think it was a blessing not to have television and videos. The beds were warmed with hot water bottles of stone or, later, rubber.

Cooking was done on a big paraffin stove with a detachable metal oven for baking. Throughout the house we had Valor Perfection paraffin stoves which shone intriguing patterns on the ceiling. Irons were made of iron (!) and were heated on the stove. In the early 1930s ours was one of the first houses to have a coke-fired Aga, which I believe was imported from Sweden. With it came flat-bottomed saucepans and a cast-iron casserole, which I still use. About this time, too, we started to make our own electricity with a Petter engine which ran, very noisily, for two hours every day to top up the accumulators.

There was another Petter engine in the well-house, which every day pumped water from the well to the tank and thus to the house. In very dry summers, we would run out of water and have to buy water from Hailsham at a farthing a gallon. Before running out, the water was a bright rust colour and I remember emerging from the bath with a tanned skin and auburn hair.'

THE CHANTRY

'In the late 1920s we rented the Chantry at Wilmington for ten shillings a week. It was two cottages then, very pretty from the outside with its thatched roof and lattice windows, but a little cramped inside for three adults, two children, a large dog and two cats. There were none of the mod cons thought essential today, and just everyday chores kept my mother busy – lamps had to be cleaned and filled, all our water had to be drawn from the well we shared with our neighbours, and then of course there was the chemical closet, situated behind a curtain off the kitchen, which had to be emptied regularly. No wonder our garden was productive – cesspits had been dug in the vegetable area for generations. A bath was an event; the tin hip bath was brought in to stand in front of the Valor cooker and I'm quite sure we all used the same water, although my early memories are of standing in the stone sink washing down with freezing water.'

HARDLY LABOUR SAVING

'Our house in the 1920s at Hurst Green was hardly labour saving. There was no electricity till 1928. Candles and oil lamps were used and cooking was done on a coal burning stove, that had to be continually stoked. The flues were brushed once a week, with a long handled brush and the sweep came once a year. There was great excitement to see his brush appear at the top of the chimney. Several houses in Hurst Green had been wired for electricity some time before being connected to the mains. On my way home from school one day, when I saw the electric lights full on in the butcher's shop, I couldn't get home quickly enough to see what ours looked like.

Running water, cold only, wasn't available till about 1930. Prior to that, drinking water was obtained from a well in the garden, which was used by the eight houses in our terrace. It had a big wheel which had to be turned and water ran into a bucket held under a spout. The water stood in the scullery, uncovered, and was baled out with a jug when needed. This would be considered unhygienic today, but no one suffered any ill effects. Rain water, for washing and for laundry, was obtained from a pump, near the back door.

Before the days of washing machines, laundry work was hard. The clothes were scrubbed in the sink, on a washboard, then boiled in the copper, which had a fire under it. Next came the wringing of clothes in the mangle, a large, cumbersome object which had a wheel and two rollers. When putting sheets through they had to be held at one end, or they dragged on the floor. Even though a bucket was in place to catch the water, the floor was always wet under the mangle. Then everything was pegged, damp, on the clothes line in the garden. If it was not a good drying day it had to be finished off indoors.'

FROM THE WELL

'At our Victorian farmhouse in Staplecross our water came from a well and was drawn up by a chain on a roller. If you let go of the handle the bucket fell back down the well and you had to get it out with a grabhook. In a dry summer when the well ran dry, water had to be fetched from a spring down a field using a yoke and two pails. The toilet was in a brick building at the bottom of the garden. It was a cesspit or earth lavatory with a long wooden seat which had one large and one small hole in it. The cesspit had lime put in it and was emptied once a year. For lighting we had oil lamps and candles. We had two cellars, in one we stored coal and in the other, butter, eggs and food.'

'Water for our cottage at Dallington was drawn from the well, great big yellow slugs slithering round the top but beautiful cold water.'

'I was married in 1929 and clearly recall a tragedy that happened at Alfriston the same year. A couple and their three year old daughter were near where the new council houses were being built when the child slipped through the cover of a well. It took some time to open the cover and rescue her. She was still alive and was taken to my mother's house. Fortunately my mother had a fire going and some warm water and the child was put into a bath of warm water before being taken to hospital, but she died three days later.

Mains water did not come to Alfriston until 1935, and many gardens still have a covered well in their gardens.'

LAMPLIGHT

'Twilight brought a refreshing peace after the toil of a busy day; then would follow the ritual of lighting the oil lamp.

The tall, slender, elegant brass lamp with its crimson globe would be carefully lifted from its place on the sideboard and brought to the centre of the dining table. The pretty globe would be removed, then the chimney removed from the lacy brass edging and laid gently on the chenille tablecloth. Small knobs at the side of the lamp were turned to raise the wick, the match struck to ignite the wick and the flame adjusted to the light required; again, with loving care the chimney and crimson globe were replaced and a warm glow filled the immediate area, while the furniture round the walls was lost in soft shadows.

The lamplight glowed on the faces of the family gathered together round its magic light to enjoy their hobbies and interests together.'

THE KITCHEN WAS A BUSY PLACE

'We had no electric light at Westfield, or mains water supply. Father used to go to the cottage next door every morning, and get four large buckets of water from the well in the old gentleman's garden. We accompanied him often, but were never allowed to go on our own, or draw the water. There was a pump in the scullery, with a long handle which, when worked up and down, brought water from the spout into a bucket or bowl. That was for washing us, the clothes, flushing the toilet, scrubbing down etc. The well water was for drinking. We had an indoor toilet, and a cesspool somewhere in the garden, which was emptied regularly by the "authorities".

For lighting, we had oil lamps, which Mother tended with professional ability. One was in the centre of the table, for writing or playing table games. It had a tall glass funnel which sometimes became blackened with sooty fumes. Mother always came to the rescue, trimmed the wick, and restored the light. Bedtime found us climbing the stairs, candle in one hand and, in the winter, a stone "ginger beer" bottle in the other. The bottle was our hot water bottle, warming our toes until we went to sleep. We usually undressed downstairs by the fire, as there was no heat in the bedrooms, even in the coldest weather.

The kitchen was always a busy place. The stove was there, called a kitchener, with an oven for baking, the top for heating kettles, saucepans, the flat iron etc, and a grill at the front which when opened up glowed with warmth and comfort on cold days. Another memory of the warm kitchen was of when the baby chicks were hatched. Mother had an old brown shopping basket, which she lined with warm flannel and in it placed any weak baby chicks until they became strong enough to return to the mother hen. To us, as children, it was a delight to watch these wet, weak, skinny morsels gradually return to life.'

WATERY MEMORIES

'There was no running water into the house, and it fell to me as one of my chores to pump water, morning and evening, into the tank in the roof space. This water supply emptied into the copper in the bathroom, and water for the kitchen and for the washstands in the bedrooms had to be carried from this source. Saturday was for us, as for many, the only bath night. On that day, my mother would heat the copper twice and we each took our baths, youngest first, and so on. Each person added a little more hot water: one cannot but envy the one who bathed first!

Water had also to be carried into the shed where my mother did the family washing, on a Monday. It was a job that took up the entire day even with the help of a neighbour. I have a clear memory of my mother having no time for us at all and of dinner being only cold meat, mashed potatoes and apple pie. The washing went through a very precise procedure. Water was carried through to fill the boiler which stood in the corner of the shed, heated by the fire underneath, and filled the galvanized baths for the rinses. After the first two rinses, the linens were rinsed in the blue, final rinse and then put through the mangle.

Not only do we take water for granted in the home, but we also expect its availability for our leisure. Today, the conscientious mother enrols her children for swimming lessons, having no doubt already taken them to the pool since toddlerhood. My introduction to swimming was at the end of a rope, in the river Cuckmere. When the warm weather arrived, our teacher would take the top class, boys and girls aged ten upwards, by bus to Shermans Bridge. We would walk along the river bank to the locks where some of those already confident in swimming would dive in. The rest of us would take it in turns to be belted up with a strip of strong canvas, much like a horse harness, which was attached to a strong rope. Thus secured, we would wade out, to be hauled in by our teacher whilst we went through the motions of "swimming". Squelching through the mud at the bank assured us of a safe return. It seems unbelievable, but I can swim and I must have learnt to do so in that harness and rope in the 1940s. The safety of the river is borne out by memories of playing with fresh water mussels at Arlington. I dare not believe that they are there now, and I would hardly dare suggest that young children wade in as we did, to find them.'

IN THE TUB

'In our farmhouse at Kingston in the 1920s and up to the war, bathing was in a tin tub until my parents had a free-standing iron bath installed in the kitchen. It was covered by a wooden lid. Every Saturday evening the copper in the outside washhouse was lit to provide the hot water. My father brought this in by the bucketful. I bathed first, then, after a top up of more hot water, my mother and finally, after another top up, my father. It was lucky that I was an only child!

The bath was emptied by a siphoning system, using a hose pipe. It was only after the war that a proper bathroom was provided. Until the mid-1920s, when mains water was introduced, all the water came from wells and rainwater butts.

Our lavatory was "up the garden" – a specially built brick edifice with a wooden seat and a large galvanised bucket whose contents were buried in the garden, usually weekly. Newspapers were often cut into squares for use as toilet paper – soft tissue paper was a luxury! I used to envy a relative's loo because the seat had a small hole and a big hole – one for the children and one for the adults.

Electricity came to the village in the mid-1930s. Until then oil lamps and candles were the norm. I remember some retired ladies, who had bought one of the old cottages, petitioning the authorities against the use of the electricity pylons over the downs.'

WE KEPT EACH OTHER WARM

'The stove at home in our cottage at Nutley, the warmer of hearth and cooker of meals, was black, and had an array of kettles on it. Apart from this fire the children kept each other warm, there being so many of them. Fires were not allowed in bedrooms except in cases of illness, and personal washing was a strip down affair with a jug and bowl, apart from bath nights.

Saturday night was bath night. The fire was made up and warm towels would be laid on Dad's lap. The bath was placed in front of the fire and into it would go the children to be cleaned and scrubbed by Mum, then hoisted out to be plumped onto Dad's lap and cuddled into the warm towelling.'

INTO THE 1950s

'From 1946 to 1955 I lived in a house at Northiam that had been built in the 1930s in the middle of a field. There was no mains water available so the house was constructed in such a way that all rainwater drained into an underground tank. From there it was hand-pumped up to the kitchen sink. In 1946 a bathroom and flush toilets were put in. This put a strain on the water supply and the tank was in danger sometimes of running dry, but the local fire brigade would come and fill it up for us.'

'When I moved to Eastbourne in 1953 we bought a three bedroomed terraced house for £1,000, the deposit being £250. Conveyance fees were £36 and our mortgage was £5 a month. There was no bathroom, only one cold water tap and an outside toilet, but we had a big stone copper under which I lit a fire to boil water for clothes and nappies and to heat water for a tin bath for the children. Adults went to the slipper baths at Motcombe once a week. I think these cost one shilling later on, when the girls were bigger and we shared. It was early 1960 before we converted one of the bedrooms to a bathroom and toilet and to a hot water system with the aid of a government grant. Bliss!'

FOOD, SHOPPING AND CALLERS
TO THE DOOR

Our diet was restricted but wholesome, and home-cooked! Village shops provided most day to day essentials, and tradesmen were regular callers to the door with everything from milk and meat to muffins.

PLENTY OF FRESH MILK AND CREAM

'My home was on the Forest at Nutley, near to my grandmother at Lavender Cottage. My parents were virtually self sufficient, having enough ground to grow vegetables for the year round, and also had the benefit of owning a cow, hens and pigs. The cow had a bell round her neck so that she could be located as she grazed on the Forest, and was naturally called Bluebell. There was always plenty of fresh milk and cream and the butter churn was always in action. My mother coped expertly with all this husbandry. When the pig was killed, joints of meat were hung in the chimney for future use.'

WE HAD NOTHING

'There were times when I was young and living in Hove that we had nothing, but were happy. Saturday mornings we queued for yesterday's bread at Gigins in Franklyn Road, Portslade with our frails (straw shopping bags) – sixpence for bread and if very lucky, threepence for cakes. Then there was food at St Richard's church hall in Egmont Road: soup taken home in a jug and rice pudding, all free. Some days there was even jam roll.

But there were Saturday morning pictures too, and the butter for tea and the smell of bacon sizzling in the kitchen on a cold winter's afternoon. I can smell it now.'

ALWAYS ENOUGH TO EAT

'Well, we always had enough to eat and as we had an allotment we had a plentiful supply of fresh fruit and vegetables at all times. Just a few minutes' walk away from my home at Lewes were quite a variety of shops – a grocer's shop, fish and chip shop, butcher's, con-

Annie Jones the milkmaid, delivering in Barcombe Mills in 1916.

fectioner's, greengrocer (who was a distant cousin of my mother), these at least remain in my memory. Milk was delivered by Mr Leney with a lovely hand-pulled trolley, complete with shiny brass churns and measures, from which he dispensed the requested amount. A greengrocer's horse and cart would come to the street once a week. On Sundays a trader would travel up the back entrances to the houses with shellfish, watercress or muffins according to the season – all remarkably fresh. Foods like beef and chicken and turkey were only really used for special occasions, unlike today, and I remember the lovely smell of jellies made for parties – with all having a stir – or with the Christmas preparations. The cake was taken to St Anne's Bakery for cooking.'

THE VILLAGE SHOP

'The village shop in Kingston sold most things for daily use. Milk, bread, groceries and meat could be ordered from shops in Lewes and delivered to your door and most people gave weekly orders because few villagers had a telephone. The shop was also the post office and a great place for getting to know what was going on in the village! It might have been termed gossip, but it meant that anyone who was in trouble would get help from their neighbours. For many years it was run by the splendid Mrs Parker but she did, until the war, have a rival – Mrs Bunce. This lady sold confectionery from the pantry of her cottage.'

'In 1913 I was born at the shop and post office in Ashurst Wood, which my parents built. Deliveries to the shop were made by big waggons drawn by shire horses which were backed up to the cellar steps. I remember the attention and excitement at the first motor vehicle Ashurst Wood saw. Mr Lacroix, a salesman from Brighton, drove a bull-nosed Morris to our shop in the late 1920s and it was much admired.

The shop served the whole village, selling coal, paraffin, groceries, ladies' clothes and shoes, men's working trousers and hobnail boots etc. It used to stay open late, sometimes until 11 pm.'

REMEMBER SAINSBURY'S?

'Can you remember Sainsbury's shops before they became supermarkets? In my mind's eye I can see the wide, white marble topped counters running both sides of the long, high-ceilinged shop, always bright and airy with a cool mosaic floor. At the far end would be the glossy wooden fronted cubicle where the cashier looked out along the length of the shop, with the ever present clock above her window.

Sainsbury's always had that indefinable but always recognisable clean and wholesome smell. There was the fascination of watching the skill of the assistant cutting out butter from huge blocks at the rear, labelled "unsalted" and "salted", deftly shaping them into neat blocks with butter pats to whatever weight the customer required, slapping them on to rectangles of greased paper, weighing them on scales with brass weights and tidily and swiftly wrapping each one.

Do you recall the blue bags of sugar, again neatly folded at the top, the cheese cut by wire on a wooden slab, bowls of pink salmon paste and of meat paste with hard yellow crusts of melted butter – again the customer could have any amount she chose – and biscuits sold loose from large square tins?

There were also strategically placed tall stools on which a tired mother could rest or where a small child could be perched to see what was going on in this exciting adult world.

There were no domestic deep freezers in those days. The frozen Christmas turkey was ordered in advance and collected several days before it was needed. It was packed in a well designed cardboard box in a nest of blue paper. The box could be opened to display the contents and refastened, requiring no string or sticky tape and it had a convenient integral carrying handle.'

CALLING FOR ORDERS

'The milkman who called at Toronto Terrace, Lewes had a cart which held a container from which he filled two large cans and brought to the door. There he measured out the milk into jugs using half or one pint measures which hung inside the cans. On Saturdays a man came pushing a barrow carrying shrimps and winkles freshly caught for our tea. An old man, Dicky Balcombe, had an allotment and he called round with fruit and vegetables in two canvas bags, a penny for a bag of gooseberries or apples, twopence for blackcurrants or pears.

Money was scarce, my Dad earned about £2 a week, so Mum paid into clothing clubs each week to buy shoes etc. There was also a club of 20 members who paid one shilling a week for 20 weeks. A number was allocated to each member, so if you drew number one you had £1 worth of goods in the first week, if number five the fifth week etc. We bought sheets and blankets this way. I took empty jam jars back to the grocer, and was paid a halfpenny for one pound and a penny for two pound jars. Sweets were twopence a quarter, so a halfpenny bought a lot.'

'In the 1930s, in the mackerel and herring season, the fishermen used to wheel a long flat handcart around the streets of Seaford selling fish. In winter the muffin man could be heard ringing his bell and shouting his wares as he too came round the streets.'

'During the 1930s in the village of Mountfield most of our food was delivered to the door. The milk came from the farm in a can with a pint measure and was put into a jug. Meat was delivered by an errand boy from Battle on a bicycle, bread was delivered from Wicks' bakery in the village and if we ran short we could knock on the bakehouse door, and they would cook a cake for customers in the bread oven if it was mixed and in the tin ready, which often saved lighting the kitchen range during the summer.

Allworks of Battle sent their representative for orders once a week and the errand boy delivered at the weekend until they had a delivery van. At this time the post office was moved from a house near the church to R. N. French's shop at Hoath Hill where they had a radio and electrical shop with some groceries at the back.

Towards the end of my time in the village a reliable bus service started and came from Gillingham via Mountfield to Hastings, but villagers still used the train a lot; I think it was cheaper in those days.

A Mr Ripley who lived in Beckley used to do a greengrocery round in the villages and came to us on Saturday afternoons. He had nine children and usually brought some of them with him, and they would run ahead to tell us he was coming. They walked from Beckley and Father pushed the fruit on a handcart and carried it in a large Sussex trug round the houses. When the cart was empty he pushed the children home. All the family lived on the proceeds. My mother always gave them tea and cakes to refresh them.'

'Housekeeping was very different at the time of the First World War. All the tradesmen called at our house in Eastbourne – the butcher with meat on a wooden tray which he carried on his shoulder; the milkman with a hand-pulled cart holding large churns from which he measured out your requirements. He came twice a day, at about 6 am and again later in the morning (there was no refrigeration to keep milk fresh). The grocer called at the beginning of the week for an order which he delivered at the end of the week. The baker came every day in a horse-drawn van. The horse knew the way and would go a few steps and wait until it was told to move on.

When fish was plentiful it was taken round the streets on a cart and the man called out his wares – twelve herrings a shilling. The coalman came once a year, delivering from a horse-drawn cart in hundredweight sacks. We used to count the bags in. Other annual callers were gypsies with baskets of clothes pegs and lace, and the onion man with strings of onions.'

'About 1922, I remember the muffin man who came round on Sunday afternoons. He rang a bell as he came along the streets of Patcham, and on his head he balanced a large tray of muffins. The tray was covered with a green baize cloth.'

AT THE BACK DOOR

'Several people called at the back door at Hurst Green. At about 5 pm every day, Mr Clarence Croft, the milkman, came with his shining brass cans and ladles to measure the milk into the jugs, which had been put out for him. The baker also came, with a round basket containing loaves. The grocer called for orders and sellers of fruit, fish (including shrimps on Sundays), and muffins, were regular callers. In the 1920s, ex-soldiers came with their baskets of tapes, buttons, mending wools etc for sale.

The tramps, or "gentlemen of the road", were frequent visitors with their cans, in which they asked for boiling water, and sometimes tea, milk and sugar to be put. It was said they knew from which houses they would receive help and marked them accordingly. My mother always gave them something. Just before Christmas one year, a tramp called. She had taken some mince pies out of the oven and put two in a bag for him. After he had gone for some time, she discovered she had only given him the tops. The bottoms, containing the mincemeat, were still in the tin. He must have been disappointed!'

FROM THE CRADLE TO THE GRAVE

We were more likely to be born, to suffer our illnesses and to die in our own homes in the past. Before the National Health Service the doctor's services had to be paid for and many families relied on home cures for basic health care. Scarlet fever and diphtheria were the scourges of childhood for many years, and a stay in the isolation hospital was a frightening ordeal for many children.

HOME CURES

'Sunday was "keep us regular" day and there would be a dose of Epsom salts for each of us – and then a fancy cake to take the taste away.'

'I used to suffer a lot with headaches. My grandmother's cure was to lay me on the settle (a long sort of chair with a slatted wooden back) and place strips of brown paper, soaked in vinegar, on my forehead. She would close the curtains and after a while I usually fell asleep. As the pain nearly always went away, I guess you could call that a cure.'

'Our family tips in the 1930s included for preserving good sight "look long distances", and to aid posture "never sit or stand like a sack of potatoes"! Medicinal tips were to mince prunes, figs and seedless raisins and take a spoonful daily (for obvious reasons); in wet or cold weather to place a good thickness of newspaper across one's kidneys to protect them (this my father did religiously); at the first sign of a sore throat gargle with salt and water three times a day; and eat slowly by chewing food and counting to 30 before swallowing. We all seemed healthy!'

'Saturday night was bath night. After the bath, in winter, Russian Tallow would be rubbed on our young chests and backs. This was a salve resembling the later Vick, and helped keep off coughs and colds. Other dosages were of ipecacuanha wine, senna pods, syrup of figs and the dreaded sulphur and treacle; all had a job to do and the results seem to have justified their use.

There was regular drill with the nit combs, intended to eliminate the possibility of fleas in our hair by eradicating any eggs. A white sheet was laid down, and the combs used over them.'

THE YELLOW PERIL

'When war broke out in 1939 I took over my cousin's bungalow in Newlands Avenue, Bexhill, and stayed there till France fell, with my son, aged four years, my father and mother, mother in law and of course my husband (when he could get away from other duties). Each day I took John in his push chair down to the front or to Edgerton Park. On John's birthday his Dad had bought him a very nice little sailing boat. This we took with us to sail on the children's lake in the park.

One day an older child came along. He knew everything and wanted to show John how to sail the boat. Somehow or another John got the worst of it and was pushed into the lake. Exit older boy.

I fished John out of the lake, took him round to the motor show-room in Sackville Road and asked if someone could take us home. By this time John was in a proper mess. Certainly, I was told, so off we went in a car. On arrival my mother said he ought to have a mustard bath.

Now, I had never given anyone a mustard bath and neither had my mother. So I prepared the bath and, being very generous, put half a small tin of mustard in. Then I dried John and put him to bed with a hot drink and half an aspirin. To my horror, next morning I found that John's skin had turned yellow and it was some days before it got back to normal. But he didn't suffer any ill effects and he still remembers the day he turned yellow.'

FIRST AID

'My grandfather was a railway signalman, and in charge of first aid. One night a platelayer stepped off the train in the dark, beyond the end of the platform, and straight over the bridge, breaking both legs. Grandad bound the legs in splints, laid the man on the carriage seat and sent him to hospital in London by train. The doctor there was so impressed by the first aid that he refused to touch the legs, and the man eventually recovered with just Grandad's ministrations. He lived to be a good old age, and walked without the aid of sticks for the rest of his life, although he did take short strides.'

THE DOCTOR

'In the 1920s at Laughton the doctor came round on set days in a pony and trap and you put a flag out if you wished him to call. The nursing association was paid by subscription. There were two slate clubs run by the Roebuck and Hall. One received ten shillings a week in illness and any money left over in the club was shared out at Christmas.'

'As there was no health service up to 1914, homely remedies were used where possible. For earache, a small onion was made hot and inserted in the ear. I have had this at times. When I was stung by a wasp in the hop-garden, on the only day my aunt did not bring an onion for this, I was promptly given a mud plaster on the spot.

Here at Rye we had two surgeries and the one most of the working folk went to charged only two shillings a bottle of medicine, the other sixpence more. The doctor who charged less was Dr J. Harratt and I have quoted his name because he is still remembered with the greatest affection by us all, who were treated by him. He was a great doctor, full of compassion for poor people and so kind to children. In *Memories of a Village*, a copy of which is in Lewes Museum, we quote an instance of where he wrapped a £1 note round a medicine bottle, which the man only found when he got home. He knew the money was needed more than the medicine. I have a friend, who is now better placed than when she was a child in a large family, and this kind doctor sent them a dinner on occasions. Whilst Dad only earned a nominal wage, my mother, due to good management, said many times, "Well, we haven't got a lot, but we have always managed to find a doctor's bill."

This same splendid doctor was also responsible for the workhouse, the little isolation hospital and was a coroner and, whilst he did eventually have a car, he was a familiar figure, walking our streets, always beautifully tailored. He never failed to come at once, when sent for.'

'I arrived in Alfriston in 1946 with my husband, who was to be the new doctor. We moved into the house of the retiring doctor, a very old house in the High Street called The Farmhouse. I had previously lived in a modern flat and was appalled to find that the only toilet was an Elsan by the back door. The consulting room was the front room, there was no waiting room and the examination couch was in the back room. There was little privacy for the doctor's family!'

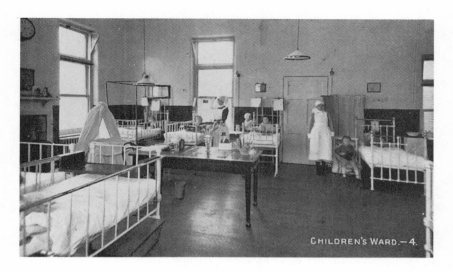

The children's ward at the Princess Alice Memorial Hospital, Eastbourne in the 1930s, spartan and unwelcoming in comparison to today's children's hospitals.

INTO ISOLATION

'We lived in Hove and my brother was sent to Foredown Hospital in the 1920s when he had scarlet fever. This was an isolation hospital and it was a good job that Mum and Dad were not allowed to visit, or they would have been as shocked as I was, when later I also was admitted with the fever, at the state of the place and the type of food we had to eat. The hygiene was awful, and there were earwigs in the porridge.'

AT THE DENTIST!

'My mother was a dental nurse for a Brighton based dentist between 1927 and 1940. She often told us children stories about things that took place during this period. One such story was how the gas that the dentists used had a strange effect on many of the patients.

Often, it seemed, their stomachs would swell, and after the dentist had finished each treatment it was Mother's job to sit on the patient's lap to expel the excess gas. Usually the patient never knew anything about it, but occasionally one would wake before she had finished.

On one such occasion a gentleman awoke early saying, "I've died and gone to Heaven." And tried kissing Mother. However he did admit to feeling very foolish when the gas had completely worn off and he realised what he had done.

Years later, in 1958 whilst travelling on a Brighton bound train with my sister, I noticed an elderly gentleman sitting quietly at the other end of our carriage. Throughout the journey he said nothing and didn't try to approach us, but as the train pulled in to Preston Park station he suddenly became very excited and insisted upon talking to us about how long it had been since he was last in the area. His fondest memory, he said, was of a visit to his local dentist! He described our mother perfectly and the story that he told was identical to the one she had told us all those years ago.'

BIRTH AND DEATH

'It was 1947 and I had come to Brighton to do my midwifery training. I was sent to an area where prefab bungalows had just been built. They had heating stoves, but unfortunately these were set flush into the wall and the only fuel they would burn was coke. It was an extremely cold winter and everything was in short supply. Before the coke arrived deep snow fell and then the lorry could not get round to deliver its precious fuel, so no one had a fire. Electricity was cut off each day from 8 am to 4 pm making it impossible to get hot water to bath the new born babies. The snow was so deep a bulldozer had to cut a path so that we could go and do our nursing. Before this had happened I missed the path and found myself up to my chest in snow. The telegraph wires were encased with ice, which became so heavy many had fallen down. I love to walk along the shore and on one occasion we found the sea had frozen as it reached land.

One day I was in a real panic because the supervisor who was a Queen's trained nurse decided to come and see that all the correct procedures were being carried out. Due to the lack of heat and water it was quite impossible to do this. One of the doctors lent me a pint size thermos flask so that I was able to bath the baby in warm water. The poor mother had to make do with cold. The mother had managed to produce one clean napkin, but our procedures demanded the use of six. When I had finished my demonstration I felt I was qualifying to be a magician not a midwife. Our one clean napkin had been whisked from place to place without the supervisor noticing what was happening.'

'When we moved to East Sussex in 1975 we found our neighbours most interesting as they had lived in the one village all their lives and their main occupation was farming.

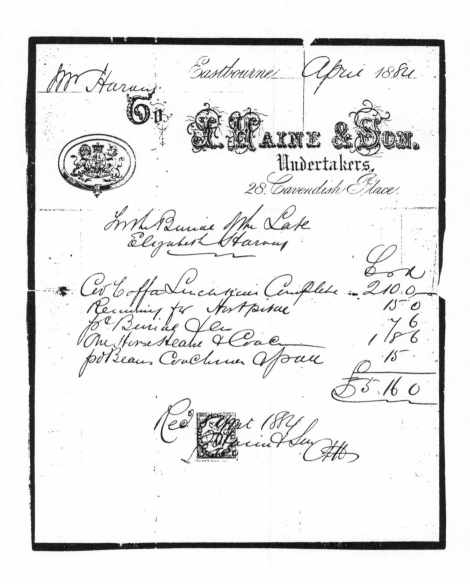

A bill for funeral expenses in Eastbourne – including £1 8s 6d for the 'horse hearse and coach'.

I spent hours with the gent after his wife died and he would often recall his early days working on the family farm. He would work from sunrise to sunset for a half-crown a week and their main diet was bread and cheese.

If you needed a doctor he would arrive on horseback, or if you went to his surgery your transport would be the horse and cart.

On Sundays they only did what was necessary and in retirement their Sunday was a day of rest. The chapel where they worshipped in their young days is now a private residence and the old tin church that was also in the village was pulled down soon after we arrived. When a local died the church was always full for the funeral, people coming from all around the country lanes and as my neighbour put it, they all met to pay their last respects to friends they had known a lifetime.'

CHILDHOOD &
SCHOOLDAYS

GROWING UP IN EAST SUSSEX

Long days of freedom marked our childhood in this beautiful county, though for many families times were hard and money scarce. We found pleasure in simple things and in a lifestyle that had hardly changed for generations.

GRANDAD'S STORIES

'My grandfather, who died in 1941, was in his eighties and I loved to listen to his stories and his songs about Sussex. He had been a shepherd on the downs above Southease between Newhaven and Lewes. He couldn't read or write and my grandmother, who had been to school, would read the newspaper to him every day. Like so many of her generation she wrote a beautiful copperplate and was a great reader. They used to say that I had always got my head in a book just like my granny and would urge me to go out and play with the other children, but I preferred to stay in and listen to the tales and the songs. To this day I can speak with a strong Sussex accent when recounting them but haven't a trace of it in my ordinary speech.

One of my favourites was of when Grandad was a little boy living in a house on the cliffs above Rottingdean which had a secret passage to the beach. Sometimes his mother would put him to bed early and tell him that whatever happened and no matter how much he wanted to look out of the window he must stay in bed with the blanket up to his ears and if, in the morning, when he got up there was a stranger in the kitchen he was to be very quiet and on no account ask any questions. Smuggling, I suppose, was a normal fact of life in Sussex in those days.

But the stories I never tired of were the ones about the Mummers who would go round the village at Christmas visiting every house and usually getting a tankard of beer for their pains. My great grandfather was usually Father Christmas – the one first through the door, saying: "Here comes oi, old Feyther Christmas. Be oi welcome or be oi be'ant?" On one occasion Grandad, grown up by this time, was playing Little Tommy Tiptoes and was supposed to follow on with the words: "Here comes oi, little Tommy Tiptoes", but he had had rather a lot of beer at the previous house and had fallen out with his father about something. Anyway Great Grandfather goes into the house with the words: "Here comes oi, old Feyther Christmas. Be oi welcome or be oi be'ant?" when in rushes Grandad with a big stick, belays it round his father's head and says, "No you bliddy be'ant, feyther" and promptly passes out.

My grandad also bore a marked resemblance to Rudyard Kipling who lived in a house by the green at Rottingdean and sometimes he would sit at a table under a large tree in Kipling's garden in full view of anyone leaning on the gate, papers spread about and pen in hand. People would peer at the "great man" going about his work while Kipling himself would watch from a window.'

HAPPY DAYS IN HASTINGS

'We had a very happy childhood in Hastings in the early 1900s, not much money, but plenty of fun. We had lots of animals, including a cat called Tinker, a light tabby, who lived with us for 19 years and had 150 kittens and we got homes for them all! A rusty black rabbit called Pa who lived for years, came in the house and once escaped and was locked up in prison. We fetched him after school, the policeman opened the cell with an enormous key and there he was surrounded by carrots and cabbages not the least upset.

We loved the sea and there were various amusements to see on the parade. The Brighton Belle, a sailing boat that gave trips, was wound up the beach at the end of the day by a pony walking round a capstan. Then there was Biddy, the tub man, wearing a battered stove-pipe hat and earrings and twirling round in the tub till he fell out! A platform on wheels, where two blind men sat, one playing an upright piano and the other a violin. Artisans drawing wonderful pictures on the dry sand. There were no bathing machines so we carried our own bathing tent on our shoulders down the West Hill and on to the beach, joining other families. We wore awful cotton meridian bathing costumes that stretched more every time we wore them and my aunt wore black stockings as well! There was no transport up Castle Hill, so my mother pushed us up the hill in prams and carried up baskets of food for eleven of us. She shopped in the Old Fishmarket, where a Mrs Swain sat resplendent in an immaculate white apron and large black hat – herrings were 14 a shilling!'

A BLEAK TIME

'During the First World War my father was in the army, leaving in Willingdon his wife Alice with five young children. On 23rd November, 1918 Alice died in the terrible influenza epidemic.

I was nearly eleven years old and can remember vividly being in a taxi riding down Upperton Road which was hung with bunting and nobody told me why. My eldest brother was sent to my uncle who had Guys Bakery at Hampden Park and my eldest sister was sent to Winchelsea near Rye to an aunt who ran a hotel there. That left me, Bertha aged nine years and Bill, four years, to be cared for in the Cottage Home, Green Street, Eastbourne.

Maisie and Sylvia, taken at the beginning of the century in Hastings.

I shall never forget the bleak empty days there with my little brother crying for his mother and only me to comfort him. A big girl told us that Father Christmas did not come there but I did not believe her, and woke up on Christmas morning to find one little box on the foot of my bed. On examination it was a grey wooden jig-saw puzzle with no colour and no picture. I cried. Christmas Day at home was full of love and joy and fun and after church aunts and cousins came and all was merry.

The big girl told us that we had to go for a walk in twos along Victoria Drive before dinner unless you were not well, so I walked about with my mouth open to get toothache, but nothing happened and I had to go. Walking along Victoria Drive we could see Willingdon church in the distance and longed for Mother and home. Neighbours brought gifts for us later and these were shut away in a big cupboard.

On the Monday after Christmas I was sent to St Mary's girls' school. The teacher said, "Write a composition on Armistice Day." Composition was my favourite lesson but whatever was Armistice Day? So up went my hand, "Please Miss, what is it?" I was hauled out to the front of the class, and the teacher said, "Here's a girl who does not know what Armistice means." Then my friend, the same big girl, went to the teacher and whispered in her ear, obviously telling her about our tragedy, and I was gently told about Armistice Day.

We were in the Home from November until March. Poor little Billie pined for his mother. Bertha could not read and did not make friends and was very unhappy. I read to the little ones, cared for my brother and sister and prayed to go home and for Father to come back.

Then one afternoon we three were tidied up and taken into the lounge and there was Mother's sister Auntie Bertha come to measure Bertha and I for black and white check dresses and to tell us that Daddy was coming home and that she was going to look after us.

Could it be true? What was the matron saying – "You can take the little boy," she said, "he cries all the time, the younger girl is a bad tempered child, but the older one is useful. She reads to the children and is useful to me." I panicked. And then I heard Auntie say, "As soon as the house is ready they are all three coming home and will be there when their father comes home."

And so it was, we went back to the little house on the bank and how lovingly she cared for Alice's children.

For three years she was Father's housekeeper and then one Saturday night when she was washing our hair and bathing us, she said, "What would you say if Daddy was to marry again?" Silence. What did she mean? In a frightened voice I said, "Is he going to?" She said, "He might do." "I'll run away," I said and Bertha said, "And I am going with her." All the time she was twisting a ring round her finger. "Supposing," she said, "just supposing he married me?"

"Oh, Auntie, is he going to, is it true?" "Yes," she said, hugging all three of us. "I'm going to be your new mummy." On January 20th the next year they were married and Alice's children were loved and cherished once more.'

A PRETTY LITTLE VILLAGE

'I was born in the pretty little village of Brede, situated between Rye and Hastings in East Sussex, in late August 1919. I was the youngest of six children, four brothers and one sister.

Our little cottage, and it was little, was called Primrose Cottage. There was a long kitchen, a living room with chimney corners and a "duck's nest" (an open fire) to cook on, also a very large pantry. There were two bedrooms and an attic, and all that was for eight of us. I remember the pantry at Christmas, when the Christmas tree was hidden in there and I used to get up early on Christmas morning, lay flat on the floor, and look under the door to see the tree. There was a huge gap, so it was easy to see. What a delight! I can still remember that tree, little fat sugar mice and pigs, then the real candles which all had to be lit at the right time. Although there were six of us, what a lot of fun we had and many a clip or two as well.

The roads were not like today, one could always play hopscotch or tops on them. The boys used to have iron hoops and the girls wooden hoops. We had no fear of traffic. There was Mr Marshall who used to own Chitcombe, he had a large car and someone to drive him around. Then Mr Palmer had a taxi, Mr Albert Crouch had a van and also Mr Oliver, who was the local baker. These were the only cars I can remember in the village.

When I look back we had a very nice life at Primrose Cottage even though we had no electric light, and the "lavvy", as we used to call it then, was up a long path up the garden. All right in the summer evenings but not much in the winter.

When I was ten years old the cottage was condemned, and we were allotted a new council house on the Northiam Road, Broad Oak. There we had electric light and we all rushed around switching on the lights; what a thrill it all was. It was a much larger house with three bedrooms and a bathroom. No hot water but who cared, at least we had a bath. We also had a large living room and a kitchen.

I started school at the age of five years, very little and very frightened. I was picked out by the headmaster to show off my nice new shiny wellington boots. I was so scared I let out a loud howl, and all the children laughed. How humiliated I was. We walked a mile to school, then home for dinner, back again, and home after school had finished. That made four miles a day. Some children had longer journeys than ours but we all plodded on.

I remember the long sunny days, going haymaking with my mother, lying in the warm mown grass, shutting my eyes so fast and listening to the bees and all the other insects. I remember that so clearly. It always seemed to be sunny in those days.

Then there was hop picking. A lot of farms used to grow hops in the village. My mother went hop-tying, then later the time for picking came round. A lot of people came from the town. They lived in hopper huts which were really just a shed. They cooked on an open fire which the children used to make outside the hut. They always brought little pieces from home to make it more homely. We walked to the hop garden, older boys helping to carry the food and with the younger children. We used to have to be ready to start picking at 7 am so that meant a very early start.

Oh, the lovely tea out of the billy-cans, I can still taste it, and bread and cheese with hoppy stained hands, but so much hard work for the mothers. We never had sandwiches, but a cottage loaf which my mother used to cut with cheese or jam on it, and a large apple pie plus a bread pudding. We all sat on the hop-poles to eat our dinner, then one by one the children ran off to play. Then the voice of the foreman was heard, "All to work" and back we all went ready to start the picking again. They were lovely days. Hop picking used to last six weeks then but the joy really came when we had the money for picking the hops.

Off to Hastings we would go to get new shoes and other bits of clothes. I always had a red coat and bonnet; I did so hate red, but my father liked it, so red it had to be. I might add I don't buy anything red now. This is the only time I remember going to Hastings.

The Methodist church in the village always boasted a good Sunday school. I still have the Sunday school large brass bell which was given me by Miss Orlow Austen. Mr Edmund Austen was the superintendent when I was small and went to the Sunday school. There were the boys on the left and the girls on the right. It was in a hall quite near the chapel. All concerts and the PSA (Pleasant Sunday Afternoons, which we children turned into Please Stop Away) were held there. We also boasted a village band and this was led by Mr Albert Crouch, whose son and daughter played in it. All the entertainment was held in the village, and a lot of concerts we had. So

97

you see we didn't have to go far to be entertained. Later this hall was sold and is now two houses.

Have you ever seen a glow worm? They are little worms that glow in the dark, and they used to be on the banks up King Woodland Hill. My brothers used to collect them and put them in the peaks of their caps where they glowed away. It was a very pretty sight.

When I was 14 I left the village school and went to Rye to work as a scullery maid. I was paid £1 per month, and I cried for my mum every day, I was so homesick. I missed my brothers very much. It was not a happy period of my life. I stayed for a little while, then attempted other jobs, finally finishing up at the Village Stores at Broad Oak, where I stayed until I was married in September 1939, the beginning of the war. I think I had a very happy childhood, such lovely memories and it has been a privilege writing them down.'

THE SMELL OF WITCHHAZEL

'The smell of witchhazel always brings it all back to me. On a warm July Saturday we were off on a school botany outing. Botany is not a subject which enthrals me, but I never missed an outing if I could persuade my parents to agree to it.

We met at Hove railway station from where a busy little steam train chugged its way through allotments and fields and the smooth, south-facing slopes of the Downs to the tiny Dyke Halt at the end of the line. From there we trudged up to the top of the dyke. This is not the summit known as The Dyke overlooking Kipling's "dim, blue goodness of the Weald", this is *the* dyke, the one the Devil dug to try to let the sea into the Weald but was beaten by the cock-crow. It is very steep and narrow and as we descended in single file round the curve of the path the scent of thyme and other wild flowers filled the air and there was the tinkling sound of sheep-bells from some hidden flock. The grass was short and springy and scattered with rabbit droppings.

When we reached the bottom there was a small spring shaded by bushes and trees, and there we searched for botanical specimens under the guidance of the accompanying teacher. A picnic by the water followed and all too soon we started back, struggling in twos and threes, specimens carefully packed into our empty picnic bags; up the steep, chalky path to the far crest, and down to the little Halt where the train was quietly chuffing to itself as it waited. A blast on its steam hooter encouraged us to hasten over the last few yards.

The result of this idyllic downland walk for me, then as now, was a deal of puffing and blowing and quantities of perspiration dripping from my scarlet face. My parents were accustomed to this phenomenon but the young schoolmistress in charge on that far off day of delight was thoroughly alarmed. I was not permitted to make my own way home from Hove station but taken back to school, still flushed and sweaty, and gently bathed with cold water and cotton-wool soaked in witchhazel.

This was not one of the remedies to be found in my mother's bathroom cabinet, and so it was unfamiliar but effective and its scent has acted for 60 years as a trigger for happy memories of a summer day on the South Downs.'

A HAPPY EXPERIENCE

'Growing up in the small village of Hartfield was a very happy experience for me, the youngest of five children.

My earliest memories are of waking up on frosty mornings to icy windows and the prospect of washing in cold water from a can in the bathroom. Piped water came later.

Then off to school and the welcome of a huge log fire burning in the infants room. At break-time there would be milk to drink, with a straw, straight from the bottle, which had been warmed on the top of the radiator.

Winter evenings at home were usually spent round the big dining table, playing games, reading and drawing, by the light of the Aladdin oil lamp hanging from the ceiling. Then off to bed by candlelight and the comfort of a soft feather mattress.

Summers always seemed to be hot. Long sunny days were spent mostly roaming the woods and fields around the village, discovering birds' nests and wild flowers and sampling the new growth on the hawthorn bushes which tasted of bread and cheese or digging for pig-nuts and enjoying their crunchy sweet flavour. Later in the summer we would get up very early and gather the mushrooms which had sprung up overnight, and take them back home to cook for breakfast.

We also loved to help at haymaking time, gathering the sweet smelling hay and then enjoying the ride back from the stack in the farmyard, on the empty horse-drawn waggon.

A local farmer would call every day with his can and dipper and deliver the new morning's milk straight into the jug and later the baker would make his daily round, bringing his big flat basket of cakes and bread to the door.

Sunday mornings we would attend church as a family and spend the rest of the day trying to keep clean and tidy in our best clothes.

Playing on the sands at Eastbourne in 1927, with little concession to 'beach clothing'.

Sunday afternoons in winter were special when we would listen for the muffin man, as he tricycled through the village ringing his bell, and there would be hot muffins toasted on the open fire and spread with real butter, for tea.

A date always awaited with eager anticipation was the annual Sunday school outing to Brighton. There was the excitement of catching the early train from the local station, the journey and the walk to the beach, past all the little curio and gift shops and then finally the race to be first to glimpse the sea.

The village itself has not altered, with all the old houses standing as before. The tall spire of our lovely old church still stands guard over them, as it has done for hundreds of years, and on a quiet summer evening one can still recapture the magic days gone by and remember things as they once were.'

COUNTRY LIFE

'I was one of a family of six children who, during the 1930s, lived in Copthorne. Our house had been a farmhouse and was surrounded by fields which, in the spring, were covered in daffodils and bluebells.

The house had brick floors in the kitchen and larder, which was quite a big one as it had been the dairy. It also had a cellar but no bathroom and no inside toilet. We had our baths in the kitchen in a galvanised bath in front of the old black stove, which had an oven which was used for cooking the meals. There was a primus which was used to boil a kettle quickly. One of the jobs my sisters and I used to do was to keep the copper stoked up in the kitchen for the baths. We also had to wash and dry the dishes and clean the brass and cutlery and for this we were given a halfpenny a week.

There was a stream running through the fields and one or other of our friends was always falling in. We used to go digging for pig-nuts which were quite nutty to eat, and we cut lengths of cow parsley stems to use as peashooters.

My mother made wine, which was kept in the cellar; we were given a farthing a gallon for the dandelions we picked and which she used to make the wine.

We went to the local church school and on Empire Day we used to line up and salute the Union flag, then on to church for a short service after which we had a half day holiday.

We loved haymaking times and building little houses with the hay and sliding down the stacks. Our fields adjoined my grandfather's and I used to go and stay on the farm and loved to collect the eggs from all round the farm, as the chickens nested in the most unlikely places. It was great fun finding the nests.

Two of my uncles had farms on the outskirts of the village and one of them came round in a milk float drawn by a pony and delivered the milk out of a churn with a stainless measure.

Before she was married my mother was a governess and was a very talented lady. My parents used to hold musical evenings and a friend would bring his violin and Mother played the piano. We children used to sit at the top of the stairs and listen.'

NEAR THE SEA

'I was born in 1904 in Sussex and for the first ten years of my life we lived near the sea, in a small terraced house opening onto the pavement, with no garden. My father was a labourer, losing all time in wet weather and getting no money when he was out of work. We took in self-service visitors, as our mother was a semi invalid and there were always doctor's bills to pay and coal to be got in for the winter. I was the survivor of four children, a little boy and a girl dying as babies and my younger brother dying when I was nearly eight.

Although we had no gas or electricity, only an oil lamp, we enjoyed our winter evenings round the fire, making rag rugs from oddments of material and on Sunday evening singing hymns and storytelling. Hot toast was made by the fire and occasionally roast chestnuts were a real treat. The crumpet man could be heard coming along the street ringing his bell, with his basket covered with green baize balanced on his head, and when in season herrings and winkles were hawked very cheaply through the streets.

Our little school was in the centre of the town, a church school divided in the centre, one half for the infants and the other for girls, while the boys were across the road further down. Each part of the school held 80 to 100 pupils. Being so near the sea, a good proportion of our scholars came from fishing and seafaring families so swimming was a very strong point at school and many times we won the local swimming shield. There were sad times, though, and I remember when one year the lifeboat capsized killing twelve or 13 of the crew, it seemed that most of our girls had lost a father, brother or uncle.

One special event I remember was a party for all the local schoolchildren held in the Kursaal in 1911 to commemorate the coronation of George V. We all had a coloured artificial flower to represent our school and ours was a mauve sweet pea. We were all given a Coronation mug.'

THE ONLY PLACE I KNOW

'I was born and bred in Groombridge. My parents came here in 1913 and Groombridge is the only place I really know. I can see it as it used to be when I was young and all my five brothers still alive. There used to be so many little shops and a brass band! The band would turn out on Hospital Sunday, which we celebrated once a year, with banners and a parade all round the village. That was a treat, I can tell you.

Times were a lot happier then, we had plays put on by the local people. The churchgoers of St Thomas always put on the Nativity and the Crucifixion at Eastertime. We didn't have radio or television but we did make our own entertainment with whist drives, Rainbow concert parties and on August Bank Holiday we had sports of every description. It was really grand. We played quoits nearly every Saturday evening on the recreation ground.

Times were hard for my parents and my Mum went hop picking to get money to see us all through the winter. My Dad used to mend all our shoes and cut our hair. We had no school dinners then but we took sandwiches and a bottle of drink, mostly cocoa.

Trains used to go right through the village from Tunbridge Wells to Brighton or Eastbourne and we had some lovely days out to the sea. We also used to help in the hayfield when the hay-making started, and take our own tea and tea for the workers. Sometimes we got a ride home in the hay waggons pulled by lovely horses from Mr R. Widdicombe's farm. Miss Widdicombe brought the milk round in a churn every day to sell at a penny a pint. Mr Mountain of Groombridge Place allowed us all to come skating or sliding on his lake when it froze over in winter.'

HOLIDAYS ON RYE HARBOUR

'I often think of the happy days I spent as a child, when I used to come to Rye Harbour and spend the summer holidays with my gran, grandad, aunt and uncle. The first time I came I was four years old. Mum was having my brother and Dad brought me over. I cried and said why have you brought me here? They didn't tell you much in those days, but after that I grew to look forward to my six weeks' holiday every summer.

When the carnival was in Hastings my Mum would send me over a parcel of paper hats, balloons, streamers and blowers. My friends and I would decorate Grandad's garden and put on a show. We made a puppet show with a cardboard box. All the kids would come ... we used to charge them a penny to come in and the grown ups all lined the fence to watch. It always seemed to be sunny in those days.

Every Saturday was a treat, because Aunt Alice would take me to

103

Rye shopping and then to the pictures. We walked to Rye and back and the road was full of pot holes, nevertheless it was fun.

But the best treat of all was when Gran would pack up a lunch and we would go down the shore to meet Grandad, Uncle Bill and Bobby Mills bouldering. We would help them to pick up the blue and white flints and fill up the trugs they carried by yokes, from the shoulders. Then when they filled up the gaff rigged boat (it was called *Sarah Elgar* after Grandad's mother) they would bring us up the river ready to unload on to the Boulder Hard. After that, home to tea of bread and dripping or jam, followed by home-made cake or lardy cake. The next day the boulders had to be picked up again and loaded on to trucks round the point. I think the men got paid something like two shillings and sixpence per ton for them. They were then taken to Staffordshire and used to make blue and white pottery, such as willow pattern china. All the boulder men had a free dinner and tea service and Gran used hers. It always seemed special to me, somehow the tea tasted nicer.

I also remember the last day of my last holiday. It was a Sunday and I was in the little Rye Harbour church and the vicar was praying at the altar, when a man walked up the aisle, tapped him on the shoulder and whispered something to him. He turned round and said in a quiet voice, "All go home children, quickly and quietly."

When I got in Gran's, my Dad was there waiting to take me home to Hastings. He said we were at war with Germany and Mum wanted us all to be together, so we biked back home. It seemed never ending to a 13 year old, but I made it.'

A FAMILY CONCERN

'The grocery shop in the village of Westfield, five miles north of Hastings, holds most of my memories of childhood. It was a large store, groceries and butcher's, on the main road, with a very large garden at the back. There were three large chicken runs, and two pig sties, but I never remember having any pigs there.

We went to the local school, which was right opposite the shop, for about the first three years. After that, we went to separate private schools in Hastings. My brother went to Kings Collegiate College at St Leonards, I went to Wellington College. At first, I did not understand why my blazer didn't have initials on it like my brother's, but perhaps it would not have been "quite proper". We travelled by the local charabanc. If it started to rain, the driver stopped and, with a little help from the passengers, pulled a large canvas cover over us all.

We did not have pocket money, but were allowed to go to the sweet counter every Saturday, and choose a quarter pound of sweets, which was our share for the week. Leisure time was spent in the large garden, or on the front forecourt where we could spin our tops, which we had coloured with crayons, with "whips", a stick with string tied to the top or skip, bowl our hoops, or just sit on the bank and take down car numbers. Occasionally, we had the little girl in from next door to play, but mainly we amused ourselves.

Quite a lot of the time, though, we "helped". We dug the chicken runs to get worms for the chickens, we gathered the eggs, and fruit from the apple trees and the two cherry trees; these were for sale in the shop. Mother worked in the office, with the help of a local girl, and I would spend hours with them, fetching and carrying where necessary. My brother's Saturday job was delivering some goods to customers, and on many occasions I would accompany him. Mother cycled round the village to get the orders, and we delivered those which the errand boy had not had time for. He had a bicycle, but my brother and I only had a box on wheels. We neither received nor expected payment for the work we did. We were a family in the real sense of the word, we had love and security, and the very best our parents could provide.'

CAREFREE DAYS

'I have vivid memories of carefree summer days in the years leading up to the Second World War. We lived in East Brighton, less than a mile from the beaches, all downhill. It seems looking back that every day of our school holidays was bright and sunny and we used to spend day after day occupied on the beaches between Paston and Ovingdean. There always seemed so much to do, with the beaches constantly changing with the tides and currents. There would be me and my sister and two or three of our cousins, and with our sandwiches packed and a drink (probably water), but with no money, we were off down the hill for the whole day.

Sometimes we walked to Ovingdean, where we befriended a local farmer. He let us play around the farm and watch the cows being milked. There was a lovely muddy pond and lots of places to make a den or play hide and seek. One day we found a ferret. I think it must have been tame, or it had just eaten, and we took it along to the farmer who was horrified and wouldn't go near it.

Once we put our sandwiches in the cow shed because it was cool. Come lunchtime we were ravenous, but to our horror all our food tasted of the cow shed. We ate it though, because we were so hungry.'

GAMES, TREATS AND CHORES

We could play safely in the roads in those days of little traffic, and our games followed the seasons as they always had done. Pocket money was a rarity and had usually to be earned, and we all had our chores to do around the house or on the farm. Days out were a great treat, even when it was to work hard all day hop picking!

SWEETS AND BOOTS

'In Withyham at the turn of the century, I remember Taylor at the blacksmith's, Snazell at the Dorset Arms, and buying a halfpenny worth of sweets at Welfares shop. A man's wages were then around 15 shillings a week and I started as a boy of twelve years old to work at Chartners Farm for only two shillings and sixpence a week cutting nettles. We used to go game beating in the season at Buckhurst, for which we were paid a shilling a day.

A yearly treat was a visit to the rectory when the Rev Sutton was there, for a special tea. I wore my mother's boots to look tidy and neat.

Our lady teacher used to tell us that if we did wrong we would go to Hell and be burned in the "fiery flames". This so frightened me then, that I have tried to live a good life ever since!'

AN ORDERLY LIFE

'Life for us in Eastbourne around 1920 was very orderly. Monday to Friday school and Saturday night polishing our shoes ready for Sunday school when we wore our Sunday best. On Sunday evenings in the summer the whole family went for a walk (no running!). My parents' favourite walk was across the golf links, which was possible because golf was not permitted on Sunday. We were allowed to play with a ball on the links but had to walk in twos in an orderly fashion along the road and parade. Winter evenings were spent doing jigsaw puzzles or playing cards and ludo.

In the school holidays we would sometimes walk to the top of Beachy Head with a picnic, or go to Hampden Park to see the squirrels in a cage in the wood. If we had enough money we would ride one way and walk the other. We had a penny per week pocket money. An annual treat was a visit to the pantomime. Other entertainment would be buskers, or an old lady with a gramophone who came along the road. In the winter the Salvation Army would have their service at the end of our road as it was sheltered from the elements. Otherwise they held their service on the beach, children by the pier and adults by the bandstand.

Rules for swimming were very strict. At first you could only go if you used a cabin, you undressed in it and left your clothes while you had a dip. This cost sixpence for half an hour. The alternative to this was to go to the far end of the parade and into an enclosure for ladies; men had a separate area. There were large notices along the parade stating "No undressing on the beach". The only other way to get a dip was to go "mackintosh bathing". You ran from your house in your mackintosh to special places, swam, then ran home in a wet costume. This was only allowed before 7 am, though later this was extended to 8 am.'

WE PLAYED IN THE STREET

'I lived near the Pells in Lewes and spent a lot of time fishing for minnows and tadpoles. In my mother's youth, 1910 to 1920, there were fairy lights in the trees, the town band played on the islands, and people hired boats, but by my day that had all gone.

I attended the Pells church school from 1927 to 1936. Each Friday morning we marched to St John's church. On Ascension Day we had a short service, then had the day off. Good Friday was even more sacred than Sundays, nobody played in the streets, everything closed down, and as a family we always went for walks over the Downs to pick primroses. On Empire Day we either congregated in the Dripping Pan with our Union Jacks or in later years at the cinema where we sang patriotic songs, *I vow to thee my country*, or *God bless the Prince of Wales* etc, a real day of celebration. The highlights of the school year were the annual music festival to sing in the choir, and the Lewes and District Sports Day in the Dripping Pan where I ran in the 100 yards sprint.

I lived in a cul-de-sac with little traffic, so we played in the street. All the traditional games, such as marbles, whips and tops, hoops (metal for the boys, wooden for the girls), skipping and ball games, plus "Touch the road you must go over", "Witches", "What's the time Mr Wolf" and many more, were all played across the road from pavement to pavement. Apart from an occasional trades-van we saw little motorised traffic; the steamroller when the road was resurfaced, the water cart in hot weather to cool the tar, but little else.

Sometimes at weekends in the summer the whole family, aunts,

The children's corner at Devonshire Park, Eastbourne was very popular in the 1920s.

uncles, cousins and grandparents, between 15 and 20 of us, would go to Newhaven for the day on the beach. There was only sand and pebbles, no kiosks, we took all our food and drink with us. The train fare was eightpence return for adults. When a large ship came into the harbour we had to hurriedly move up the beach or the wash would swamp our belongings. Holidays were a luxury. My Dad was in the Territorial Army so loved camping out. We spent most of our holidays in a tent at Pevensey Bay. One year we could not afford to go away so we spent nearly a week on the Downs above Lewes, till rain forced us home.'

DIFFERENT TIMES

'I look back to 1922, to a very different, quieter life. I was born in a small village cottage in Mountfield. My parents were young and the country was only just settling down after the First World War. My father then worked on a farm, and there was competition from returned servicemen trying to rebuild their lives.

I was a delicate child and my parents were told I might not make my first birthday; looking back, this must have made them poor as in those days every doctor's visit and bottle of medicine was charged.

Christmas was saved for all the year with W. C. Allwork of Battle, paying an amount when the grocery bill was paid. A few days before Christmas my mother would choose the Christmas fare, a special iced cake, a Tunis cake, fancy biscuits and ham.

We had good books and board games; I had lots of dolls, including a gollywog and a black baby doll which was one of my favourites. At this time children would walk to school in groups two or three miles and play in the woods in groups quite safely.

If we had a real treat we were taken to Tunbridge Wells for a day, two shillings and sixpence on the steam train. I joined the Girl Guides while still in the village and attended the Wesleyan chapel Sunday school. Our outing once a year was a trip to Bexhill on the train and our treat as soon as we arrived was an ice cream cornet and a bottle of lemonade which we had with our sandwiches after games on the beach.

There was great poverty in those days. I remember going with Miss Connie Collins, an elderly, silver haired lady who ran the Sunday school, to take a can of hot soup to a couple living in a tent in the wood at Eatenden Lane. The man was terminally ill and they had been put out of their tied cottage and had nowhere else to live. I also remember children at school who had no shoes or if they did the toes had been cut out when their feet got too long for them. One family I knew sent the eldest daughter home with me from school with a note asking my mother if she could spare any food or cast off clothes. My mother had just done a week's baking of pies and cakes and she gave the girl a meal and sent her home with clothes and much of the cooking she had just done.

Jumble sales in those days yielded very little, as children passed down clothes and they went from one family to another and were altered if they didn't fit.

Friday evenings after my father returned from work, the whole family would walk into Battle and all had our weekend treat. My mother visited her sister in the High Street, my father went for a drink with work pals and we children had four pennies each to spend in Pallets shop next to the old chapel in the street. This shop was a wonderland for children, where it was possible to buy many items for two pennies. There were many counters as well as sweets hanging from the wall and even the ceiling – there were Spanish bootlaces and belts, sherbet suckers, sweet cigarettes, gobstoppers, huge lollypops in bright colours, raspberry creams with a nut on top, sugar mice and clocks, pigs all colours, chocolate purses and many more, very few wrapped as today. Boiled sweets were always in large glass jars, unwrapped.

On Sunday we often walked many miles as a family and we were sometimes given a bag of sweets extra to our pocket money from a little sweet shop which was next to Johns Cross Inn. The sweets were displayed behind white mesh with polished brass rails on top and we children would peer through the mesh and choose our assortment of sweets.'

A SENSE OF SUMMER

'We all tend to colour happy memories with blue skies and sunny days. When I look back at my childhood, growing up with my four sisters and brother in Berwick, I am no exception. I have a definite impression of well marked seasons and an overriding sense of summer. I can remember the edge of Sunday afternoon Sunday school being dulled with the delight of riding my bike over the warm bumps of tar, bubbling in the heat. The resulting pops were proof of skilled, aimed cycling.

The seasons were also marked by the ritual of changing from one set of clothes to the next. My mother would bring down the suitcases containing the summer clothes and we would begin the trying on of dresses to find whose fitted whom this summer. And of course when summer arrived so did the ice cream man. Waiting for his arrival on a Monday is a tactile memory; I still clutch the coins, feel the hardness of the step I waited on and experience the delicious anticipation of his bicycle and box coming into view.

There are also the memories of sensation and sound; the feelings of freewheeling my bike down Common Lane, the agony in my arm as I pumped air into the organ in Selmeston church each Sunday, my schoolteacher's voice reading the newspaper headlines to us each day during the war and calling us "cold rice puddings" when we displeased her.'

IN AND OUT OF SCHOOL

'I was born on 3rd April 1916 and lived in Leicester Road, Lewes, and in the three following years had a brother and sister. We had a very happy childhood. I, being the first grandchild, was made a great fuss of and went to a nursery school in Bradford Road (as did my brother and sister later for pre-school tuition), after which at five years of age I attended St Annes' school. Later I moved up to Western Road school where I stayed until I left school.

We used to go to Lewes Dripping Pan for our annual sports – a good idea even if one wasn't sport minded as it got one off school lessons. We could have swimming lessons at the Pells. Although I

110

chose to go it was somewhat frightening. After initial instructions on strokes we would get down the steps at the deep end and, with a webbing waist loop and tow line, we would be towed across a corner. Oh, the panic if the towline was slackened – which it was! As we progressed we would go down to shallower water and be towed across the width. Then would come the dreaded day when we had to swim a few strokes across the corners, but we made it.

We also played stoolball and the boys indulged in football and cricket. We played various games in the playground such as tag, leapfrog, five stones, marbles and ciggy cards, with boys and girls in separate playgrounds.

Out of school hours took many forms. My family used to go on picnics on the Downs, and blackberrying at Breaky Bottom, where raspberries were also to be found. Many a day was spent on wild flower picking, mainly around what we named Shiffners plantation for bluebells and primroses. We used to play on the Downs and I can recall the lovely smell of wild thyme which was so plentiful as to be crushed underfoot. Our family would frequently go to Newhaven sea-shore, which was gorgeous with its sandy shoreline. As we got older we used to go and play in the seaplane sheds near Tide Mills, which were lovely for climbing and hide and seek. We also used to push small trucks around and travel on to the ruins of the Tide Mill village. We sometimes went grass sledging down the steep hill just on the outskirts of Offham; it was not overgrown with trees and bushes in those days. I had a very fast sledge as my father made it and it had mahogany runners which were kept well rubbed with dripping – we had many a tumble over hillocks but it was great fun.

Sheep fairs were held at the foot of the Downs by Lewes prison and we enjoyed the excitement, animals and noise. Also race days were great. We used to sit at the foot of the hills beside the main road and watch all the people going home, particularly enjoying the charabancs.'

BEST OF ALL

'The best thing of all was riding back down from the fields after hay-making, on one of the horses' backs. They were always sweaty and when you got off, your legs would be all wet and covered in horse hair.'

POCKET MONEY AND CHORES

'I had twopence a week pocket money and was expected to save a penny of this. I was lucky, for most children I knew at Nutley got nothing at all. A penny went a long way before 1920. Aniseed balls were ten for a penny in the village sweetshop kept by the two Misses Carr.

We were kept busy at home with a multitude of tasks. Needlework was an important skill and from the age of about twelve girls were expected to make their own socks and stockings and to be expert darners. One girl remembers she came home from school with a hole in her sock. "Darn that before you go to bed," she was told. She was bored with mending, so she just drew the edges of the hole together instead of making a neat darn, and then went to bed. Unfortunately for her, the sock was inspected. She was woken up and told, "Now do it properly before school in the morning." And she did.'

A GREAT PLACE TO GROW

'Nowadays you can approach Seaford Head from the seafront without fear of meeting the Giant, although the foundations of the house where I was sure he lived are still there, as are the imprints of a child's imagination.

Just a few years before the Second World War our family moved to Seaford, when I was five years old and my sister just two years old. It was a great place to grow up in.

We had one of the wooden beach huts right on the edge of the "Prom" and early morning swims were followed by cooked break-fasts over the primus stove, shared with the family from the next-door beach hut, delicious aromas carried on the salt wind. Summer seemed to go on for ever then.

We could roller skate around the Martello tower, dodging the shingle thrown up by the tide. The ice cream man cycled along the Promenade displaying the familiar sign "Stop Me and Buy One". My favourite was the three-cornered, cardboard wrapped, forerunner of the iced lolly, especially the lemon flavoured one.

But when we strolled along past the jetty, where all the locals tried their luck at sea fishing, and up on to the Head we had to pass the big red brick house and go through a narrow passageway with a high wall on each side, and into which there was a gate which gave access to the house.

My heart pounds now as I walk again the narrow aisle, my step quickens as I approach the gate and listen for the slightest sound. The enormous hinges would surely creak if the handle was turned. You see the gate might open and the Giant grab me inside.

My younger sister had no such fears, she had run ahead and I had to pluck up courage and pass that gate.

Faster and faster my heart pounds and faster and faster I fly by safely into the sunshine beyond, to follow the edge of the golf course, skirted by a blaze of yellow gorse bushes, to watch the cross-channel ferry leave Newhaven harbour.'

GOLDEN DAYS

'My childhood, like that of many people of my age, was interrupted by the 1939–45 war, but after a time as an evacuee in Yorkshire, I returned to Brighton.

As a family we had always been encouraged to enjoy the country-side, and we would set off on our bicycles with Shandy the dog sitting in my cycle basket. We would visit Patcham, Rottingdean, Arundel, Amberley, Eastbourne, and if we went to Seaford we could go in the sea, as that was one of the first places where the barbed wire barricades were taken away.

My favourite destination was Brown's boat yard at Barcombe Mills. I wonder how many people will remember the Brown family with their interesting little tea rooms on the river Ouse, just beyond Lewes. Dogs, cats, rabbits, hens and ducks wandered freely among the chairs and tables, and they even had a parrot in a cage suspended from the branch of a tree.

Tied up at the water's edge were the small boats. They could be hired for an hour or two, and there was nearly always a queue. At last Mr Brown would signal that it was our turn, and hold the boat for us as we clambered in. Our dog would spend the entire journey at the helm, guiding us on our way. The river was very narrow, and round bends we went, ducking to avoid overhanging branches, and bumping into the bank, always wondering what would be around the corner. Cows grazed in the fields, and it seemed to us that we were a thousand miles away from civilisation.

All too soon it was time to turn back, with a promise of newly laid boiled eggs for tea. What golden days they were, and did it ever rain?

Years later I took my children to Brown's. They didn't care for it very much. They had been to a real river – the river Thames!

I wonder if it is still there. I won't go back to see. I would rather remember those magical days when the sun always seemed to shine.'

WE STARTED YOUNG

'I was one of seven children living on a small dairy farm in Polegate, where my parents worked extremely hard. As children we all had chores. My brothers helped with the milking, by hand, the milk then

Children worked on the farm from an early age. Stanley Field had been out wooding in 1927 at Herstmonceux.

going through the cooler. From the age of four I would help my father to deliver the milk each morning and late afternoon by pony and trap. I had to knock on the door, call out "Milk" and ladle the milk from the churn by half pint or one pint measures into the customer's jug. When we had finished the round we went to Grandma's to tell her who had had milk and how much as she kept the ledger and knew the amount to charge at the end of the week.

Polly, the pony, always received a sugar lump each night and I was rewarded by a penny each Saturday. Sometimes we would be stopped in the street by a Weights & Measures man who would test our milk to make sure we had not added water and that our measures were correct.'

GOING HOP PICKING

'I was born and grew up in Wadhurst, and my most vivid memory is of hop picking time. From a very early age we enjoyed the excitement of getting up early on misty, sharp mornings and being collected by a big lorry which had benches inside to sit on. You held on for dear life as you travelled down to Bomans Farm, where we picked. It was not all play, my brother and I had to pick the hops into a box or upturned umbrella before adding them to Mother's bin to earn pocket money. As we grew up this was the way we earned our first bike or doll's pram. We did play too, though, and one day I was found by my mother poking an adder with a stick. I was soon taught the country code.

The big treat came in the afternoon when Storm, a huge grey horse, was brought into the hop garden by the farmer's wife and we were each given a ride along a grass track to a charcoal burning area. This held a great fascination for us kids, but not quite as much as the stories we were told about what lay further on down that same track. There was a house called "Great Showsmiths" which was reputed to be haunted and local people were said to have seen and heard a coach and horses cross a bridge at midnight, also tales of highway men and smugglers. Looking back I think it was our mother's way of seeing that we did not stray too far, and every night we returned home tired, very dirty but oh so happy.'

SPECIAL TREATS

'I was not born in Brighton but from early days, about 1913, when I was seven, I was taken to Clapham Junction station and put in charge of the guard for collection at Brighton by my aunt who lived by Hollingbury Park. Here my cousins and I with friends, enjoyed various ball games and races, also leapfrog, handstands and cart-wheels. On firm ground skipping, hopscotch and tops were favour-ites. The tops we coloured with crayons and whipped with string which had a small knot at the end, the winner being the one who kept it going the longest.

We often visited Black Rock and at low tide scrambled over the rocks holding jam jars with string under the rim and a handle added, then with a small net on the end of a stick fished for shrimps and tiddlers. It was necessary to avoid those rocks covered with green weed as they were very slippery and it was so easy to fall into the clear pools. At the top of the cliff were two derelict houses which, with erosion, were very near the edge and these we pretended were haunted, as often odd noises could be heard. On the slope heading down to Marine Parade bathchairs were stationed with attendants to push elderly ladies along the seafront, and also goat carriages for small children.

On the beach we enjoyed the Punch and Judy shows and also the Pierrots. We also paddled with our dresses tucked into our bloomers and after rough weather looked for long brown streamers of seaweed with a stem at the end that had broken away from outlying rocks. These we took home to hang up outside to act as a barometer – if wet they were limp and clammy, and dry, quite crisp.

As a special treat we travelled to Devil's Dyke by the old single track railway where we picnicked and flew our kites. These we made from split bamboo cane with a short crosspiece to which coloured crepe paper was stuck to make the kite shape, with small pieces for the tail, then string would be attached to the other end, as long as we could obtain, tied and twisted round a short piece of wood for holding. We were always encouraged to make our own toys and to use our imagination.'

SCHOOLDAYS – THE BEST YEARS OF OUR LIVES?

Strict discipline, starched white pinafores, long walks to school, slates to write on and fires in the classroom – memories of schooldays in the first two decades of the 20th century.

A GOOD GROUNDING AT RYE

'For me schooling at Rye was in the building which is now part of the County Library. The whole of my education was in that building, from the age of five until I was 14. Despite the large classes we had, I still think, a really good "grounding" in education, since we had to learn to read and write and "do" arithmetic. Us girls had to learn to sew, to patch and to darn and, by the time the Great War started in 1914, we could almost all of us knit socks for the troops and also a kind of mitten-like gloves. We also had to make our chemises of calico, hopefully trimmed with lace, and for a period we had to take stockings, usually black woollen ones, to mend on Friday afternoons.

When I first went into the "big" school at seven years old, we had a well-to-do lady run a penny bank. She called once a week and I had to be sure to take the little book in a bag with twopence to save entered in it and I imagine that was about the amount other children saved.

Holidays weren't so long as children get now, the longest being arranged to cover the time needed for hop picking. If we stayed away from school, even for illness, the school attendance officer always called to know the reason.

The heating in each, rather large room, was simply by a coke "bogey", which was far from ideal.

A medical attendance man (I presume a doctor) called only occasionally, as did the school inspectors, which we all dreaded for they seemed to us children to ask the most awkward questions, but really they were checking up on the education we were receiving.

On one or two occasions we danced the maypole on the Salts and, I think, at Winchester. Also on a very few occasions we were taken for a short country walk to nature study. The cookery classes for my age were finished in 1914, due to the war, but they had been part of the school programme prior to this.'

TWO GENERATIONS AT WITHYHAM SCHOOL

'Extracts from the archives of St Michael's church school, Withyham:

29th January 1912: On coming into school at 8.35 am the fires had only just been lit, and the temperature of the main schoolroom was only 27°F and the infants room was 29°F. All efforts failed to raise the temperature above 30° by nine o'clock and therefore as it was quite impossible to use the school in that state, the children played organised games until 9.40 am in the hopes of getting the school warmed by then. The temperature of the main room was on 49°F by midday but the infants room stayed at 39°.

28th July 1913: Miss Fanny Louise Penn started as headmistress.

22nd January 1917: We find great difficulty in procuring coal as no men are available in bringing it out of the mines.

10th October 1917: Still great difficulty in obtaining coal for the school fires.

11th October 1917: The school boys have today carted ten cwt of coal from the station, as we cannot find any farmer able to do it for us.

29th November 1917: Received today one ton of coke, with five tons more to follow, as a gift from Mr Follett who is also having a new stove placed in the main room.'

'I came to Withyham in March 1919, and of course to a different school, which was not easy to accept. For a start there were only two rooms. Infants were taught by Miss Kingswood, juniors and seniors by Miss Penn who was also the headmistress and very strict she was.

There were about 56 children of all ages. The forms were the old iron type, with very hard seats and no backs, which made you sit upright. We were made to sit boy and girl to a seat. This was done to keep us out of mischief, for the headmistress knew the girls would tell on us. Then look out, for the two foot long rule came down on your knuckles without warning!

The playground was in two parts, one for boys and one for girls, and if you were caught or seen on the wrong side of the fence then you were for the cane, by Miss Penn who used to lay it on strong! You were not allowed to shout or misbehave in any way, we thought she was a so and so! Little did we realise at the time the good she did for us.

There was only one holiday per year, eight weeks for hop picking September until October.

Lessons started at 9 am and finished at 3.30 pm and often as not, some of us had to stay an extra 30 minutes if we did not do our lessons properly. You had to look after yourself, because there were some rough ones and fighting always broke out after school was finished.

The rooms were fairly warm in winter with one combustion stove, and a coal fire in the big room.

Sunday school was held in the main room and you had to learn the collect of the day and repeat it to Miss Penn.

The times I think we most looked forward to were prize giving and our summer holiday. Prizes were given for best attendance, and progress for the year, also for essays on Empire Day.'

'I was a pupil at Withyham school from 1930 until 1936. There were only two rooms then, the small one for infants, taught by Mrs Kingswood, and the large room for juniors taught by Miss Ridley and seniors taught by Miss Penn, the headmistress, who had her desk at the end of the room.

The desks seated two pupils each and had iron frames so that the seats and desks were all in one piece and not very comfortable. There were combustion stoves to heat the rooms.

Each morning started with assembly which consisted of a hymn, prayers and the collect which had to be learned off by heart each week, and said on your own at each playtime until you could say it without being prompted. Many used to learn it over the weekend in order to say it first thing on Monday mornings and thus lose no playtimes. Assembly was followed by the register, and then we all had to stand with our hands out while Miss Penn came to look and see if our nails and hands were clean. If they were, we received a little gold coloured star which we stuck in our book, five stars to a page, and periodically these books were checked and if we had more than a certain number of stars missing we had 200 lines to write ... "I must keep my hands and nails clean".

We had our little bottles of milk each day for which we paid twopence halfpenny a week and during winter, if we paid threepence a week, we could have the milk made into hot malted milk. There was no canteen then so we took sandwiches for our lunch as we could not get home, and used to eat them at our desks. We always sang grace before leaving the classroom at noon and again when returning for afternoon lessons.

In the morning and after each break the bell was rung for us to go back into school and we had to form a straight and orderly line outside the school door and then we were brought to attention and marched in, in proper military fashion, but then Miss Penn was rather like a sergeant major and the discipline was as stringent.

The cane was used daily, sometimes more than once a day, and although I have several times seen a boy grab the cane as it reached his hand, and break it over his knee, there was always one to replace it ... she seemed to have an inexhaustible supply of canes! Strangely enough I never managed to taste it, but many times had the ruler over my knuckles while writing, because my pen was not pointing at my shoulder or I had a blot on my blotting paper, and several times too, for not wearing a thimble when sewing. Another sign of dis-approval was shown by a prod in the back as she crept up behind you and looked over your shoulder at your work.

Although Miss Penn was exceedingly strict, I must in all fairness say that she was a very good teacher. Although I never thought so in those days, when I look back and think, she had very few pupils who failed their scholarship which was a great credit to her.

We had an anti-litter league and taking our turn, in pairs, we had to take a spiked stick and collect any litter lying around the school. This was done in our dinner hour.

There were about ten school gardens. The boys had about seven and the others were for the girls, where we grew vegetables which were sold to buy seeds for the next year.

The only game the girls played was stoolball and we didn't play that very often as we were frequently told that arithmetic was more important.'

PENNIES AND BOOTS

'When the master at Dallington had his birthday all the children were given a penny each, and proud of it they were.

If he saw a boy with worn out boots, Mr Peploe sent him to the shop to get a new pair and paid for them himself.'

EAST DEAN DAYS

'Most village schools were church schools and East Dean was no exception. The vicar, Rev Evans, visited the school once a week and taught the children their catechism and about the Bible. On Ascension Day the children would attend church and then the rest of the day was a holiday.

The boys were taught gardening and the girls knitting and needlework. The children had to bring sandwiches to eat and would walk sometimes as much as three miles or more from the outlying areas. The girls played skipping, wooden hoops, rounders, hopscotch and stoolball, while the boys played conkers, marbles, steel hoops, tops, cricket and football in their seasons. Boys generally wore short trousers and jerseys.

Mrs Davies-Gilbert would drive over from the Manor House, Eastbourne in a pony and trap once a year and present the children with a new penny and a currant bun each.'

THE HIGHLIGHT

'In the 1920s the highlight of each year was our school treat, when 40 to 50 of us went from Preston Park to the Orchard Gardens at Hassocks. We met at Brighton railway station for the journey, which was thought quite a long way in those days. Mothers usually came too. When we arrived there was plenty to amuse us, with a huge lake and boats we could take out for a row. We took a picnic lunch but had tea in a large barn which had already been prepared for us. We arrived home later that evening, tired but very contented.'

UNHAPPY DAYS AT CHAILEY

'In January 1924, at the age of three and a half years, I came to live in East Sussex. I am a polio victim, contracted at eleven months and three weeks old. I was sent to school at Chailey Heritage, a school for disabled children; in those days, of course, we were called "crippled children". My parents were advised to send me there to receive medical treatment and an education. My father was in the Army and had to pay seven shillings and sixpence per week.

Chailey in the 1920s was beautiful country, no fast cars (not even slow ones), just horses and carts. There were no main roads, just country lanes. There were violets, primroses, cowslips and lots of other wild flowers in the hedgerows.

We children were not supplied with wheelchairs. We were bundled into long spinal carriages and pushed along the lanes for nature lessons.

The Heritage was founded by Dame Grace Kimmins, who was the Commandant. There was the boys' school on one side of Chailey Common and the girls' school at the other end. We were not allowed to mix. We were in trouble if we looked at them in chapel on Sundays.

We lined up outside the dining hall for our meals and when the music started we marched around the long tables to our seats. When we reached the top of the first table we had to salute the flag.

Discipline was very strict. When our meals were finished we had to clear the tables by numbers, eg one – place your hand on your knife, two – pick it up, three – pass it to the end of the table, and so on until everything was cleared. We were not allowed to talk unless given the order.

We all wore the same uniforms and a red braid band around our heads with elastic at the back to keep our hair away from our eyes. We all had short hair.

Visiting was once a year, Easter Monday. We had five weeks holiday at Christmas and seven weeks in the summer. I was lucky, I had a good home to go to and loving parents, but many of the children had no homes and had to stay at Chailey.

When it was time to go back to Chailey a special train would pick us up at London Bridge – we would all be crying and so would the parents. None of us wanted to go back, but our parents had signed for us to stay until we were 16 years of age.

After seven years at Chailey I went home in such a terrible condition, with septic chilblains up to my thighs and my boots two sizes too small. My toes were bent under, so my parents decided to try to get permission for me to leave. This was granted provided that I attended an orthopaedic clinic once a month. So with joy I left Chailey and East Sussex, hoping never to see the place again – I was ten years old by then and attended an ordinary school with able-bodied children. From then on I never looked back. I worked until I was 60 years old and then retired.

In 1983 my husband and I came to live in Pevensey Bay, East Sussex. It was not long after that I decided to visit Chailey Heritage.

What changes there had been and how differently it was run. Out had gone the old army-type discipline and kindness had taken its place.'

HURST GREEN VILLAGE SCHOOL

'I was a pupil at Hurst Green school from 1921 to 1928. There were about 90 children altogether, aged from five to 14 years and three teachers, so each class contained a wide age range and very mixed abilities. Bright children were moved up the school quickly, often "jumping" a standard. Those who had difficulty in learning sometimes stayed in the lower classes for long periods.

The infants class, with its 17 year old, uncertificated teacher and children from five to eight years, was housed in its own room. A door, with glass panels at the top, covered by a bead curtain, led into what was known as the "big room", where the rest of the school was taught. Another door led outside. In the corner of the room was a round, coke-burning stove with a guard round it. Often one of the older boys came in to make up the fire, or fill the coke scuttle, if necessary. He was only a few years younger than the teacher and was often rather cheeky to her. My earliest memory of my infant days is drawing an apple, from a model put up in front of the class – not very creative! I remember my little hand holding a red pastel, going round and round to get the shape of the apple. The highlight was when the headmaster came into the room and did conjuring tricks with the apple, making it vanish up his sleeve.

The "big room" had its two classes separated by a dark green curtain, which did not reach right across the width of the room, but children and teachers got used to the inevitable noise that came from the other class. A bell, on the headmaster's desk, was pressed if the noise got too loud. There were two stoves, one in the middle of the room and one in the far corner.

Lessons were very basic, but thoroughly taught. I enjoyed the 3Rs, with arithmetic, composition, dictation etc, but my least favourite lesson was needlework, when all the girls in the two classes met together with the assistant teacher (the headmaster's wife) whilst the boys had drawing with the headmaster. In needlework we made garments, pinafores, knickers and nightdresses and we knitted vests, in four plain, four purl rib. I was a clumsy child with my fingers and the order, when showing my work to the teacher, was often, "Unpick!" We learnt how to make buttonholes – again a mystery to me, to patch and to darn, when a sock with a hole in it was brought from home for that purpose. If none was available a hole was cut in

The infants class of St Andrew's school, Eastbourne in the 1920s.

a good sock. We also made baskets from cane and raffia. Some excellent specimens were turned out, but mine were usually woeful.

Physical education, or drill as it was known, took place in the playground and exercises were done in straight lines to commands given by the teacher. Boys played football and cricket and girls, netball and stoolball.

The lavatories were dreadful, just buckets under wooden seats, which I used as little as possible.

There were no school dinners. Children who lived near enough went home and Mum was always there. Some children lived long distances from the school and walked from their homes, but there was very little danger then from traffic, or unsavoury characters. An older child would be in charge of the younger ones. On wet days they arrived soaking and their coats hung all day in an unheated cloakroom. They brought packed lunches to eat at midday.

Discipline was strict and the cane was wielded often. I remember the infants room door frequently opening, its bead curtain swinging and a hand pushing through some miscreant, usually the same boy, who spent some time propping up the wall and grinning at the children in the top class till he had to make his excuses to the headmaster. Retribution was swift! In later years, he admitted he deserved his punishments.

Christmas concerts always took place and on Empire Day (May

123

24th) the whole school went to the village cricket ground where a suitable display was given for parents and friends. This consisted of patriotic songs and recitations, also dances, often round the maypole. Some children were dressed to represent the countries in the British Empire and an older girl always took the part of Britannia.

A real treat, just before Christmas, was when everyone walked to a big house in the village, the home of a lady who was a school manager. Strict instructions were given beforehand regarding behaviour. The lady gave us a festive tea, after which we adjourned to the next room where there was an enormous, decorated Christmas tree, bearing a present for every child and for the teachers, too. We all walked round it, each child looking for their present, for they were all labelled. After the receiving of presents, we sang a carol and gave three cheers for the lady. On leaving, each child received an orange.'

FEES PER TERM

'In 1926 South View, Western Road, Hailsham was described as being a girls' school situated in the most healthy and beautiful part of Sussex. The fees for boarders were eight guineas per term, daily fees were four guineas per term (two guineas for under-tens). Use of school books and stationery cost five shillings per term.'

A STARCHED WHITE PINAFORE

'My earliest childhood memories are of living at Beddingham and starting at the local school in the early 1920s, wearing a white starched, embroidered pinny. We used slates and slate pencils and also sand trays for writing. We played with tops and hoops and marbles. In winter we wore muffs to keep our hands warm and kid leather button boots on our feet.

Outings were in a big horse-drawn waggon. In summer we were taken to Newhaven and at Christmas to Firle Place, the home of Lord Gage, where in the large front hall was a huge Christmas tree, beautifully decorated, and we all had goodies to eat and something from the tree.'

NO NONSENSE

'We walked two miles to the village school at Nutley. The whole school was warmed by a big iron stove, and on it was perched a bath of water containing the bottles of school milk, warming it through for break time. The milk cost a halfpenny a bottle. Toilet facilities were

very basic and I still shudder at the thought of those bucket lavatories. There were oil lamps for lighting, suspended from the ceiling.

One teacher taught every subject and got to know the children
well. It was hard luck if there was a personality clash. When Mr
Walker was the schoolmaster he was known as a man who stood no
nonsense.'

THE SCHOOL CHOIR

'Life in the village of Chiddingly, when I was a child during the late
1920s and 1930s was quite different from today. Cars were owned by
just a few well to do people. Many children probably never left the
village, except when travelling to neighbouring villages for school
sporting events. Therefore an event such as the Music Festival, held
yearly in Lewes, was indeed something special. The Women's Institute were responsible for organising this, thus giving encouragement
for a great competition, but more important, keeping alive so many
of our old English folk songs.

The headmaster of our school, Mr Oswald Sturdy, was of Welsh
origin, and singing was his great pleasure in life. We learned and
practised the songs set for the festival with great enthusiasm. We set
off on the day in a bus hired for the occasion, in high spirits for the
eight miles to Lewes. The Corn Exchange and Town Hall seemed so
large and other children with their teachers all appeared so confident.
Standing on the stage we felt less certain of our singing than in the
school classroom. We cannot say we did our best, but we got
through our ordeal, though it must have been a very lukewarm performance. Worse was to come!

Each choir had to take a simple sight reading test. This took place
in a smaller room. Our knowledge of sight reading was very rudi-
mentary, so it was with relief that as we tentatively sang the first
three notes, they seemed familiar. Yes, we knew it, and with no hesi-
tation completed the tune of *While shepherds*, feeling extremely
pleased with ourselves. Our joy was short lived. One glance at our
poor headmaster's face was enough, not to mention the scornful
expression on the adjudicator's face. The latter in his summing up in
the main hall to everyone, left us in no doubt that we were complete
dunces. He spared us nothing – we would have liked the earth to
open and swallow us up.

The homeward journey was most subdued and we wondered what
would be in store for us the next morning. We soon found out. He
would teach his choir to sight read if it was the last thing he did, or
the last thing we did for that matter. Every morning – without fail –

125

we did our sight reading exercises. We became so note perfect that absolutely nothing could deter us.

Our second visit to the Lewes Music Festival was an entirely different story. Not only had our confidence in singing on stage recovered, but we came top for sight reading, not one mistake. Our jubilation was even more complete when we found it was the same adjudicator as the previous year. He gave us enormous praise, congratulating our master on his splendid achievement.

Needless to say our return journey that year was one of conquering heroes!'

SCHOOLDAYS INTO THE 1930s AND 1940s

Little had altered in Sussex schools for the next generations of children, though war was to bring changes for us all.

TWO MILES TO WALK

'We lived nearly two miles from the school at Guestling. This meant walking across two fields and through a wood before reaching the main road. Sometimes there would be tramps in the woods, with their smoky fires and billy cans of tea. Some frightened us and most of the children walked in groups. The wood was halfway between Rye workhouse and Hastings workhouse and the tramps would walk from place to place. If my brother and I were late for school we would be kept in after the rest of the children had gone home and we would never walk through the wood alone.

School was great fun and I loved it. Each Christmas we had a party, when an elderly lady would give us each an orange and a cracker.'

VISITS TO THE DENTIST

'Through the school we visited the dentist in the Simmonds Institute hall at Seaford. There would be a number of us on benches in the main hall awaiting our turn. Those who were being treated could be heard crying, and they would come back into the hall with bleeding mouths. It was all quite frightening.'

GETTING THERE

'My sister and I had to walk nearly three miles to school. A long way when you are only five years old. We lived at Ashburnham, near Battle. We walked through Ashburnham Park, and down the drive which had been the road to London in the days of the coach and horses. Further up the drive was the milestone telling the miles to London.

I remember being allowed to sit in the actual coach which belonged to Lady Catherine Ashburnham. It was a beautiful coach, all red velvet plush inside and a little step that came down from somewhere. We passed the stables, where the coach was kept at Ashburnham House, on our way to school.

We met other school friends on our way, including Marjorie whose mother lived at one of the lodge gates. She had to open the big gates when someone wanted to come through. No washing was to be on the washing line if someone important was expected. Then there was Mary, the head gardener's daughter at Ashburnham House. Not forgetting our next door neighbours Peter and Pauline who began our journey to school with us. Our mother always allowed one hour for us to get to school.

Peter and Pauline's father had a chicken fattening business and he also owned a car with a dicky seat. He used this to take his crates to market and if he could, when it rained, he would come and meet us from school. We all wanted to sit in the dicky seat even though we still got wet.

When the war came we had evacuees from London to stay with us. They couldn't walk all that way to school! So a taxi came for them and it took us too which was great while it lasted but the day they went home the taxi stopped. Can you believe it.'

'When I was twelve I attended the church school in Battle. It was quite exciting as we had to walk through Battle (we had previously lived in a quiet country village) and if it was very wet we got a bus to school. In those days children had no school dinners, but the schools were beginning to organise hot drinks, mostly cocoa, for the children who brought food from home. We would call at the cake shops on the way to school and get a penny worth of stale cakes to eat in the play break, sometimes getting four or five cakes in the bag.'

BISHOPSTONE VILLAGE SCHOOL

'I was born in East Sussex and in 1932 my family moved to Bishop-stone village, where I attended the school which is now the village hall. There was a headmistress and an infants teacher and approximately 56 children.

The infants teacher was tall and slim, and she had her hair in coils over her ears. At five years of age I thought she was very old, I now realise she had probably come straight from sixth form at the grammar school! In the infants classes we were taught to knit and sew as well as all the normal classes. I still have a handkerchief sachet I embroidered then. Little boys who used bad language had a short, sharp lesson. They were marched into the cloakroom and she washed their mouths out with soapy water. They never did it again!

At seven we graduated into the next room. We sat at desks facing the headmistress. Her desk backed on to a big coke burning stove with its oval guard fastened to the wall. On winter mornings the bottles holding a third of a pint of milk warmed on the hearth. A cane lay, ready for use, across the top of her desk.

Boys were taught leatherwork, made seagrass stools and edged cork tablemats with beads. The girls did smocking, needlework, knitting and simple weaving. The crafts were entered in the village summer show. Our headmistress came from Northumberland. She taught us folk dancing, folk songs, sword dancing and poetry. We played netball, stoolball and shinty.

It was a Church of England school and the vicar took assembly every Wednesday and most saints' days. Our day started with prayers and grace was said before and after the lunch break. Some of us went home at midday, the rest brought sandwiches. During the winter they were allowed to toast them in the top of the coke stove, spiked on a long fork kept for that purpose.

Children then attended the village school until they were 14, but just before the war eleven year olds and over had to go to school in Seaford. Those who passed the eleven plus examination went to Lewes grammar school.

My fondest memories of my schooldays was of Friday afternoons and the last lesson of the week. How I loved the stories read to us by our headmistress. *Jungle Book*, *The Wind in the Willows* and many other books came alive in the sleepy silence of a class of spellbound children.'

I CAME TO TEACH AT LAUGHTON

'In 1933 I left Dover to come to Laughton to teach in the village school and live with my aunt and cousin. You can imagine my surprise when I found we had oil lamps or candles, oil stoves for cooking and water brought to us by a neighbour, two buckets a day for the three of us. We were allowed another bucketful at the weekend when we shared a hip-bath (in turns) with water boiled on the oil stove. Sanitation was in a hut in the garden.

During the war we did fire-watching in turns. At this time I lodged with a family where Land Army girls were also billeted. We had a few evacuees but were considered too near the coast for organised schools, although at neighbouring East Hoathly they had a school for a time billeted around the villagers.

Laughton school, luckily, was a short walk from our cottage. We had three classes, five to 14 year olds, and I had the middle class. Here again we were short of water. This was brought by the caretaker twice a week in a zinc carrier on wheels from the local inn. Heating was by open fires lit by the caretaker about 8 am. In winter the children often had to sit in their coats until the classrooms warmed up. I remember going in one spring morning to find hyacinth bulbs growing in water were frozen in the jars, so we put them by the fire and then I was called by the children as they were now "boiling".

The children walked across fields and were often poorly clothed. Some came on their mothers' bicycles and a few who came for nearly two miles came on their own bicycles. We played cricket and stoolball against local schools – East Hoathly, Chiddingly and Ripe. To get there we either walked or shared the few bicycles. This of course took a whole afternoon.

We were fortunate in being able to give our children a hot meal at lunch time. This was cooked by a local lady and the children paid a penny halfpenny, twopence or threepence according to their age. In the autumn the children picked blackberries and these were made into jam for the winter.

During the war we were reduced to two classes, the older children going to Ringmer school. We had two Anderson shelters built into the school playground. Luckily, although the school was damaged one night, we had to use the shelters only once.

At Christmas time we collected food from nearly all the villagers and gave the children a party with a small gift. All the village came to these parties and it was a great social event. Once during the war we had some soldiers billeted in the village and so they came to join the celebrations. This you can imagine was a great success, enjoyed by the children and young soldiers.'

'I AM A THIEF'

'We went to St Mark's church school at Arundel Place in Brighton, next to the gasworks. The teachers were very strict and the strap was used for punishment. I remember a child having to walk around all day with a large notice on his back and front saying "I am a thief", after stealing a few sweets from another child's desk.'

ROTHERFIELD PRIMARY

'At Rotherfield primary school we enjoyed playtimes with marbles (my favourite), leapfrog, handstands (I couldn't), hopscotch, kiss chase, chainey, conkers and skipping. In school I remember passing "love letters" in class and talking too much! I never got the cane but had to stand outside occasionally. I also had my knuckles rapped with a ruler.'

IN THE MIDDLE OF THE FARM

'The girls school at Mile Oak was built in the middle of Mr Broomfield's farm and girls who lived close by used to walk to school, through the unmade up farmyard and lanes. This was all right during the summer, but when it rained there was a great deal of mud to be negotiated. Our route passed the cow stalls and the farm horse stables. Many times the way was blocked, until the animals had passed by.

The girls who lived further away arrived by bus which stopped at the end of what is now Chalky Road.

There was no such thing as street lighting and when the school put on the end of term plays the lane up to Mile Oak Road, from the school, was highlighted by a line of hurricane lamps.'

I KNEW YOU COULD DO IT

'I was five years old when the Second World War started. My father had bought a new house – I believe it cost £750 – just north of the Old Shoreham Road in Portslade, near the old village, and we moved there in 1938 from our previous house nearer the coast.

My schooldays began at the beginning of the war in the new infants buildings of the St Nicholas church primary school. My

Forest Row Scouts collecting the District Camping Shield in 1953 from Group Captain Harvey Pack.

mother took me, together with my sister and brother who were younger, and we walked the half mile from our house, partly along the Old Shoreham Road. On some occasions other mothers from the vicinity would take all the children, thus giving mothers like mine, with small babies, a rest.

The classrooms were light and airy, although rather formal compared with those of today, and we had coat pegs with pictures and suitably sized toilets and wash basins. I found no difficulty in reading, in fact I cannot remember learning to read, and I was usually allowed to choose my own books. There was a hall, and we would go there for music sessions and PE. The thing I remember most about the infants school was spending long periods of time in the air raid shelters, reciting nursery rhymes and, later on, multiplication tables, which we did not understand at the time!

The transfer to the junior school was rather a shock. It was housed in the original Victorian building next to the infants school, and the lavatories were at the other end of the playground. The classrooms were high and draughty, some divided by wood and glass partitions which could be pulled back when necessary, and the cloakroom space was minimal. We sat in double desks with iron frames and lift-up seats, in rows facing the front and usually a boy with a girl. However, even if the surroundings were rather intimidating, the tea-

131

chers were, on the whole, very kind and good at their job – at least that is how it seemed to me, but then I enjoyed school and was probably not much of a problem!

I can remember needlework lessons, when we took turns to read to the other children as they worked, and playing the piano to the class once when I had learnt something quite difficult. We were taken to the local park occasionally for games and sports days but I cannot remember doing much PE in school. We always went to church on Ascension Day, and then had the rest of the day off, and on Empire Day we went to school in our Guide or Scout uniform. There were no school dinners then and we went home at lunch time, by ourselves when we were older, but at first our mothers met us and returned us to school, and gave us a meal in the hour or so allowed. This meant four walks each day, and must have been very time-consuming for mothers with younger children.

In the last year at the junior school it was suggested that another girl and myself should sit the entrance exam for the Brighton and Hove High School as well as doing the eleven-plus. My mother and father were keen that I should do this (my father was at this time in the army in France) so I took the exam and was offered a place for September 1945. I had a lovely letter from Dad, eventually, saying "I knew you could do it!" '

MEMORIES OF SKOOL!

'The Brighton & Hove School was indeed fortunate to number me amongst its pupils. I must confess, though, that scholastically I did nothing for the image of the school. Those were the days when spelling counted and all mistakes were marked 'SP' in red and had to be written out three times. Hockey was OK though – goal keeper dressed up in pads, kickers and gloves. School colours! I remember the day the award was announced in prayers and I had to walk up on to the platform to have my hand shaken by the headmistress as she pressed the precious square of yellow and green material into my other hand. I must admit, though, that she and I did not see eye to eye on much and I spent quite a bit of time on the form outside her study door waiting to be interviewed about some wickedness or other. She was, without doubt, a wonderful woman, totally dedicated and immensely erudite.

School also meant bright green marrow jam tart for school dinners. Revolting. But the third of a pint of milk and the buns delivered to the school in great batches by Davis and Cowley of Seven Dials were super! One penny for a plain bun and two pennies for an iced bun.

THE WORLD OF WORK

The Smithy

ON THE LAND

Generations of Sussex families have farmed the land and until the 1950s their way of life had changed little since Victorian days. Horses were still the power on the farm and children helped their parents in what was usually a family concern. Farming was a way of life and involved whole communities, lives revolving round the seasons.

MOST MEN WORKED ON THE FARM

'I was born in East Sussex and in 1932 my family went to live in Bishopstone village. Most of the men in the village and some from the surrounding district worked on the farm.

The carters worked, and looked after 16 shire horses, a few breeding mares with foals and broke in the young horses to work in harness. There was a forge on the farm where the blacksmith made cartwheels, horseshoes, and all the other ironwork was done. He also shod the horses.

Long summer days were spent as children taking cans of hot tea and sandwiches to the men in the fields. We rode empty Sussex waggons up to the hay or harvest fields and under the watchful eye of the carters, led the horses and full waggons back to the stacks. At the end of the day, a carter would put us up onto the horse's back, to ride home to the stables. The carters and their teams did a lot of the ploughing. There were also steam engines, one at each end of the field which pulled the plough to and fro on steel cables. A steam engine drove the threshing machine to thresh the corn from the sheaves. This was a noisy and dusty job.

Before the war the fields were full of crops. Cabbages and mangolds to feed the cattle, linseed, flax, wheat, barley, oats, grass and clover, all grown in rotation.

A big herd of Guernsey cows were hand milked twice a day. The cowmen started work at 4.30 in the morning and milked again at 3.30 in the afternoon. Every morning a churn of milk was delivered to the back door of the village shop. As children we did a milk round, not a paper round. We collected cans from the houses and took them back to the shop where the postmistress poured frothing milk into them from a measure which was hooked over the edge of the churn. We then returned the full cans before going to school. The

Walter Harwood, farm foreman and head carter on a farm at Little Common in the 1930s.

rest of the churns were taken by horse and trap from the farm dairy to the dairy in Seaford.

Before the Sussex bull was moved, one of the men would walk down the village street, shut all the gates and warn the children to stay in the garden. This enormous creature was led by two men holding a pole each, which were attached to a ring through the bull's nose. In the spring cattle were driven on foot down to the Pevensey marshes and were left to fatten up before being sold at the market, which was by Pevensey Castle.

Large white sows wearing leather harnesses were tethered by a long chain to the front of their triangular houses, which were dotted over the fields. Their litters were born in the houses, and the piglets ran freely over the field when they were big enough. The big white boar was kept behind the barns in a walled-in enclosure with a five bar gate at the end. One weekend the boys decided to have a rodeo. All the younger children sat on the wall and the bigger boys took it in turns to ride the boar, and run for the gate. My father was doing his rounds and heard the pig roar and came to investigate. Boars are dangerous animals when aroused. Children scattered as he too, roared in horror. I jumped off the wall into a cart rut and fell, sprain-

135

ing my ankle. I was the only one caught and got the full fury of a very frightened man! Life on a farm is never dull.

When I was a child the life of farming families was not always a very settled one. Men were employed by the farmer, or the bailiff, and the family moved into a cottage on the farm. If the man disagreed with his employer, or was not a good workman, he was dismissed. Usually he was given a week or a fortnight's notice which meant he also had to vacate his cottage in that time. Some men were employed on condition their wives worked in the farmhouse or vicarage.'

A WORKING FARM

'I was born in Northiam in 1909, a daughter of the village doctor. One of my earliest memories is of the sheep fairs which were held twice a year, one in spring and the other in autumn. These were held on the village green where sheep pens were erected, and as these were only temporary they were made from hurdles. The sheep were placed in the pens prior to auction so that local farmers could inspect them. The actual auction would last about two to three hours.

At the end of the auction the pens would be dismantled and within a few days the green would be back to normal, leaving no trace of the event. Unlike the cattle market which was held each week next to the Station Hotel, now called the Rother Valley Inn. Cattle pens were permanently there and it was an ideal place to hold the market as the railway was just down the road so transportation was easy. After the cattle had been sold, people would sell their garden produce, eg beetroot, carrots, cabbages etc, and this all helped to supplement their income.

Gate Court being a working farm, we had 50 cows which had to be milked by hand and that had to be done by a certain time to enable the milk to be taken from the farm by horse and cart down the road to Northiam station, where it was then taken by train to London via Robertsbridge. We also kept sheep, pigs, hens and turkeys on the farm.

We had six cart horses which worked on the farm. Every morning at 5.30 a horseman would arrive to feed the horses and then return an hour later to harness up the horses ready to begin work at 7 am. They were used for ploughing the fields and bringing in the hay and general farm work. Hops were also grown and the same hop pickers came every year from London and stayed in wooden huts on the farm. The hoppers were paid according to how much they picked and a tally was kept.

During the war when German planes flew over the local people

Rick building was a craft, as these stacks at Halfway Cottages, East Dean in 1950 show. Later the corn would be threshed, an intensive few days' work.

took no notice of them, but for the London hoppers it was a different story. One day when a London hopper was having her hops measured, German bombers flew over and when we turned to speak to her she was nowhere to be seen – we found her laying face down in a ditch petrified. She thought that they were about to be bombed – meanwhile the local hoppers carried on working.'

HEAD CARTER

'As a child I lived on a farm where my father was the farm foreman. He was also the head carter which meant he looked after all the horses, most of which were shires that were used to work the fields. I was born in one of the cottages on the farm so I was used to all the animals at a very early age. When I was three years old my father sat me on a hay-turner and I held the reins to drive my old friend Knobby, the cart horse, home, closely followed by Father driving another horse and cart. The old horses knew the time of day and did not need any driving but I was too young to know that and thought I was doing a great job for my Dad.

Also when I was three I went missing and my mother found me sitting in the bend of Knobby's back legs. I have been told she nearly died of fright!

By the time I was going to school, Father used to give me sixpence to clean his horse brasses, of which he had quite a lot.

There were events Father took the team to each year: the Bexhill Horse Show, the Hastings Carnival and the local Sunday school outing. All of these occasions meant that Father had a lot of hard work to get things ready, so my brothers and I had to help. I used to shampoo the horses' legs and dry them with pine sawdust. It made the hair beautifully white, soft and fluffy. We did not mind helping since we all enjoyed these events.

One night my mother woke to see a light in the stable. She woke up Father, who quickly dressed and went to investigate. Knobby had broken loose, found out where the light switch was and rubbed it with his nose to switch it on. He was a real rascal, always up to something!

The horses always enjoyed a treat after a busy day at work. Father kept a box of sugar lumps and a bottle of aniseed oil in a chest in the stable. He used to put a drop of aniseed on a sugar lump for each horse and the children also joined in. If you have never tried this, I can assure you it is jolly good. You may guess that Father had to lock up this little treat.

We moved away from the farm at Little Common when I was

twelve and came to live in Catsfield, on another farm. My father died in 1978 and I was left some of the horse brasses I used to clean so carefully.'

I LOVED EVERY MOMENT

'I was born in Uckfield in 1910, but my family, who farmed at Downlands on Snatts Road, moved to Penshurst in Kent when I was only a few weeks old. Links with the Uckfield area were still strong, with relations and friends still there and my grandparents still farming in Uckfield. Grandpa gave up work at 82 years old and they retired to Buxted, looked after by one of my aunts. After she died, at 22 years of age I volunteered to go and look after them for a few weeks – and stayed with them till they had both passed away, four years later.

At first there was no electricity in the cottage and we used oil lamps, which gave a lovely light, and of course cooked on the kitchen range. Grandpa had a pension of ten shillings a week, which he gave me as wages, and on that I felt really independent.

Mascall's Farm, next door, was owned by a Canadian, Mr Dart, and after a while he asked me to help on the farm occasionally, knowing that I came from a farming family and was interested. This I did regularly, while still keeping house for the grandparents. Mascall's Farm was much bigger than it is now, and was mostly strawberry fields. Eventually I was working there every day and it was very hard work, especially during the hot summer days, but I loved every moment of it.

When my grandparents died Mr and Mrs Dart asked me to go and live at Mascall's, which I was very happy to do, as they treated me like a daughter, having no children of their own. They gave me full board and ten shillings a week, and bought all my clothes, but for that I did all the cooking and housework as well as farmwork. This included haymaking. We had a very old tractor-mower, and it was my job to sit on the mower to work it while the tractor pulled it along. The mown hay was raked into wind-rows and left three or four days to dry. We had a mechanical rake to turn it and I had to sit on this too. Then the hay was picked up with forks and passed up to me on the waggon, to be taken to the stacks. These were thatched by a specialist who did all the stacks for miles around. I remember once during haymaking I dropped a cigarette stub in the field and started a fire! I got a terrible telling-off from Mr Dart, who forbade me ever to smoke again while haymaking – and I never did. Another thing that happened was the spiked iron tractor wheel going over my foot and the spike going between my toes. I was lucky my foot wasn't crushed, but still suffer with it sometimes today.

When the war came in 1939 things changed on the farm. We had to plough up all the strawberries and plant sugar beet, wheat and barley – things we couldn't get so easily from abroad any more. We grew all our own vegetables as well, and the main thing I remember from that time was that it was work, work, work. There were only Mr and Mrs Dart and me, and Mr Durrant who was 84 years old and as good as any youngster, to look after about 180 acres.

Mr Dart had a large dug-out built (which still exists today) and I used to do my stint of fire watching every other night around the farm. We had to report anything we saw by telephone from the farm, but the nearest thing I ever saw was a shower of incendiaries over Uckfield, one of which burned down the photographer's shop in the High Street.'

NEW ROOTS

'Apart from the war years, my husband had, for 40 years, lived the life of a "townie". He was the fourth generation of a family of builders in Essex. When he announced that he was packing up building and going into the country to start a smallholding, everyone thought he was "nuts". He knew nothing about rearing livestock or growing crops, and my knowledge was minimal, but as he was so determined I agreed to go along with the idea.

We decided that the sooner we started to prepare the way the better, and so we went to classes to learn the basics. There we were assured that once we had acquired a smallholding, the experts at County Hall would come to our assistance and help every step of the way. In the event, they could not have been more helpful.

But where to go? East Sussex, of course. Where could one find more beautiful scenery, and nowhere was too far from the coast. My favourite relatives lived in and around Eastbourne, so our minds were quickly made up. I spent hours in Southend Library studying the lie of the land and soil conditions. I found that the Heathfield/Crowborough area had the most favourable loamy soil.

Very soon, "properties for sale" leaflets started piling up on our doormat. One grasped our attention. It was described thus: "The garden cottage of a large estate, with kitchen garden, greenhouses, orchard, walled garden, stables, pig sties, outhouses and bothy with 3½ acres. In a state of neglect, needs a lot of repairs to be done." An additional tempting item was "750 feet above sea level, magnificent views". It sounded quite a challenge, and the price was reasonable.

140

Right away, we set off for the Mayfield area, conscious that we were part of a queue of cars heading for the same direction. A mile out of the village we turned into a private lane, passing a 14 foot wall surrounding the estate.

Going through the gate, we stood in wonderment at the glorious views, with the High and Over near Alfriston in the distance. Above were clear blue skies, drifting down below were clumps of fluffy white clouds. It seemed too good to be true. Then we faced reality. The dilapidated cottage with grey mould on the walls, the greenhouses with few panes of glass left in them, the broken down sheds, and the weeds shoulder high. Someone said, "One year's seeding, seven years' weeding". We faced a formidable task, that's for sure.

We drew up a list of priorities. "Reglaze the greenhouses, repair the sheds, buy some scythes and rotovator, and get cracking". This was February 1957, and there was no time to lose. The cottage would have to wait. We would have to slum it for a bit, after all we had to earn a living.

Other potential buyers were swarming around, no doubt with similar thoughts to our own. Then the estate agent arrived. "The first to sign will get it," he said. No time for a survey, we had to take a chance, so we got into the car, dashed off to Mayfield and were first in the queue. We signed.

Back we went to Essex to put our bungalow on the market, and prepare the way for disposing of our building business.

Once we took over our mini-estate, it was all stations go. We cut down the weeds, and found the soil in remarkably good condition. Then we rotovated it in preparation for salad crops. We quickly repaired the propagating house, so that I could sow seeds and start up bedding plants. The largest of the greenhouses needed completely reglazing, and this is where I grew 1,000 tomato plants. In the smaller lean-tos we grew cucumbers.

With so many empty outbuildings, we decided to use them for deep-litter laying birds, and we invested in 400 of them. Some were allowed free range. We went to market and bought a Friesian calf and six pigs. Our pigs we intended to sell as baconers, but swine fever in the area delayed their sale and they ended up at market as fat hogs. We overfed the Friesian and she became "blown". We walked her around, slapping her backside, thinking it was "wind". An ex-army land girl said, "Stuff her mouth with broken egg shells." We had to admit defeat and off she went to market too.

The next calf we bought was a Guernsey, from a local farmer, and he advised us how to rear her. We had her artificially inseminated, and found our names in the Herdbook. A fortnight before calving, we sold her to a farmer. We were beginning to realise our limitations.

Due to our inexperience, we had great difficulty in buying goats. We fell in love with some beauties in Buxted, but no way would they sell to such novices. In Hurst Green we discovered a herd of British Sanaans and the owner took a chance on us. We arrived home with a mother and her daughter, Sunset and Evening Star. They both produced kids and we were there at the birth. Their milk was a bonus, we used it ourselves, sold to neighbours, and made ice cream and cheese.

The pair were great characters. They would climb up on to outhouses and crunch any fruit which they could reach. I remember going into the stables one day when my husband was milking them. He had put his pipe on a shelf whilst milking Evening Star, and there was Sunset, awaiting her turn, pipe in mouth and puffing away.

We needed a household pet, so we went to Buxted and bought a Sealyham, Susie. She had puppies and we kept the pick of the litter, Sally. Susie was very useful, going out every evening to the house of the free range chickens, bringing in the eggs one by one in her mouth, rarely cracking any, and we rewarded her with scrambled eggs for supper.

We grew corn the old fashioned way, scattering the seed over the ground, and at harvesting, stooks were erected and the hens busied themselves clearing the grain. When ready, we tossed the stooks into the henhouse for the birds to kick around to make litter as they scratched for food. When we moved later, they came with us and died of old age.

By the time we were into our second season, and things were going fairly smoothly, we decided to increase our chicken population. We thought it would be economical to buy day olds. One hundred and fifty arrived and four days later the same number disappeared. Where? Under the floorboards of the bothy where we had housed them, taken there by rats. We sent for the ratcatcher, who put down poison and we watched in amazement as an army of rats staggered drunkenly to their death. Thinking that we had solved the problem, we sent for another 150 day olds. The apparently secure infra-red lamp slipped its moorings and the second batch met an untimely end. So it was pullets for us in future.

Living off the beaten track, there was no passing trade. We supplied my Eastbourne cousin for her hotel with eggs, salad crops, soft and hard fruit. We bartered our produce with the butcher in return for meat and the grocer in return for his goods. Bedding plants went to Heathfield market and the rest to wholesalers.

After four years' hard labour, and corn bills piling up, we had to take stock. There was no fun in our lives. It could not go on. A sudden legacy solved the problem. My husband had achieved his dream, but reality claimed us.'

TIED TO THE FARM

'I was born at Foxhole Farm, Netherfield in 1922. At three months old we moved to The Model Farm, Normanhurst.

Lady Brassey lived at Park Gate, Catsfield and once a year we were asked to take our savings books to school and she used to arrange with the post office to have money put in our books, starting from one shilling to five shillings till we left school, to encourage us to save.

Before the war the new Kitchenham Road was made and I remember my Dad helped to do it. He had to hire horses and carts from local farmers and to get extra men to help. My Mum used to wait outside the Union (which is now Battle Hospital), where the tramps went in for the night and were turned out at 10 am, to see if any were willing to work for a few weeks; they were fed and paid and slept in one of the outbuildings.

My job as a child was always, when I got home from school, to get the kindling wood in ready to light the fire in the morning. The ashes had to be cleaned out and the stove blackleaded; it was the only thing we had to cook on. We had to have lots of hot water to wash up the dairy things.

When I was old enough I had to start milking the cows, and we were allowed to sell milk to our neighbours; I think it was fourpence a pint. We used to take it out in a can with a pint measure and fill the jugs which were left outside, no bottles in those days and they got milk twice a day. As time went by our milk round got bigger and then bottles came in, so then I had a pony and trap. One pony I remember very well as we had to put a muzzle on it as it would snap and bite.

When I left school I wanted to be a nurse. I went and saw Lady Brassey, who was one of the head ones at the Royal East Sussex Hospital in Hastings. I wasn't quite 16 then and she said they don't usually take probationers till they are 16 but you look a strong healthy girl. One day a letter arrived for me from one of her staff. My Dad said, "What's that about?" so I told him. He soon put a stop to that, we want you on the farm! So I went and saw her ladyship to thank her, but that was that.

When Dad mowed the corn with a mowing machine, we had to make the bonds. We would get a good arm full of wheat or whatever, laid it on the bond and twisted it round and tied it up. We stood them up in sixes or eights to dry before stacking them. Another art was making a corn stack. You had to make a round stack. The bottom started off with faggots (thin wood), then you laid the

Shocking up corn near Robertsbridge in 1936, when the harvest was still largely a manual task involving whole communities.

sheaves of corn with their ears inward, side by side in a round. When it was so high you gradually drew it to a point, then a man came in to thatch it. The stack had to stand there for some time, until the threshing machine came round. That made quite a noise, you could hear it when it was on the farm next to yours. Then I was sent to see how long it would be and are you coming to us next? We wanted to know because we always supplied them with tea and something to eat.

We grew our mangolds and swedes; I remember pulling them when it was very cold, for the cattle. I had to get a big trug and fill it with the mangold and swede. I put them in a mangold cutter, turned the handle and put the trug underneath to catch it, then feed the cows with it. In the winter we brought the calves in a shed, and you didn't clear the straw out, you kept putting clean on top. When the weather got better and the calves were turned out the shed had to be cleaned out and I had to get a hay knife to cut it out, get the horse and harness it up, fill the dung cart, take it out to the fields, put it in lumps and then go and spread it, which was quite hard work.

Normanhurst was a private house owned by the Brassey family. Eventually it was turned into a young ladies' school. When the war came they were evacuated and the army took it over. The woods all around made good camouflage for the army lorries. Bringing the cows home to be milked one evening my Mum was with me (only because of the soldiers about) when they said they could do with a glass of milk. My Mum being a businesswoman said, "Well come up to the farm about 5.30 and you can buy some." Whilst we were doing the milking she went inside and cooked some buns for them to buy as well. Then of course one told the other and we were getting more than we could cope with. Because tea and sugar were rationed, off she went to the Food Office in Battle to get a permit to run a canteen.

We had a long trestle table in the backyard and wooden seats, which was all right in the summer but when the winter came they came inside our tiny kitchen. They took it in turns to do the toast and we were out in our little scullery cooking eggs and heating beans. We used to have twelve dozen cakes sent out from Hastings every day on the bus. Then Mum got a tobacco licence to sell cigarettes. We only had a primus stove to work on. The toasting fork went missing one day so Mum wasn't very pleased about that and closed the canteen until it came back. Another time the mirror on the wall went missing so Mum reported that to one of the officers when he came for cigarettes. "I will put it up on the notice board," he said, and that came back too.

We had an air raid shelter dug out of the bank. We had a lot of incendiary bombs, about the time we had been threshing the corn and they dropped in amongst the shavings which was rather dangerous, but the soldiers were soon there to help. Another time when the doodlebugs were over our planes tried to bring them down in the sea, but some got through, and one they brought down landed amongst our milking cows. A lot were killed. They were in a field behind a row of houses at Catsfield and by the time I got there "Butcher Smith" was coming away. He was the butcher in the village. He said, "I shouldn't go up there, it is a terrible mess. I have been there with my humane killer." We got compensation but nothing like the cows were worth.

I was working in the fields hoeing, quite away from home, and there was a dog-fight going on, our planes against the Germans. The empty shell cases were falling down about me. I began to get frightened. My hair was full of curlers with a scarf on, so I took the curlers out and went into the wood so they couldn't see me if they came down! I expect I had a date that night and wanted to look extra special. This was all happening in my teens.

When we got to 20 we had to register for one of the services and I thought I would like to join the WAAFs. I didn't say anything to my parents, and I got as far as having my rail warrant to go to Brighton for a medical when they found out. No way was I going to Brighton, they put a stop to that, "You are wanted on the farm." Mum went to the Agricultural Office in Battle to say I was more help on the farm than going in the WAAFs so there again I was stopped. There was no arguing the toss, we had to do as we were told.

Eventually Normanhurst was taken over as a prisoner of war camp so the canteen finished, and in the end was demolished which I think was a pity.

Once I said to my Mum I wouldn't get married until I was 25. She said, "I will give you £25 if you don't." We got out of the farm after 25 years there and they bought a small chicken farm which took all their money and when I was 25 and still at home there wasn't the money to give me, but she said "You can have the single bedroom suite", and never told Dad. When Mum died he had a sale about two years after, as he was getting married again and that was sold, so I didn't get it. I got married myself just before Dad in 1948 and food was still rationed, but Dad had kept a pig which was killed and he gave me half of it and a crock of lard which started me off very well.

When we had the farm we always had a pig killed every now and then and I can remember these sides of bacon hanging on the walls covered with butter muslin. When we came in late at nights from haymaking or harvesting, Mum always had a good supper waiting for us.

I well remember Battle Fair day, the gypsy women used to get drunk and fight. That was the one day my Dad would come home the worst for drink. In spite of everything I loved him and we got on well together.'

ON THE FOREST

'Colemans Hatch is a small hamlet situated on the edge of Ashdown Forest and in the early part of the century consisted mainly of two or three estates and several smallholdings employing most of the residents. Many of the people relied heavily on the forest for grazing and bedding for their animals and for firewood for their homes. Most of the village was without electricity until the 1950s and many properties drew water from wells in their gardens or springs near their homes on the forest.

My father was a smallholder rearing his animals on the forest. He cut litter and bracken to use for bedding for the animals during the winter and also rushes for thatching the haystack.

My earliest recollections, in the 1940s, are of Mother cooking on an open fire, a large kettle always hung on a chain over the fire for hot water for all uses. We had no services except for a cold water tap and bathtime, whilst we were small enough, was in the tin bath in front of the fire. Lighting was by paraffin lamp and candles to go to bed.

We seemed to have proper seasons in those days, very hard winters with the fields frozen solid for weeks and thick ice patterns on the inside of the windows in the mornings, but these were followed by glorious hot summers. As I grew older these became hard work when haymaking time came around, because having no brothers I had to help in the fields and as we only had a few acres everything was done by hand. In those days the hay was not baled but stacked and thatched and then in the winter it had to be cut in slices from the stack with the hay knife – not a pleasant job when covered with snow and frost. Although I was expected to help with the farmwork it was never a chore, I loved it and of course I had my favourite animals, at one time a pet black sow I took for walks in the forest, another time a bullock I used to ride and my last, before I married and moved away, a Highland cow.'

FARMING LIFE

'Shorthorn cows were being milked in the cowsheds in 1948, when my husband left school and became totally involved in the farming done by his father and his grandfather. The cowmen would be at work by 4.30 am and each one put on a long, white overall, fastened by ties at the back, and a white skull cap. Milking was done by hand, each man dealing with twelve cows. This took place twice a day, early morning and mid afternoon, as it is now. Although some milk was bottled in the farm dairy, with edged cardboard caps being manually pressed over the larger topped bottles, milk in the small hamlet of Barcombe Mills was delivered in two large cans carried by hand. For a short time I had that task, and enjoyed it. Calling at each cottage I would normally find the back door wide open, then into the kitchen I'd step and find the jug, or basin, and I would proceed to ladle out the milk with a one pint or half pint measure. Prior to 1940 two such deliveries a day were made, but during the war the milk was rationed to half a pint per day.

On my rounds I'd sometimes meet carters, each one leading a horse drawing a cart of dung. Those heaps of dung were dropped, strategically, out in the field and later three or four workers would go with large, long pronged forks and scatter the dung from each pile to fertilise the whole field. Hoeing was another "gang" job, where several men would be bent over each allotted cant singling out the sugar beet. They would work methodically, tediously and back-achingly throughout the whole day. But there was a lot of jolly chat and leg-pulling ... and when they were serious, they were certainly putting the world to rights better than any politician. The companionship was close and comforting.

Harvesting was a pleasurable, hard slog creating enormous appetites in the workers. No wonder they were given extra rations of cheese and butter during the war! Although it could be extremely scratchy, there was something rewarding about clutching sweet smelling sheaves of corn to you and getting the pair to stand in a shock (or stook). Best of all was a ride on top of a waggon load of straw or hay. Dry hay can be very slippery stuff, though, and my husband's grandfather slithered from the top of one load when he was 88 years old, fracturing his skull ... but he lived to be 92.

In the early years of our marriage, at the time of the Queen's coronation, corn was stored in neatly built stacks. They were not complete until the skilled thatcher had roofed them, with tightly bound straw, to keep the weather out. The thatcher would usually have a mate helping him with the selecting and dampening of the straw. Later, the threshing gangs would set to work, using "chattering" machinery which worked away at separating the corn from the straw and creating great clouds of choking dust. Not only was the dust and dirt thrown around but so also were the dozens of mice who had made their homes in the stack, and they would dart crazily into the men's shirts and trousers! This caused plenty of annoyance, entertainment and laughter. Farm jobs of that era were companionable. Now, the men are isolated in their air-conditioned tractor cabs with their radios; they have to resort to CBs for company.

When we were married in 1953, we had no electricity in our farmhouse, and it wasn't until our fourth child was born in 1961 that the electric current reached our home. Prior to that, the oil lamps had to be lit every night. One of the most difficult things to do was to carry a small child upstairs to bed whilst holding the oil lamp, at full arm stretch, with the child trying to reach forward and grab it! Lamp light was certainly warm, cosy and flattering. I can remember another light, too, out in the garden – my husband was too busy farming by daylight, so his gardening was often done in the dark with a candle, in a two-pound jam jar, at each end of the row he was digging.

Up until 1960 there was a thriving, effective Rabbit Clearance Society in East Sussex. The farmers would also contribute money towards the payment of someone permanently employed to keep the rabbit population down. The sudden onset of the dreadful myxamatosis disease in rabbits eliminated the need for such a society. Rabbit casserole was always a popular meal. Pigeon pie is still a great favourite with us, but by far the most delicious pie was rook, which we don't get nowadays.'

THE FARM WAS MY LIFE

'I can't remember a time when I didn't love the farm. The farm was my life, the world was my garden. As a small girl I lived on a farm at Beachy Head called Black Robin. There was quite a little band of us, my two sisters and the Coastguard's children and other farm workers' children. We walked down a winding path we called a twitten, crossing a zig-zag road twice on the way to Meads primary school. We ate our lunch sitting on forms in the cloakroom leaning against damp coats. On days when the fog came early someone would say, "Perhaps the hill children had better go", and we wandered off together, sometimes getting a lift in the post van.

On hot, sunny days the school took us on to the beach and we learnt to swim in the sea. Such was the freedom and security that surrounded us as children. We were able to walk down to the beach alone and pick cowslips and wild raspberries on the way, skirting carefully around fascinating dewponds. Occasionally Mother and Father would leave me with my small brothers and sisters and they would take a stroll. I remember one night waiting for them to come home, and as it got unusually late I lit the paraffin lamp and wondered where they were. They were actually on top of Beachy Head lighthouse. It seems someone told them at Holywell that because of the special spring tide they could walk out to the lighthouse, so they did and were invited up to see the light. The lighthouse keeper was sorry he couldn't light the lamp as that, he said, was against regulations. Years later, after the war, I walked out with a young man and stood on the green slimy steps of the lighthouse, but visiting was not allowed thank goodness. It was terrifying to look up at those cliffs.

I remember the red poppies bobbing in the corn, the little white sails bobbing in the blue sea, I remember people talked of war, they said it wouldn't come, but it did.

My young brothers were now at school. We moved out of the machine gun zone right into the path of the doodlebug, in Herstmonceux. I saw my first doodlebug at five o'clock one morning as I stood in a cow yard, it was eerie.

The farm was now my job. I was too young to be in the Women's Land Army, but my father had agreed to train me to work on the land. My father was a master craftsman; starting as a carter boy, his expertise in farm crafts included making faggots for sea defences, and he could thatch a stack or barn and lay a hedge. He taught me to scythe and cut a swath of hay from a haystack with a huge hay knife. Now in the middle of the war he had charge of a famous Red Poll dairy herd, three land girls and a very grateful 16 year old daughter.

I cried when my father sat me under my first cow with a bucket. The milk wouldn't come out. "Please," I said, "can I use a machine?" "Not until you can hand milk," he said, "you'll be glad you can one day." I remembered his words when two years later I had charge of my own herd of cows. One frosty morning I went into the engine shed to start my petrol milking machine. I pulled the cord, it spluttered and stopped, I tried again and flooded it. I picked up my bucket. I was glad I could milk by hand, no tears this time.

The war was still on and the Land Army girls were doing a marvellous job, but I was a freelance. I earned £4 10s a week, 5 am to 5 pm seven days a week, Tuesday afternoon off.

I worked with what was known as a Gascoigne Milking Parlour, the very early forerunner of the modern milking parlour. Some parlours were towed around and used in open fields by Land Army girls. My cows, 70 plus in number, stood in a concrete yard and waited their turn to come in to the parlour. Open to the weather at the back and roughly surrounded by corrugated iron sheets, a centre door pushed open and one by one without haste or hassle those lovely beasts came in to be milked. It took about an hour and a half to clear the yard, and what joy if at the end of milking there was a clean yard.

There were three machines used each side alternately. Above the machine a hopper, at the pull of a noisy metal handle, released food, the udder was washed and checked for mastitis clots and the machine applied. The milk travelled along a pipe down an open cooler into a churn, and when full a label was written and attached to the lid bearing the guarantee that this was TT Attested milk, no less!

Oh, those long lovely days and the mornings when the spilled milk froze in the gutters. The doodlebugs always seemed to come over just as I stood in the middle of a field of kale with swap or hoe.

Between 5 pm and 5 am we found time to dance and ride in jeeps, join young farmers' clubs and learned to skin rabbits, draw chickens, iron a shirt in seven minutes and lectured on the 'aspirations of a young farmer' to anyone who would listen. I don't remember green wellies but I remember we had a whale of a time.'

HOP PICKING

'Hop picking was and still is to this day an absolute joy to me. My mother first took me to the hop gardens when I was only two years old. She did not have, as so many other mothers did with children, a box on two wheels with two straight handles. My father carried me part of the way before going to work and I have been told other kindly folk did the same, since it was quite two miles or more to get to the hop gardens. However, as I got older I had to carry the two umbrellas, whilst Mother carried a loaded basket with food and drink for the long day.

Usually it meant leaving home at 6 am to get to the hop gardens at 7 am in time for the call, "All to work". Mostly the grass we walked through was wet with heavy mist and, on occasions, Dad "painted" the edges of my boots with mutton fat. When we got to the hop garden everything was wet, but we still had to pick.

The hops were picked into bins, made of the same kind of coarse canvas material as the hop sacks. This material was suspended from the wooden frame, which could be closed and carried by the pole-puller to another set. My aunt had one half of the bin and my mother the other half and each half would have held anything up to ten bushels or more. There were four bins to a set and a pole-puller for each set. In between "pulling" he could and did pick some hops. It was also his job to see that each bin was correctly placed, to give each the same amount of "hills" to each picker. The "hills" were the clumps of hop-poles. The hops were measured two or three times a day so that the oasts were always well supplied for drying them and a waggon was used to take the ten-bushel bags for this.

We had to wait to have dinner until the call "All to dinner" came, but this was usually about midday and about 15 minutes before this every other bin made a fire to boil the billy on, the wood having been collected mostly by us children beforehand. This billy was similar to a large upright tin, with a handle over the top and the tea was added when the water boiled and given a stir. *Everyone* who has ever tasted "hop-garden tea" agrees there is no other tea to compare with this, it's the best cup of tea ever! Another job we children had, in preparation for dinner, was to arrange a stack of poles (from which the hops had been picked) to form a kind of arch, softened by lots of used bins. Dinner usually consisted of sandwiches, boiled pork seemed best, or meat turnovers and sometimes fruit pies made in saucers, as well as buns and cake. All the baking had of necessity to be done at weekends, if possible.

My mother and aunt always wore "wrapper" aprons (a kind of sacking material) to protect their skirts, since hop stains, brown, cannot be removed. The black stains on the hands, caused by the pollen, were best removed by washing the hands with soap and runner bean leaves, which removed the dark stain easily. The money paid for picking was, all the time we went, as far as I can remember, one shilling and threepence per dozen bushels! Our farmer was always slightly lower than some in paying.'

'Hop picking around Burwash was a way to earn money to buy winter clothes and boots. Hops were picked into a canvas bin supported by wooden legs, a man with a large wooden bushel measure going to each bin two or three times a day. The hops were then put into a large sack called a poke and the number of bushels picked was recorded in a book. I remember the dreaded upturned umbrella which had to be filled with hops before being emptied into the bin and a clip round the ear if you didn't keep picking. It took a long time to pick five bushels, for which a shilling was paid.

Lunch was eaten sitting on the hop poles, with that awful bitter taste from the hops. Jam and Marmite sandwiches with a bottle of cold tea, cocoa or lemonade (made with Eiffel Tower crystals bought in a small bottle costing fourpence, which made about one and a half pints when diluted with water).'

Spraying the hops at Staplecross in 1935, using soft soap.

153

MILK AND BUTTER

'I was born in a Victorian farmhouse at Staplecross. There was a large pantry which held the separator for the milk; the cream was made into butter which was sold locally or taken by cycle to a local market. Skimmed milk sold for twopence a pint, butter was ninepence a pound. Some butter was salted down in large crocks for winter use.

All the work on the farm was done with three horses. I used to cut chaff for the horses and turn the handle on a machine which cut slabs of linseed cake for the cows and swedes and mangolds for the animals.

My uncle used to dry the hops picked by the village people, six to eight bushels for a shilling. When the hops were drying, coal had to be got in to keep the fires going and they worked all night. When the hop pockets were full they were loaded on waggons and taken to Bodiam station, then loaded into covered trucks and taken to London.'

FREE GRAZING

'I came to Ditchling in 1928, when there were very few cars on the roads and children were able to play on the roadside. We were quite near a farm where milking was done by hand. You heard the milkman calling the cows very early in the morning, and they had to cross the road from a field they were in to the milking sheds. At that time there was free grazing for cows on the common and we often saw cows lying by the side of the road, with no cars to worry them. Sheep were moved from field to field, travelling on the roads, and this was all part of country life.'

IN SERVICE

Many young girls found that going into service was the only form of work available to them when they left school, in those days when most farms and many middle class homes employed at least one servant and the big house or estate gave employment to whole communities.

FROM FRAMFIELD TO LONDON

'I was born in 1890 in Framfield. My father was employed at the "big house" and we lived in a cottage some distance from the village. We were a family of six girls and two boys, a happy family.

After I left school I went into service in London. We were a large staff with butler, footmen, cook with her staff, housemaids and parlourmaids, coachmen and grooms, who cared for the horse-drawn carriages, and there was a nightwatchman. When the family were more than twelve for dinner the butler and footmen would wear silk breeches and powdered wigs. It was lovely to see. The table always looked beautiful with cut-glass and gold plate, and the ladies very fine in their evening dresses. We did a lot of entertaining. It was a rich household, and the houses were full of beautiful antique furniture. Sir George loved antique furniture and sold it. When visitors came I had to show them to their rooms, and look after them. We were happy and treated well. I enjoyed London. I was lucky as one of my sisters was also in service in London, so sometimes we were able to meet if we had a day off at the same time. We had a day off each week. I was in Piccadilly when news came through of the relief of Mafeking. I went to see King Edward VII lying in state. As a household we went to church, either morning or evening, so that there was always someone in the house to carry on the duties.

After I retired I returned to Framfield, but was persuaded to join the household of Lady Thornton as cook. I had to teach myself, but I enjoyed it. I had two kitchen girls to help me. We got all the food locally and from the farm. I had lots of good food to cook with, for instance 20 pounds of butter a week. Lady Thornton, as a local benefactor, would give twelve cloaks each year, for six village boys and six village girls. These were made by the lady's maid. In my spare time in the evenings I loved to crochet and made many white cloths with deep crochet borders. I was happy and content in my years in service and to this day members of my old families keep in touch with me.'

A YOUNG GIRL OF 15

'Life wasn't exactly full of excitement when I came to Hove in 1928. A young girl of 15 knowing nobody, I came to work in St Aubyns, Hove, to be trained as a house parlourmaid. What a joke. It turned out more like a maid of all work, as another girl and I had to clean a five-storey house, as well as looking after the Mr and Mrs and a granddaughter.

We did have a daily cook, but we two had to do everything else including cutting the old boy's nails. There I had my first taste of rationing – and freedom. We were allowed out one afternoon a week, from 3 pm to 9 pm, one Sunday off 11 am to 1 pm and the next 3 pm to 9 pm – and for the princely sum of £1 3s 4d a month. Often on my day off I had no money for entertainment, so I used to walk into Brighton and back, just looking at the shops, and if it was raining I went back to the house, where at least it was warm.

I stuck this for six years, then as my health was going down due to the poor food I left and found another job for £1 a week. Now my life began to get a bit more exciting. I had a boy friend who eventually became my husband for 47 years – and I began to go about with another girl.

We had a lot of fun together, and one great pleasure was to visit Sherry's Dance Hall, at the bottom of West Street, to sit up on the balcony watching the dancers below. It was a long time before we could afford to go down there and join in. But still there was the occasional splash out for the Hippodrome, ninepence upstairs, where we saw Max Miller (The Cheeky Chappie) and many others. I remember too, tea dances at Staffords, a big store in Western Road, and Sunday afternoon dancing at the Regent Ballroom; dancing the night away at the Dome and Corn Exchange in Brighton to the music of three big bands, and the biggest thrill of all, dancing at the end of the pier, with the sea gently lapping below. It seemed as though a full moon was always shining down on us.'

NOTHING ELSE TO DO

'I have lived all my life in East Sussex and most of it in East Hoathly, where I was born. My father was a coachman at Beliman's, one of the big houses and, in 1927, earned 35 shillings a week.

I went to East Hoathly church school until I was 14, when I left to go into service. I remember the headmaster as being kind, but strict, and all children looked up to the staff. I enjoyed needlework and made a nightdress just before leaving school. On that day I remember the vicar's wife, a formidable woman, coming to the school and asking me what I was going to do, was I going to be a nursemaid? "No," I said, "my mother says a nursemaid never gets any peace." To which the vicar's wife replied, "You don't expect any peace if you're going into service." Most of the girls did go into service, there being nothing else for them to do in the village. Occasionally the odd clever boy would go off to the grammar school in Lewes.

I remember the squire of the village, a Captain Clements, dying. He used to go to Buxton to take the waters and one year whilst he was there he slipped and broke his neck. My mother took me to watch the funeral, standing by the lychgate – we curtsied to the gentry.

We didn't go away for holidays, but Whit Monday was a special day in the village and was known as Club Day (the club being what the men paid into in case of need – a form of insurance). The men gathered in the morning and, headed by the Blackboys Band, marched to church for a thanksgiving service. Then they retired to the local inn for lunch. In the afternoon, the families gathered in the recreation ground for games and races and a picnic. For this day the girls had new dresses, usually made by their mothers.

After leaving school I went into service as a housemaid at Chalvington rectory. Besides myself there was a parlourmaid, a cook and a nursemaid. My mother had to provide my uniform – a print dress, apron and cap for morning and a black dress, white apron and cap, which I changed into to serve in the dining room and wore in the afternoons.

I then moved to Eastbourne, where I progressed to being a parlourmaid. I was there when the First World War ended and remember the family giving the servants the day off, so we all went to a service at St Saviour's and then celebrated. We could go down to the beach to swim without taking a "hut", but only between 6 am and 7 am. We would put a coat on over our swimsuits and then dash to the beach for a swim, put the coat back on over the wet suit and dash back to the house.

I moved back to East Hoathly to one of the big houses, this time as cook. I can remember the mistress of the house discussing the meals for the day and then the parlourmaid would use a French phrase book to translate it into French, before putting the menu in the dining room. Eventually I left service when my mother died and I had to look after my father.

157

We were never rich, in fact I guess we were poor, but my mother was a good cook and we were well looked after and were happy and content.

One further story again concerned the vicar's wife, who ran the Mothers Union. The ladies would pay something each week into a club, to buy things for their family – good, warm, wholesome, no-nonsense things. Once a year they would tot up what they had saved and decide what they wanted from the village shop. (There were two of these, one which catered solely for the gentry and one other for everybody else!) These things would then be parcelled up, but with one end left open, and sent to the vicarage, where the vicar's wife would inspect them, to make sure the money had been well spent. Only then could the ladies have their parcels!'

ESTATE AND BIG HOUSE

'In most villages there was a Squire and his family, who were the main employers. When a boy left school he generally followed in his father's footsteps and worked on the farm or on the estate. The girls went into domestic service in the big house. After the war, and with further education and easier travel, the drift from the land into town jobs began to take place. Tractors took the place of horses on the farms and as new machinery became available, the numbers of men working on the farms decreased. So the farm cottages were not needed and many have been sold.

Up to the 1940s most of the men and women in East Dean were employed by the Gilbert Estates and Forestry Commission.'

'The big houses of the area – The Vachery, Chapelwood, Chelwood Beacon, Oldlands, Pippingford and a few others – provided employment in Nutley as children grew up and left school. They could train as gardeners, chauffeurs and domestic servants, and these occupations were the mainstay of paid work apart from agriculture, as there was no commercial undertaking for many miles.

In earlier generations we worked hard for a pittance. The men who worked in the village grocer's shop earned twelve shillings a week and had to spend ten shillings of it in the shop. Poaching and other illegal activities were resorted to. Food seems cheap in comparison with our own times – sugar, for instance, was one shilling and threepence for a 14 pound bag, but this had to be balanced against, say, a nurseryman's wage of eleven shillings for 54 hours, rising to 14 shillings in summer for 63 hours. These meagre earnings were paid on Saturdays, so the village shop was kept open until 10 pm that night.'

VILLAGE TRADES AND CRAFTS

Every village had its own tradesmen and craftsmen, from the local blacksmith to the shopkeeper, and all were at the very heart of community life.

THE VILLAGE BLACKSMITH

'The forge at Wivelsfield Green was built in the Victorian era and demolished in 1968. Children would wait for the school bus in the warmth and shelter of the buildings, while later in the day the older men would call in for a rest and a chat, making it a place that was sadly missed.

The blacksmiths always wore leather aprons, a necessary protection against oil, grease and grime. Inside the shop horseshoes of every size hung along the heavy beams and beneath the benches, among the many implements in for repair, the curly, oily iron filings would gather from the drilling machine.

Two forges stood side by side with powerful heavy bellows keeping the coals glowing ready to heat the horseshoes. These were held by long iron tongs until they were red hot, when they were taken to the anvil to be shaped by blows from the hammer, showering sparks in all directions and scattering onlookers to a safer distance. At the end of each forge were long troughs of water for cooling the iron shoes before taking them to the penthouse where the horses were tied up. The shoe was fitted to the hoof and amid a singeing smell and cloud of smoke the shoe would be hammered on to the hoof. Heavy cart horses, hunters, riding horses, ponies and sometimes donkeys all arrived for the blacksmith's attention.

A huge grindstone stood outside the shop and was used for sharpening implements of all descriptions; strength was needed to turn the wheel when spade, scythe or hay knife was pressed hard against it. There was a tyreing platform at the front of the shop which was used when putting iron tyres onto wooden cartwheels. An iron cutter also stood outside which again with great strength applied, would cut through iron bars easily and swiftly. With all the heavy implements, plough, harrows, rakes etc it was not unusual to see a child's tricycle or scooter waiting to be repaired.'

IDEN STORES

'The shop at Iden was a typical village grocery, drapery and post office stores as I remember it 80 years ago.

As you entered the double fronted shop, the grocery counter was on your right, drapery and post office on your left and provisions at the back. On a wooden pillar in the centre of the shop was a clock which my father wound up on Saturday nights. I vividly remember 1916 when the clock was adjusted for Summer Time for the first time.

In front of the grocery counter were large glass-topped biscuit tins. Hanging from the ceiling were banister brushes and broom-heads, also a black metal holder for a ball of twine, the end of which hung over the counter to tie parcels. Father tied bags of sugar etc with a slip knot.

Nothing was individually packaged in those days. Tea came in large boxes and was decanted into large black canisters which stood on a shelf behind the counter. Sugar was kept in a drawer under the counter. It was a frightening experience to open the ill-fitting sugar drawer in the wasp season.

On one end of the counter was the till, next to it the scales. At the other end was a desk on which stood the day book and bill books. Next to this a glass sweet cabinet and the brass sweet scales. The

Horses were still providing the power on the land, as here at Herstmonceux, until the 1950s, keeping the village blacksmith busy.

toffee came in half pound slabs and had to be broken with a small toffee hammer before weighing. No toffee can be as tasty today as that was. Behind the counter were drawers holding rice, desiccated coconut, pearl barley etc and on narrow shelves above were cigarettes and tobacco. For one local farmer, Yankee Plug – an evil smelling tobacco – was specially stocked. At the window end were shelves holding medicines – Beechams Pills, Friars Balsam, cod liver oil, ipecacuanha, syrup of figs.

In 1913 the bakery, which was nearby, came up for sale with the post office attached. Father bought it from Mr Baker (yes, he really was a baker) and transferred the post office to the main stores, keeping the old shop as a lock-up for crockery and storing poultry and pig food at the back of the bakery.

The post office was a box-like desk with a sloping lid. Stamps, postal orders, sealing wax for registered letters and parcels were kept in this. Along the edge of the counter beside was a brass yard measure. Newspapers were laid out here with magazines and comics on a shelf behind the counter. I was often reprimanded for borrowing magazines to read before customers collected them. The only paper my sister and I were allowed was *The Children's Newspaper*.

The drapery shelves held rolls of calico, cotton prints, aprons, men's shirts etc. Under the counter were small items – ribbons, lace, buttons, cottons. Also red spotted handkerchiefs in which farm labourers carried their bread and cheese when they went to work.

On the provision counter stood cheese – only Cheddar and Dutch – and bacon. On a shelf close by were lard, butter and margarine placed on large round dishes. Father cut rashers by hand. It was a red letter day when he bought a bacon slicing machine.

At the back of the shop stood the large flour bin. Father was very security conscious. At night he took the post office cash-box upstairs and put it under the bed. But if we all went out when the shop was shut he would put it in a paper bag and bury it in the flour bin, or some other place.

Hobnail boots with other things were kept in a spare room upstairs. In sheds behind the garage coal, coke and paraffin were stored.

There was no self-service. But there were two chairs for customers to rest on while being served. Every householder in Iden was a customer until the International Stores in Rye started a delivery service to the village. The only village competitor was Mr Pettit, butcher and greengrocer. There was an unspoken agreement between the two shops that certain goods would only be stocked by one or other of them.

Most customers had their goods delivered, at first by pony and cart. Later a Ford van was bought. The roundsman had three days of driving instruction and then he was on his own. The old cart shed was turned into a garage for the van. I wanted to drive the van and I pestered Lewis Bryant, the driver, until finally he let me have a go. It wasn't easy going up Rye Hill with a heavy load. You had to keep your foot down hard. I was just twelve at that time. Nobody worried about driving licences then.

From an early age my sister and I helped out from time to time. When rationing came during the First World War Win delivered the first ration books (and I, being smaller, trailed along behind). She was just twelve then. On one occasion there was a mistake in Father's sugar allotment – he got a hundredweight he didn't order so customers trusted to keep quiet got an extra pound.

After the war, when rationing ceased, no one would buy the war-stock jam which came in large tins. It was so stiff it had to be melted before it could be decanted into jars. So Mother took all the tins of different jams and melted them together and sold it as Mixed Fruit Jam – it went like hot cakes.

Mother used the copper for jam-making. A good clean after the week's washing and it was ready for use. Her speciality was goose-berry jam. One early summer day, two of the village women would come to pick, top and tail the gooseberries and the copper would be filled. Three hundred pounds of jam was made in one day. In those days customers returned their jam jars to the shop and got a penny refund, so containers were not a problem. The idea of using the copper for jam-making was taken up by Miss Carter in the village. She originated the nationally known Dorothy Carter Preserves.

Mr Tooth, the baker, lived in the cottage adjoining the bakery. Often he had a small piece of dough left over and he would make me a tiny cottage leaf, sometimes with a currant in it.

There was no electricity in Iden until the early 1930s. Before that three large oil lamps lighted the shop. One Tuesday afternoon (early closing day) we were sitting indoors having tea, when the postman, who had come to empty the letter box, knocked on the shop door to see if there were any parcels or registered letters. Father went to let him in. As it was dusk Father called out to bring a light. My sister took a candle and went into the shop. She held it up high so the light would shine on the opposite side of the shop. The flame ignited the brushes hanging above. The postman quickly pulled the brushes down and stamped out the fire.

Iden had no mains water. We had a well in the garden and two 200-gallon rainwater tanks. Drinking water was fetched daily from

162

the well at the bakery as it was thought more pure.

The shop windows protruded from the front wall and there was a flat roof. My bedroom window was above this. When I was nine years old, new windows were put in and a new roof put up. Before the workmen finished I put two Kilner jars in the space behind the fascia board. In one was a letter I wrote to the finder. I don't remember what I wrote. The other contained a copy of the *Children's Newspaper* edited by Arthur Mee.'

ALFRISTON POST OFFICE STORES

'The Post Office Stores was an essential part of Alfriston life during the war, providing a meeting point and centre of communication. The population of the village was small but the shop was a busy place and, together with Waterloo Stores, essential for the supply and storage of food for Alfriston and the surrounding villages.

Although there was a regular bus service, petrol rationing kept people in their villages and it was necessary for the store to stock a wide range of goods. Apart from the post office and groceries, there was a bakery supplying bread and some cakes, stationery and newspapers, ironmongery, wool and haberdashery, and also coal and paraffin and even corn for the many families who kept a few chickens!

There was a full time staff of five men and three women besides the paper boys and girls and an errand boy. Deliveries were made to the outlying villages and accounts sent out monthly. Coupons had to be collected for all rationed goods – it was time consuming counting and packaging these and then working out what could be purchased from the wholesalers. Most goods were supplied in bulk and had to be weighed out and bagged. Sugar came in sacks, tea in chests and biscuits loose in big tins. Butter and cheese came in 28 lb blocks which had to be cut and wrapped – when rations were only a few ounces a week this all made a lot of work.

The mail came to the village by bus, the mail bag padlocked to one of the hand rails. It was sorted at the post office and delivered by the postman on his bicycle. The mail box was emptied in the evening, the letters franked and put into the mail bag which was sealed and put on the five o'clock bus.

The telephone exchange, which was not automatic, was also at the post office. Although there were not many subscribers the exchange had to be manned 24 hours a day and several people from the village helped out during the night. If there was a Red Alert the air raid wardens had to be notified immediately. During the latter part of the war, when there was a risk of an invasion, a soldier on sentry duty was posted in the square.'

ICE CREAM AND PETROL

'In 1933 Conny left her native Yorkshire and arrived with her husband in Alfriston. They moved into the house above and behind Ye Olde Tea House, which was next to the Star Inn in the High Street.

She remembers serving teas and light lunches and selling sweets, chocolates, cigarettes and ice cream in the shop. This ice cream she made herself from local milk. She made it by hand at first and stored it in a container packed round with ice, which was delivered by the fishman. When she made a batch of ice cream there was often a queue outside the shop to buy a small cone for one penny, a large cone for twopence or a sandwich for threepence.

Outside the shop was a hand-operated petrol pump, from which Conny served petrol. However, after much grumbling to her husband, he installed a Wayne electric petrol pump – one of the first in the area. After the war cars often double parked across the road in

Hoping for an ice cream at Ye Olde Tea Shoppe, Alfriston.

order to fill up with petrol and other users of the road had to wait till the transaction was completed! Although the pump has now gone the petrol tank still exists under the pavement.'

UDIMORE VILLAGE SHOP

'My parents kept a small village shop for years where everything was stocked which people needed. As well as grocery and drapery, corn and paraffin were sold. The trade was mainly done by calling on people in the nearby villages and delivering the goods. Prior to the First World War these goods were taken round in a horse-drawn covered van thus protecting the driver and goods from the weather. Some of the customers were small farmers and made their own butter which was very good, and this was bought for resale. The accounts were usually paid for on delivery but occasionally there were arrears.

In those days groceries were not packaged as now and butter, margarine, lard, sugar, tea and coffee and soda etc were bought in bulk and all had to be weighed and packed. Cheeses were sometimes "ironed" for customers to taste: a small steel iron, shaped like a hammer with a hollow steel handle, was pushed into the cheese and pulled out with a small amount and offered to the customer to taste in the shop. Bacon came by the side and was cut into rashers and joints for boiling.

At Christmas time currants, sultanas, raisins and dates came in large boxes and had to be opened and cleaned in a large sieve, stalks and other rubbish being removed. These were stored in drawers under the counter and weighed and packed as needed. Figs came in hessian bags, but better quality figs and dates were sold in boxes.

As well as the usual items of grocery we sold bread which was ordered from a baker and delivered to us by van. Brushes and brooms, buckets and baths, saucepans and kettles and other iron-mongery, coconut matting and mats were also stocked as well as drapery and stationery.

Tea was kept in large canisters and weighed and packed. Candles came in three-pound packets and were sold in three, six, or twelve as ordered; short ones were called twelves and long ones eights.

We sometimes had an assistant who lived in and was taught the trade. The men in the shop wore white aprons – no overalls as now.

A bicycle was used to deliver locally and the goods were taken round in a large wicker basket fitted to the carrier on the front of the bicycle.'

ON THE CASH DESK

'On leaving school in 1923 at the age of 16, my first job was on the cash desk of a butcher's shop in Eastbourne. My wage (a good one at that time) was 15 shillings weekly from which I had to give my mother ten shillings. The rest was mine for leisure activities and clothes. Until this time my mother had made my clothes but decided that with her advice I must now make my own. We usually managed a weekly visit to a film or the theatre and an occasional game of tennis.

At the shop were the owner, two men assistants, two errand boys, and a Saturday morning boy. The errand boys did various jobs in the shop and were gradually learning the trade. Trade bicycles which had very large baskets at the front were used for the delivery of the meat. I had to write the necessary information tickets which were then attached to the orders.

Men who delivered meat to the shop carried carcases on their shoulders, even forequarters and hindquarters of beef. Large meat hooks were then attached and the carcases hung on a steel rail. The hindquarters had the suet still attached. (How good it was to have fresh beef suet!) Cutting up the meat was done on a large, very solid wooden block, using knives, saws, and choppers. Before being scrubbed the block was scraped with a "brush" which had strong metal prongs, and all surfaces in the shop were always thoroughly washed. Sawdust was spread on the floor. Meat which needed to be stored was kept in a huge ice box which was like a small room.

We worked till late evening on Saturdays and until 11 pm on Christmas Eve, when there were bargains to be had. Leading up to Christmas was a very busy time, with poultry to be plucked, extra orders etc.

A local firm, noted for their cooked meats, bought brisket of beef from which they made delicious pressed beef. Shin of beef used for stews and beef tea (a nourishing drink for invalids) was only a few pence per pound, about sixpence I think. Today it is highly priced in line with other cuts of meat.

The men in the shop used a language called backslang, words spoken backwards, eg the word "back" would be pronounced "k-cab".'

MASTER BUTCHER

'My father was a master butcher in the county town of Lewes before and during the Second World War. My brother and I were born there and lived with our parents behind and over the shop. The accommodation consisted of three bedrooms, two living rooms and a kitchen, no bathroom, and the only toilet was outside across a backyard. We had hot water in the kitchen only, heated by electricity.

Before the war it was common practice for butchers to have their own slaughterhouse nearby. Father's was about 200 yards away, just off the High Street. Father would go to Lewes cattle market every Monday morning dressed in his market clothes of jacket, cloth cap, cord breeches worn with leather boots and leather gaiters kept in place with buckle straps, and in the winter, an elderly Burberry. These garments were kept in a special cupboard, near the cellar, because Mother said they smelt of the market animals and she refused to have them with other clothes. I don't think they were cleaned very often, if at all.

Once at the market, Father would select the animals he needed to buy for that week. In the afternoon, two or three of the shopmen would be sent to market to collect the animals and lead them through the streets to the slaughterhouse. Once there they would be put into pens and fed and watered and bedded down for the night. The next morning Father decided which of the animals were to be slaughtered that day. This work wasn't done until the afternoon, because in the morning an enormous copper had to be filled with water and a fire lit, which had to be stoked from time to time as it was essential to have plenty of boiling water – this took the whole morning. After the animals had been killed, dressed and hung, the slaughterhouse had to be scrubbed and cleaned down, knives and choppers put away ready for next time. The next day the local authority sanitary inspector would come and inspect the carcase and agree it was fit for human consumption. The sides of beef, lamb or pork then had to be humped on the backs of the shopmen round to the shop and placed in the refrigerator until needed. In the early 1930s Father had a freezer put in – I think it was the first one in Lewes.

Most of the animals Father bought were for slaughter and human consumption, but he was extremely fond of pigs and from time to time he bought several very young ones and kept them for a number of weeks before they were sold on again. Obviously, when they were in residence at the slaughterhouse they had to be fed and watered every day and the pens cleaned and fresh bedding put down. Sometimes my brother and I would go with Father and help and this is when we were taught that pigs are very clean, fastidious animals and extremely intelligent. In fact, Father was heard to remark many times that his pigs were far more intelligent than some of his customers!

Of course, not all the meat sold in the shop was home killed. Some mornings Father would leave at 6 am to drive to Brighton meat market where he would select beef, New Zealand lamb etc for delivery by carrier later that day.

Long hours were worked in the shop, 8 am until 6 pm, half-day closing on Wednesday and late closing on Friday and Saturday until 9 pm. After each day's trading all benches and counters had to be scrubbed down, and the floor swept ready for fresh sawdust to be put down the next morning. Meat was delivered daily to customers by a young man on a trade bicycle and on Friday and Saturday the van made deliveries to villages such as Cooksbridge, Plumpton, Ringmer, Laughton and Firle.

In 1939 Father had eight young men working for him. After the declaration of war this rapidly reduced to one, the others all having joined the Forces. All private slaughterhouses were closed and meat was delivered from government meat markets. Food rationing followed and life became more and more difficult. At the end of the war the old private slaughterhouses were not allowed to reopen. Father's slaughterhouse was sold for land value, pulled down and a private house now stands on the site.'

COAL AND CAKES

'Elijah Cresey (known as the Mayor of Hollington) was the local coal merchant at the end of the 19th century, and he also owned a small farm with 18 horses. He used to haymake nearly all the local fields. His wife started the little shop just over 100 years ago at Hollington Corner, as it was then known, on the main road to London. This little shop sold just a few groceries, eggs and bavins (special bundles of firewood). In the shop was a large beech mangle and people would come and press their washing. If they did it themselves the cost was one penny, if Mrs Cresey did it the cost was twopence. At the back of the shop was a large brick oven, heated by faggots, where bread and cakes were baked.'

'My father was a baker and confectioner, who firstly worked for his father at The Broadway, Crowborough, but later had his own bakery shop in London Road, Bexhill. My father worked long hours, sometimes very late into the night, and then after a few hours sleep returned to start baking the daily bread, sometimes as early as 4 am. Then after that it was on to the morning cakes. Afternoons were devoted to icing and decorating birthday and other special cakes. Most of us, sons and daughters, worked with my father for the beginning of our working lives.'

INDUSTRIOUS VILLAGES

'From the turn of the century the proprietor of the little village shop cum post office at Colemans Hatch could be seen walking around the scattered community delivering his bread and other goods and he continued to do this until his death in his eighties.

Milk was delivered to the door by the farmer's daughter. Their farmhouse backed on to the village shop. She carried the milk bottles in bags on the handlebars of her bicycle! Her father was not only a farmer, he was also the local blacksmith, working from the forge beside the Hatch Inn.

Another smallholder also delivered milk which he carried in a churn resting in the sidecar of his motorbike.

The village had its own telephone exchange operated by one of the Divall family. A team of postmen delivered mail. The shop was situated off the road itself but in 1950 the Misses Divall, daughters of the original proprietor, opened another shop on the road near to the church; this continued to trade until 1990 although the Divall family retired from it in 1967. An alternative to the shop was the gentleman who carried goods around on his bicycle.

Two brothers were the builder and the undertaker. They also had the contract to keep the church in good repair. There was also a thriving brickyard until the late 1940s.

The post office stores at Colemans Hatch, run by the Divall family.

Until the 1960s the village consisted of three large family estates employing many people. Smallholders lived nearby on the Ashdown Forest where they grazed their sheep and cattle.'

'When I came to live in Buxted in 1936 it was a wonderfully self sufficient village with two flourishing grocer's shops in the centre and another general store and a tiny bakery (with a wood-burning oven) at the top end. We had a butcher, a baker who would cook Sunday joints for his customers, a haberdasher who also ran the threepenny lending library and the post office. The letters were sorted there and you could call in and see if anything had arrived for you in the afternoon. There was a hairdresser (Caroline, the blacksmith's daughter from the next village, Hadlow Down), a little newsagent's in a cottage front room, a corn merchant, and farmers with a local milk round who would also deliver eggs and ready dressed poultry.

Mr Ede and Mr Milhouse in the village were spare time "snobs" and would mend the children's sandals or patch their boots for twopence or threepence. Many cottages with large gardens were pleased to sell their garden produce, flowers as well as vegetables.'

'Chailey is a large, long village and back in the 1930s was known as South Common, South Street, Chailey Green and North Common. There were general stores North and South, but at that time Chailey Green had a post office and general stores, a butcher, a tailor, a builder and undertaker and also a haulage business. The butcher's shop had a parrot that used to whistle at us as we walked to school. There were other businesses too, namely the Chailey potteries, builders, wheelwrights turned builders, a baker and a traction engine firm with threshing equipment.'

'There were three grocers at Dallington in the 1930s, one of which had the post office, one baked bread and the third, ours, sold everything from feed corn to toys as well as the usual groceries. The majority of people who lived in the village worked locally, mainly on farms or in the shops supplying the village and surrounding area. Other local shops were two butchers, one snob, and a garage where we took accumulators for the wireless to be recharged. Two bakers delivered bread three times a week and milk came from the local farms.'

OTHER WAYS WE MADE A LIVING

There were, of course, dozens of other ways we made our living in the past. Here are a few memories of working life – from fisherman to nurse, from auctioneer to postman.

CANVAS AND JAM JARS

'My father, grandfather and mother started a canvas producing factory in St James's Street, Brighton and as it became more successful and they needed a bigger factory, we moved out to Hove. My mother ran a small shop in Mortimer Road, Hove and there was an alley at the side which led to a factory around the back. The factory produced painted canvas which was made into suitcases.

The shop was full of huge jars, each containing some form of food which had to be transferred to the customer's containers when they came to buy. Pickled onions or even jam were sold loose and each customer had to save jam jars and have them refilled. It was much the cheapest way to buy your food.

We even made our own ice cream in a machine which looked very much like a barrel, but worked on the basis of a thermos flask, with an outer and an inner shell. In the middle was ice, which kept the whole process working and maintained the temperature good and low.'

LONGSHORE FISHERMAN

'My father was what was called years ago a longshore fisherman, which meant he got a living on the sea there at Rye Harbour. He used to put out a line at low water, and then go down after the tide had been over the lines which had hooks on them and fish it, which means he would take the fish off the hooks, that's if there were any. He also used to go shrimping and cockling, then go out selling what he had caught.

He bought a secondhand errand boy's bike, then cycled to Hastings fish market every morning, getting there by 6 am when the fish started to be sold. He would then go to different villages selling it (there was no fish market in Rye). Later on he bought a motorbike and sidecar, then a few years later he got a car which meant that he could go further afield.

Bobby Mills and 'Old Relic' John Milgate, aged 78, bouldering at Rye Harbour in the 1920s. The boulders were used in the Staffordshire potteries.

I can just remember sitting by the river watching the men of the village loading up railway trucks with what were called "blue boulders"; they are flintstones and were sent up to the Potteries to be used in the manufacturing of china.

Also on the sea shore men used to go on the sand with "keddle nets" catching fish. My favourite was seine net fishing. Women and children used to join in with this. There was a very long net, and people waded into the sea with it and made a large semi-circle coming back to the water's edge, walking up the beach with the whole net out of the water.

One of our pleasures was going over the river by means of the ferry, which was a small clinker-built wooden rowing boat which cost one penny each way, and if the ferry man was having a pint in the pub any village lad who could row would do the job for him and of course keep the money.

We would spend hours watching the fisherman making nets, and we often used to get paid for loading up their needles with the twine they were using.'

THE ICE MEN

'Mondays and Thursdays were high days in Brighton when large lorries used to arrive at butchers' shops and dairies with ice. There were no domestic fridges or freezers then. The men hacked away at huge lumps of ice in the lorry, then wrapped it in thick sacking, slung it over their shoulders and delivered it to the appropriate shops. There it was chopped into even smaller pieces to surround meat and dairy produce. The unit where the ice was made was in a building by the Brighton station.'

TRUG BASKETS

'In times past there were several Sussex trug makers in the local Herstmonceux area. As the years went by towards the 1950s there were only two registered trug businesses: Messrs Theo Smith and Sons, the earlier dated one, and my family's firm, namely R. Reed and Son which was formed before the turn of the century.

It paid to make batches of similar style baskets. We dealt with both wholesale and retail customers, such as horticultural sundriesmen, seed merchants, and bazaar organisers all over Britain in the category as wholesale buyers.

Soon after the General Strike we sent consignments to California. The goods had to be entirely hand-made and hand-cleft otherwise the trade would have ceased. The petrol engine, saw bench and planer in the Field Lodge could not be used at all, but as the price was good we carried on until the Wall Street Crash put an end to things, with no further negotiations with that particular wholesaler.

The word "trug" is derived from the Anglo-Saxon word "trog" meaning a wooden vessel or boat shaped article.

First of all the wood has to be acquired from which to make the trugs. A cant of sweet chestnut of about ten years' growth, with clear butts, is cut during the winter months. The coppiced trees' lengths are then brought to our field and this sweet chestnut is split with a long-handled axe, the cutting edge of which, instead of being parallel to the handle, is set at right angles to it. The chestnut wood is then stacked and stored for ensuing use.

Later some is taken to the trug workshop further along the main road at Coopers Craft and pieces are smoothed with a draw knife using a wooden horse, an ingenious contrivance forming both a seat for the worker and an adjustable vice to hold the lengths of wood required.

The chestnut is then steamed, very necessary, as it is a hard wood and is bent around wooden formers to become the rims and handles, fixed at right angles with nails.

The next process is preserving willow. Once it has been obtained, it is stored in pyramid fashion or laid in piles for seasoning (green willow would warp). The seconds of cricket bat willow is sought after, being usually free of knots. Other kinds procured are sallow willows, nicknamed "sally", and trug boards are cleft out, smoothed with a draw-knife and the ends tapered.

Seven boards are needed for larger trugs and five for small. These are dunked in water to make them pliable. The widest board over-lays the base of the handle and is nailed to it, then the ends are curled and fastened to the rim. Continuing thus the gradual narrower ones are added in clinker style, until the trug is formed. Feet are added, and bands are attached for large trugs.

The common rectangular shape were used mainly by farmers for sowing corn, scattering the seed up and down prepared ploughed fields. Obviously there are other shapes to mention such as the oval square and round made in different sizes. The doubled handled cucumber trug is made in two sizes and there is just one standard size for the walking stick trug.

The rims and handles could have the bark left on, or be peeled leaving them white. The latter could be stained and varnished, or painted or have designs done in pyrography (poker work).

Rupert, my brother, made a model aeroplane from willow trug basket boards. The propeller would be placed pointing into the wind when in the garden. John Player bought it for ten shillings in the 1930s. Rupert made a few more, but trug making was his work.

One Sunday morning in the 1930s, a lady came to our Coopers Croft trug shop for two small size painted rim trugs. My mother did not wish to sell on a Sunday. There was a stationary car further along the road and the lady said that she was the Nanny to the two little princesses in the car, Elizabeth and Margaret Rose, and they wanted to have the trugs to play with on Cooden Beach, so Mother succumbed and a sale was made.

Around 1942, Canadian soldiers stationed in woodlands nearby were driven to distraction trying to sleep with the continuous singing of the cuckoos.

Some of these soldiers played a trick on us by climbing up about twelve feet to our sign of three walking stick trugs. One was taken down and posted in the letter box at Magham Down post office. A local policeman returned it to us the following day.

As well as having the trug basket manufacturing business we had a cycle shop and sold petrol in cans.

On Wednesdays Father loaded up his pony and trap with an assortment of Sussex trugs and went to Herstmonceux Castle and sold some to visitors who came mainly from London.'

THE POSTMAN

'My grandfather lived with us in Rye and he was a postman. He used to get up in the morning at four o'clock and do his gardening and then go to work. He walked from Rye to Camber for a penny for a telegram.'

LADIES UNDERWEAR DEPARTMENT

'I was just 14 when I left school at Easter 1939 and went to work as an apprentice in a ladies' underwear department in a big store in Eastbourne.

Quality shops then were lovely places to visit. The customer was the most important person. A commissionaire would greet you after alighting from your chauffeur driven car, with "Good morning madam, can I help you?" and inside the shop walker was not far away ready to give directions and help. Many ladies came every day to meet their friends and take tea or coffee in the first floor restaurant, resplendent with potted palms and a string orchestra.

Throughout the shop was a system of air tubes which took carriers from counters to the central cash desk and change was sent back. At times a mistake was made and the carrier would go the wrong way. A series of curt little notes would fly along the tubes to hurry up with so and so's change, followed by a flipping of the lid at the counter end designed to upset the cashier at the other end!

Before my first day I dreamed of learning to sell lovely pure silk underwear trimmed with hand-made lace. In fact, folding and tidying stock was an apprentice's job, not dealing with customers. Most nighties and petticoats were pink or peach with sometimes an odd daring black creation or white for the "bride".

My second choice would have been the dressing gown section. Woollen housecoats for about 65 shillings or Shetland wool bed jackets lined with pure silk chiffon and swansdown trimming.

The knicker department didn't sound too good. Imagine selling nothing but ladies' directoire celanese knickers (with a double gusset!) every day. Half a crown a pair at sale times and in any colour.

The penultimate horror was the woven counter, dealing in vests and combinations. The latter came in several weights, wool for winter, mixtures for in between and spun silk or sea island cotton for summer wear. One could not do without one's combs even in the summer, it might get chilly! These grotesque garments which are pantees and vests all in one, had a slit from waist to crotch at the back to facilitate visits to the toilet and a flap of fabric to cover the offending gaping hole. The worst problem came with keeping stock of combs. Some had short sleeves and long legs, short sleeves and short legs or long sleeves and corresponding choice of leg lengths. Quite a complicated matter to fit madam out with her desired requirements.

At this point I can say unequivocally that should a particular garment throughout the department not be in stock a telephone call to the London warehouse before it closed would ensure delivery the next day. Sent from London by early train it would arrive at the store by opening time!

However, you guessed it, I ended up in the corset department. I didn't cry on the job but saved it up until I got home. My mother said, "Give it a try, you may find it interesting." I did, and it proved fascinating if hard work for very little return.

I soon learnt about two-way stretch roll ons, not a lot of use for figure control but comfy and warm and they kept your stockings up. Lacing corsets were still very much in vogue, front or back lacings, bought two sizes smaller, the laces then pulled up as the garment wore and stretched. These monstrosities were heavily boned and fastened at the front with a busk, a formidable metal contraption which stuck into your chest or groin when you leaned over. However, it taught you to bend and lift correctly all of a piece and consequently there were not so many back problems. Though I never wore one, devotees say they were the most comfortable and satisfactory corset ever made.

The "semi step-in", as the name suggests, had to be stepped into and pulled up. Mostly made of elastic and top of the price range. Problems came because most ladies wanted to wear their "stays" over their vests. The trick was to get them to put on their celanese directoire knickers (elasticated at the waist and the knee) capturing the lower edge of the vest, shoes off, step into garment, cross legs and up she comes just a bit too high, down with the knicks and pull corset into position, vest daintily frilled at the bottom edge.

Stays, as they used to be called, were boned originally with whalebone but later on with steel which rusted. Therefore stays could not be washed, hence the over-the-vest cult. Imagine never washing your corsets, but even in 1939 this was very much the habit. We spent a lot of time assuring customers their garments should be washed along with all their other underwear every week. By this time bones were coated and did not rust, or were made of a plastic substitute.

The brassiere was in its infancy in 1939 and many people wore nothing but Kestos: two triangular pieces of fabric with cross-over elastic across the back and buttoned in front. Not a lot of uplift there. Bust bodies were designed to suppress the bust, very strong, long and tight. I suppose we sold as many of these as Kestos. With the advent of Hollywood stars with amply supported busts the uplift garment became popular, but again was not effective if worn over the vest!

After a three year apprenticeship I eventually graduated to being a corset fitter, although the war prevented me from taking a fitting course in the London corset houses.

After war service I returned to the same department and in nine years lived through interesting developments in the corset world. There were all-rubber garments (did the resulting sweating reduce the inches?), padded bras, blow up ones, lycra and many ingenious inventions all bent on improving the flesh that is there, not necessarily reducing the inches. I am glad I stuck it out all those years ago.'

HOT SEAWATER BATHS

'Grandad was a plumber and decorator in Seaford and in the early 1900s he decided to open a hot seawater baths establishment for Grandma to run. His three children had to accompany him every morning to fetch seawater in buckets on a handcart before going to school. They must have been very relieved when the venture was not very successful. Later on his son joined him in the business and when he went to France in the war, my mother took her brother's place, becoming one of the first lady painters and decorators in the area.'

TRAINING AS A NURSE

'In 1947 I commenced training to become a State Registered Nurse. We signed a four year contract. The Royal Sussex County was a voluntary hospital before the NHS in 1948. It changed little during our year there and was very fine indeed.

Most of my set were barely 18 years of age and extremely naive girls. The work was arduous and very different from the "high tech" training of today. The student nurses did everything, the first year being the most menial of course. Orderlies and auxiliary workers had not appeared.

We cleaned everything twice daily including mopping floors every morning. All the chairs were taken on to the balcony and turned upside down to scrape the blanket fluff from the chair legs! Some wards had coal fires which had to be kept burning on cold winter nights. Everything had to be carefully saved, washed and sterilised. The word disposable was never used. We really "nursed" the patients and as most of them were "warded" for at least two weeks they became very helpful as they recovered.

We were not allowed to accept any gift from grateful patients or relatives, not even a sweet. The night nurses cut and buttered the bread for breakfast, as sliced bread had not been invented. We were never allowed to sit down on duty. Our uniform was very important to us and we were not allowed to wear any of it out of the hospital area. We were especially proud of our navy cape lined with scarlet.

Our monthly salary was £12. We had to queue for it at the board room. Out of this we had to provide ourselves with uniform style stockings and Clark's shoes from Hanningtons. However we really did feel proud to be training at the RSCH. The years spent there prepared us for anything that might follow.'

ESTATE AGENT AND AUCTIONEER

'Once seen, my father's office could never be forgotten. He ran the family estate agency and auctioneering business from our home in Beckley. A front room was the "office". A large oblong table stood in the centre which, except for small spaces where my father and his clerk worked, was covered in piles of paper at least six inches deep. Round the walls were more papers on every possible surface – bookcase, mantlepiece, roll-top desk, horsehair sofa. Precariously balanced, if one slipped a whole pile would fall. The floor was covered too, apart from the smallest gangways, with piles up to 18 inches high. There was a system. Ask for a particular piece of information and my father would unerringly go to the right pile and extract it.

While this room was called the office, the business actually took over the whole house. My father's writing table was in the sitting room, the typewriter lived in the dining room, catalogues were duplicated in the kitchen, old papers dating back to 1902 were kept up the steps in the kitchen storeroom. A whole bedroom was full of papers and mysterious odds and ends – unclaimed leftovers from furniture sales.

In 1902 the business was started by my grandfather. Those were the days when livestock still travelled to market "on the hoof". With a journey of six miles to Rye or even further to Cranbrook, he, as a newly arrived farmer in the village, decided to start a fortnightly market at the new railway station at Northiam. By the time I remember, more than 40 years on, the market had become weekly. Livestock sales were in the morning. Animals were shipped off by train or lorry to the slaughterhouses and in the afternoon vegetables and other produce were sold for the local housewives.

Wednesday, market day, had a regular routine, starting with the loading of the car at 8 am with the market stationery in an ancient Gladstone bag and produce from the farm and garden – apples, tomatoes, whatever was in season. Just after the war it was rabbits. Many a weekend the family "outing" would be rabbit catching over the farm. My parents busied themselves with rabbit nets and preparations while I stood around, getting cold and bored stiff waiting for the ferrets to do their stuff. Happily most of the rabbit catching on the farm was done by two men and their dogs, often getting 50 at a time.

In the mid 1950s the Ministry of Agriculture's increasing paper load and new regulations for weighing machines finally defeated this small market and my father closed it.

When my mother married, she was expected to become part of the business and it was only through her insistence that the first (and last) modern technology came to the office in the late 1940s – a 1915 Underwood typewriter and an equally basic duplicator. Its top speed was as fast as the ink dried on the sheets spread out over the rest of the table. Previously all letters, catalogues and house particulars were handwritten and the letter press stood like a grim instrument of torture in the corner of the office to make the office copy.

Everyone in the house was involved in the business activities – sheep fairs, underwood sales, furniture auctions, selling houses, farm valuations. I remember as a very small child sitting under my father's desk and checking the arithmetic on valuations and forms he dropped down to keep me quiet. My father and grandfather were blessed with loyal support from their clerk, Mrs Comport, who joined at the age of 18 and, except for a few weeks off at the birth of her daughter, never had a day off in 40 years.

The busiest time for showing houses was the weekend. Meeting the London bus was a regular event and taking prospective purchasers to see the houses. Houses which today sell for £50,000 and more were sold for £100 in the 1950s.

Furniture auctions were fun, but hard work. All our auctions took place in village houses and cottages. The preparatory cataloguing and organising lots was followed by viewing days when the often small houses were crowded out. The sale itself was generally out in the garden because of the lack of space but I don't remember much rain. Sometimes it was not fun. Like the cottage in Northiam where my mother went to help catalogue the linen and looked down to find her legs covered in fleas.

At another cottage in Beckley, where the owner had died, unopened parcels were discovered – linen, corsets – enough to start a drapery shop. Viewers hayed over the lots so much that the sale was delayed while my mother and the porters frantically tried to put things back in order. The final result was more lots than they started with!

Just after the Second World War things were in short supply. This was a good time for furniture sales. A pastry bowl sold for 39 shillings and a secondhand blanket for £15. Village rivalries came into play. Mrs Player and Mrs Skinner would always bid against each other and the price could get ridiculous. Like the not very good grandfather clock which went for £19, a lot of money at that time.'

DAD WAS A GAMEKEEPER

'I grew up in rural surroundings as my parents lived in a cottage across Piltdown Common, and my earliest memories are of wandering along a grassy track between gorse bushes, this path being used by the local farmer as commoner rights to drive his cattle and sheep to the fields behind our house. Many times these animals trespassed into our garden trampling vegetables, for which we claimed compensation.

With complete regularity the butcher, baker and grocer delivered their goods regardless of weather; if they were late it was a talking point among neighbours, but of course they had a chat with customers, knew their needs and if they were in trouble, or ill. This contact was so important to women who lived in isolated places, as many did across fields and in woods on farms. Dad was a gamekeeper keeping very long hours, leaving at about 7.30 am, returning at about 6 pm and at rearing time going back until late in the evening. I used to walk through the woods and fields always accompanied by spaniels and retrievers to take his meals, without fear.

Our leisure was taken on Sunday afternoons, as a walk through the fields and woods on the "rides" as the paths were called (trimmed and cut out regularly). We were shown nests and wildlife that Dad had observed the previous week, so simple, but our whole world. I wandered free, always with dogs, through the brooks where I checked Dad's fishing line he had set up and left for trout as he went through, and dropped my own fishing line in the special small

Broody hens incubated the young pheasants for this gamekeeper on Piltdown Common.

pools known to us, to leave and check on my return. These brooks were full of cowslips in the spring, and the woods were carpeted with wild daffodils which we had a procession of local people walking by the house to admire.

On shooting days Mother cooked many sausages, on a tiny range, which with loaves and bottles of beer were carried out in hampers to the keepers' hut in the woods for their lunch. In bad weather our small sitting room was used by the shooting party, which was composed of mainly medical specialists, Members of Parliament and the professions from London. Every Christmas we received a hamper from Harrods, great excitement ... another era.

When the farmer made his hay we children rode back to the farmyard on top of the waggons. Haytime and harvest drew us like a magnet and we played many games weaving in and out of the sheaves stood up in sixes and called "shocks".

In the spring our meadow below the house was filled with coops of broody hens. Dad had canvassed the local farmers for miles around for these, which were lent to incubate and brood the baby pheasants. Every day the hens would be taken off their eggs, tethered lightly by their nests, fed and watered, then returned. Then came hatching when each coop had a little pen for rearing. The pheasants were later released in the woods.'

ALFRISTON'S STABLES

'In the early 20th century Alfriston was well known for its large racing stables called the Wingrove. It was owned by Mr Bathos. He trained racehorses for many people, including the notorious Horatio Bottomley who lived nearby.

I was born in a cottage opposite the stables 84 years ago and my family was closely connected with the stables. My grandfather was a stable boy and two of my uncles were travelling lads, who went with the horses to race meetings. In 1912 Bathos's horse *Long Set* won the Lincoln, and Bathos had a huge party on the Tye for all the village to celebrate. I was only two at the time but my family talked about it for years.'

WAR & PEACE

THE GREAT WAR 1914–1918

When the men marched off to war in 1914, times were hard for those they left behind and those years have left scars on many Sussex families. Peace was welcomed, but it was not the end of the suffering.

THINGS WERE GRIM

'After the war started, notifications were put in head post office windows, just typed notes, which all crowded round to see. In those days there was no television or radio and very few working people saw daily newspapers. Very soon men from Worthing were being called up for service, and food began to get scarce. Rationing was not brought in until later, so it meant telling each other when food was available and having to queue for many foods in short supply.

At school we got very sore fingers from making up sandbags of rough hessian. All school scholarships were cancelled for several years. As the war dragged on and more men were called up, we were also ordered to keep a blackout. Gradually families, one after another, lost loved ones, and as it was the custom then to wear full black for mourning, things seemed very grim. Then we had the Zeppelins over, causing destruction.

When the war ended on 11th November 1918 there was great excitement everywhere and people went rushing to the shops for anything red, white and blue. When all the flags, bunting and ribbons were sold, anything the right colour went, even to flannelette.'

VILLAGE EFFORTS

'Canon Humble-Croft's son Cyril was Eva's godfather. When he came home on leave to Waldron from the Great War Eva, along with the rest of the household, had to line up and wave a Union Jack to welcome him. He was killed shortly after he returned from leave.

Cyril's brother Arthur was married to Madame Margaret Cooper, who was a well known opera singer. She came to Heathfield and sang at a concert to raise money for the war effort. Eva had to be lifted on to the stage to present her with a bouquet of flowers. Many concerts were held in Waldron to raise money for the soldiers. At one of the concerts someone gave a donkey as a prize, and the Canon's daughter won it. Eva was allowed to ride it until she fell off and broke her arm. Her only recollection of rationing in the Great War was when a scruffy looking van would arrive in the village, and the children would run after it shouting "the rations have come".

Eva's mother would go haymaking in the summer and she wore a long black dress. Several of the village men who were too old to go to war formed a volunteer brigade called the Gibraltar Watch, named after the Gibraltar Tower which stands in Heathfield Park. They would cycle to Heathfield and form a lookout at the top of the Gibraltar Tower because of its view over the countryside.

One day a German plane crashed in Waldron and the Gibraltar Watch had to guard it until it was recovered by the Royal Flying Corps.

On the day the Great War ended, the news arrived in Waldron by telegram to the post office.'

THE ROYAL PAVILION

'During the war the Royal Pavilion in Brighton was used as a hospital for the Indian wounded. Those who died were cremated on Tegdown Hill at Patcham on a "burning ghat" and later the Chattri was built as a memorial and unveiled by the Prince of Wales in 1921.'

Wounded Indian soldiers were cared for at the Royal Pavilion in Brighton during the war.

185

THE BLUEBOYS

'Between the Downs and Summerdown Road in Eastbourne a soldiers' convalescent camp was established in about 1916. It was known locally as Summerdown Blueboys Camp and was for wounded soldiers. The soldiers, dressed in bright blue flannel suits, white shirts and scarlet ties, were seen walking in the vicinity. My mother had a confectionery and tobacconist business in Church Street and as a four year old the soldiers were familiar to me sitting round a marble top table having soft drinks from the soda fountain and ice cream.

I attended the "babies class" at St Mary's infants school opposite and the only occupation I remember is being given loose woven woollen material to pull out the threads to make stuffing for cushions for the Blueboys.

After the Great War, what was probably the first council housing estate in Eastbourne was established at Victoria Drive. Known as "The Hutments" it consisted of black huts, which had probably been moved from the camp by the army. A few years later the huts were replaced by brick-built houses, the nucleus of the large council housing estate which exists today. At this time the camp site was developed for private housing – now Old Camp Road and Pashley Road.'

TAKING THE HORSES

'When I was eight years old, during the war, I remember soldiers coming to the family farm at Dallington, inspecting the farm horses and taking them away to war. There was very little compensation paid.'

LIGHTING THE BONFIRE

'My father was a doctor and too old to serve, so he examined many recruits daily and set up a first aid post in the Mepham School. He was also head of the local St John Ambulance. I just remember Armistice Day – our house at Hastings was ringed with fairy lights and my brother Richard, "the doctor's fat boy", lit the enormous bonfire on the West Hill.'

AN AWFUL TIME

'I was a small child in the early 1920s and at that time men were coming back from the war. There was an awful lot of poverty and

So many did not return, leaving a grief that for some has lasted a lifetime.

unemployment and men would come round the streets singing. If they were lucky people went out and put a copper or two in their cap or tin. I remember one day a man was singing *Where is my wandering boy tonight?*. I ran indoors sobbing bitterly and told my parents there was a man outside who had lost his little boy. I needed a lot of consoling and convincing.'

A LONG TIME

'I met my love in 1914, just after I moved to Portslade. He was in the 91st Field, Royal Engineers, and they were trained in Portslade during that year. I remember the day they were all photographed and how the man who took the photographs promised to let me see them when they were developed.

My love never came back and I never married. I was just 20 years old then and now I'm 99. It's been a long time with only a photo to keep me company.'

THE SECOND WORLD WAR 1939–45

Once again we were at war and this time we were all in the front line, dodging the doodlebugs and spending our nights in the air raid shelters.

BATTLE IN DOODLEBUG ALLEY

'As I was entering my teens the war came. The previously quiet town of Battle became suddenly full of soldiers, houses were commandeered and even our school was moved overnight. My father joined "Dad's Army" and my mother worked in the Toc H canteen. As the war went on life changed, when boys we had grown up with joined up, some never to return. There were plenty of dances to go to, I remember curling my hair with pipe cleaners and pressing my dress with flat irons heated on the kitchen range before going.

Rationing was not too bad in the country and the local butcher or grocer could always be relied upon to have something under the counter for special occasions.

There was a strong community spirit among the cottages during the war, sharing a shelter during air raids, clutching unwilling dogs and cats and flasks of hot tea until the all clear.

I left school at 14 and after a while obtained employment in the local council offices where I stayed until I was married. During that time in the war I was in the Civil Defence although not strictly old enough, and took my turn in the report centre during raids and set the siren going.

Battle was to discover that it was what was known as Doodlebug Alley, this part of East Sussex suffering very badly. I had a narrow escape when one decided to drop at the back of the council offices. I was cycling to work when a bomb dropped in Battle High Street killing Mr and Mrs Giles who ran the local newsagent's. A bomb also landed inside the gateway of the Abbey but failed to explode, which was very lucky for the town as there was a lorry loaded with gelignite standing nearby.

I shall never forget the morning of D-Day. My parents and I were awakened by a terrible noise. Two Martin Marauder aircraft had collided and one, in an attempt to rid itself of its bombs, was not only too low for the crew to bale out but was a blazing inferno. It crashed not far from our cottage killing all those on board. After the war all the bodies were returned to America for reburial except one who remains in the American Cemetery near Cambridge. My husband and I have been to visit his grave.'

BOMBS AND GERMANS

'Mr Sweet was the only working cobbler to remain in Brighton and Hove during the Second World War. As he was deaf and dumb he had been excused military duty. Being in much demand in the area, he worked at different shoe shops on different days of the week.

On one occasion, whilst cycling between shops, Mr Sweet assumed he was having a giddy turn, and got off his bike for a moment. He was travelling up West Street at the time, when he felt he was experiencing flashing lights before his eyes. Then, after a moment, they stopped and he got back on his bike and continued his journey.

Imagine his surprise when later he heard that a small advance party of German soldiers had been captured in that area. Their first statement was to recall their amazement at the bravery of a lone man seen cycling through their line of fire.

They had thought that at one point he was going to give himself up, when he got off his bike. So they stopped firing, but to their amazement he had got back on his bike while they just stood there and watched.'

'On a gloriously sunny summer afternoon in 1941, whilst walking along The Kingsway, Brighton, my mother found an unexploded bomb. She was pushing my sister's pram at the time and didn't realise quite what she'd found. Thinking that someone might fall over it, she removed my sister, who was still asleep, from the pram, laying her gently down on the pavement. It was a bit of a struggle, but finally she managed to get the bomb into the pram, and carrying my sister gently in her arms she proceeded to the nearest police station. When the station officer told her that he thought it was a bomb – and that there was every chance that the bomb was live – mother fainted.'

'In 1939 the Army requisitioned Old Orchard at Waldron and Mrs Bains moved away. Because of the war, children were sent to Waldron from London to escape the bombing. They were sent to Waldron school and were collected by local people who took them home to live and to look after them.

The ARP were based in a room at the rear of the greengrocer's shop in Cross-in-Hand. When they were notified of an air raid, the greengrocer's wife would run up and down the village with a tin hat on her head blowing a whistle.

The first air raid over Cross-in-Hand was on 15th August 1940. One bomb fell in Beaconsfield Terrace and cut off the electric and water supplies. A Dornier bomber was shot down and crashed in the woods at Back Lane. The pilot landed unharmed by parachute and was arrested by Mr Stan Herring, a special constable, and was taken to the ARP room at the back of the greengrocer's.

The Foord mineral water factory at Cross-in-Hand had an underground shelter which was open to anyone while an air raid was on. All women were expected to do firewatching at night.'

WE DIVED UNDER THE TABLE

'I looked after two children while their mother worked in the canteen in Preston Park, where Canadian soldiers were stationed. It was my job to take the children for a walk after tea, then wash them and put them to bed.

One day I had them both sitting on the kitchen table, washing them. Without warning a bomb dropped on the railway viaduct, behind the house. We all just dived under the table. The house shook, the window blinds shot up and down and the glass in all the windows blew in. After it was all over, I walked them down the road to my mother. We were absolutely black, covered in the soot that had shot down the chimney. But we were safe.'

THE RAIDS GOT HEAVIER

'I was born between the wars and lived with my parents and my brother in Newick, a village some nine or ten miles from Lewes. In 1939 I went to school in Lewes which meant a cycle ride to the station and a journey by train. The trains were two coaches long with no corridors and of course they were steam trains. After Dunkirk we children got used to the dog fights taking place in the skies above us during the Battle of Britain and in fact used to collect the shiny brass bullets and shell covers which rained down around us. From our back garden we could see the glow in the sky from the blitz in London almost 60 miles away. We also got to recognise the distinctive sounds of the different aircraft and were well able to recognise "one of ours" and "one of theirs".

Later on, the raids became heavier and many a German bomber

unable to reach his target would off-load his cargo of bombs over Sussex on the way back to France. Some time during 1943 or thereabouts four of us schoolgirls were coming home from school on the train. I think it was probably a Wednesday (early closing day) as a lady called Mrs Wilkins was in the carriage with us when a lone German aircraft flew over the train and strafed it with machine gun fire. Mrs Wilkins pushed us on the floor and laid on top of us. When it was all over I remember pulling the communication cord to stop the train. Mrs Wilkins's face was pouring with blood and she subsequently lost her eye. When we got home my friend Bunty and I found splinters in our clothes and there was a piece of glass sticking in the top of my school satchel. My mother never got cross about the splinters and dirt, she just sat down and cried.

The whole of our part of Sussex was a Restricted Area and nobody was allowed in or out without a permit and travel was also restricted. Apart from the train to school we went everywhere on our bikes. My Granny and Grandad lived in Seaford and my best friend Hilary lived in Newhaven. On one of my holidays with my Granny I biked over to Newhaven to see Hilary. Neither of us took much notice of the activities of the Canadian army as we were used to them being about and anyway "Careless Talk Costs Lives" and we had had it dinned in to us that in wartime spies were everywhere.

However, even we couldn't avoid realising something was up and very soon we were watching as streams and streams of men on stretchers were carried off the ships and laid gently along the pavements and streets all round the harbour. It was all very orderly with not a lot of screaming or shouting, just lots of nurses and people and all those lovely friendly Canadians who used to give us chocolates and rides in their armoured cars lying around with bloody bandages. Then along came an officer who shouted, "Get these children out of here" and we were hustled away. But by this time we had heard where all the wounded men were coming from – Dieppe. I had to stay with Hilary and her parents for an extra night because only ambulances were allowed out of town.'

WE TOOK OUR CHANCES

'I came to live in Portslade in 1938 where I ran a general store in North Street. North Street is situated one road behind Wellington Road (the seafront road of Portslade) and during the war both were restricted areas for a while. I had to report "out" at the police station in St Andrews Road if I planned to leave the area. Likewise, I had to report "back" upon my return.

I looked after the shop and my small son while my husband was away. The shop sold everything, including food which was being rationed, and we stayed there for eight and a half years in all.

I remember one Saturday evening, while putting up the wooden shutters in front of the shop windows (for protection), a German plane came flying low over the Aldrington Basin, just a little way along the coast road. It was machine-gunning, and it killed a butcher's boy who was making deliveries to some boats in the harbour.

I had my bedroom windows blown out one night by the explosion of a land mine, and I once had to attend court because I forgot to pull the blinds down at one of my upstairs bay windows. I can't remember how much I had to pay, but the maximum fine was £3.

On D-Day the noise was terrific from the planes with the gliders at the back. Everyone was outside looking at them. Nothing much was done that morning because everyone knew what was happening. For one thing, the 1st Guards division was stationed along in Hove, and Princess Elizabeth had been to inspect them earlier. All their stuff was moving off at that time, so you knew something big was happening.

When the war first started we used to use the air raid shelters, down one of the side roads between North Street and Wellington Road, but we got fed up with sitting in them all night. So we used to sit underneath the stairs during an air raid, but then my family insisted that we had one of those awful table shelters. During the last part of the war though, I just used to sleep upstairs, because I got fed up with having to keep going downstairs. So at the end we just took our chances.'

OH, BY THE WAY!

'We did not escape the war unscratched and had our share of bombs where we lived outside Lewes, but on the whole we were relatively safe. We used to sit with our three little evacuees on the steep staircase, which was enclosed and had no windows, during night raids.

Three little girls, farmer's daughters from Great Streele Farm, came one morning, very excited, with a dead owl they had found in their attic. After it had been duly admired and exclaimed over they casually said, "Oh, by the way, a German fighter plane came down in one of our fields last night"!'

DOGFIGHTS AND DOODLEBUGS

'On 28th September 1940 my neighbour witnessed a dogfight in the air over Dallington. The pilot, an RAF officer, was shot down and his plane landed in a field near Padgham Corner. A wooden cross was erected in the field and later this patch of land was handed over to the parish council and the cross adopted by the Air Force Association.

Of course, the area had its share of doodlebugs, one of which fell in the same field at Padgham Corner, where pieces remained for some time, and another at Prinkle Farm. Local people remember running away from German planes machine gunning the fields, though luckily only a cow was killed.'

LIFE GOES ON

We still had to bring up families and keep everyday life going, though changes came to even the smallest villages as a result of the war. We got used to seeing soldiers about and to making do, and to worrying about our loved ones overseas.

WARTIME IN BISHOPSTONE

'In 1939 children from London were evacuated to the country. The vicar at Bishopstone was the billeting officer. We had two little sisters and their brothers went to another family. I can remember my mother sorting out a change of clothes for them. They were two very frightened little girls with only the clothes they were wearing. They had never seen farm animals or fields before and had no idea where milk came from. The evacuees spent most of their time sitting on the grass on the village green. They did not like the quietness of the countryside and soon returned to London. After Dunkirk, with the risk of invasion, it was our turn to be evacuees.

Early in the war the Devon and Cornwall Regiment were under canvas in a field in the village. Then the Canadians came. They commandeered all the empty houses in and around the village. The vicar acted as chaplain to the local forces and with the army chaplain he held services in the church. The vicar's wife had a canteen and a quiet room in the vicarage.

One of the ladies in the village held "open house" for the young soldiers (after the war she received an invitation to go to Canada for a holiday from the parents and relatives of the soldiers she had helped and befriended when they were so far from home). Socials, dances, whist drives were organised. The village postmistress and her sister in law made the back rooms of the shop into tea rooms. They put tables and chairs in the garden and in the small garden across the road. The story goes that they spent most of the night before the Dieppe raid baking and a lot of soldiers on that raid carried a paper bag full of home-made scones. It was a sad time for the village. For weeks after the raid socks and underwear stayed on the lines behind the houses where the missing Canadians had lived, in fact until the Canadians cleared up and pulled out.

Fuel tanks were then built in and around the village and pipe lines laid down to the beach at Tidemills. This was in the build up to D-Day for fuelling the landing craft and smaller boats. The coastal roads were full of tanks and army lorries.

I was, at that time, travelling to Lewes every weekday. The boats from Normandy began to bring in the prisoners of war. I vividly remember Newhaven Harbour station platform packed with German soldiers waiting for a train to take them to POW camps. The last uni-formed soldiers billeted in Bishopstone village were four German POWs sent to work on the farm. They lived with an elderly man and his sister until they were repatriated after the war.'

MICROGRAMS

'As the war progressed, mail from the troops was very difficult to send from far away places and took up too much space in the ships coming home. Then someone came up with the ingenious idea of the microgram. After mail had been censored, each letter was photo-graphed and made into a negative of postage stamp size, so one sack could take hundreds, possibly thousands, of letters.

On their arrival in Great Britain, the negatives were developed onto a piece of paper roughly four inches by three – small but quite readable, with just the serviceman's name and rank, no address, and his censored letter.'

Clearing up the debris after another air raid in Eastbourne.

WAITING FOR LETTERS

'Every day was one long day of worrying about where the men were, what they were doing, and if they would ever come back. It was a nightmare. I'd be working in Portslade, and every day when I got home it was always, "Is there a letter?" If there wasn't a letter from my boyfriend (as he was then), I'd get in a panic. Few today can possibly understand what we went through and I pray no one ever finds out what it is like to be separated from your loved one because of a world war.'

GETTING A JOB

'On leaving school at the age of 14 in December 1939 my first place of employment was in a small draper's shop, Carpenters at Seaside, Eastbourne, opposite Christ church. The proprietor was a Miss Horwood. The shop sold baby wear, haberdashery, millinery and also carried out alterations to ladies' dresses and coats on the premises. This work was part of my training, and we also made, by hand, iron and kettle holders etc. Unfortunately, due to the evacuation of coastal towns such as Eastbourne, the shop had to close in September 1940 when non-essential people were asked to leave the town. I accompanied my mother and brothers to Lewes where we stayed until December 1940.

On returning to Eastbourne, virtually a dead town, it was difficult to obtain employment for a 15 year old. I was fortunate in obtaining hairdressing training at Roselands Hairdressing Salon, Seaside (Archery). I well remember my mother being used as a guinea pig for my Marcel waving experience, on one occasion losing some hair due to me having the irons too hot. (Father did not know, I was able to cover up my mistake by rearranging the parting.)

While working at Roselands one particular memory is of a morning in August 1942. Just before 9 am I looked out and saw two German FW 190 fighter bombers coming in from the sea. We all dived for cover as they dropped their bombs; one hit a boiler in the power station about 200 yards away, shattering our shop windows, and the other bomb dropped on houses in Marlow Avenue.

From the spring of 1942 I served as a warden in the Civil Defence, my duty post being only round the corner from the shop, in a building next to the Archery Tavern.'

FLOATING POUND NOTES

'A cold and drear day in February towards the end of the war saw me aboard the 11.45 am train from Victoria, bound for Eastbourne. My sister and brother in law had returned to Guernsey to retrieve what they could of their home they had so hurriedly had to leave in 1940, when the Germans invaded the Channel Islands. Their daughter, Valerie, was at a boarding school in Eastbourne, and as it was her tenth birthday I had been asked to take her out for a birthday treat. I was in the WAAF, billeted in London, and had managed with some difficulty to obtain a weekend pass!

The journey was slow and tedious, the train arriving late at Eastbourne, leaving me very little time to find the small hotel near the station I had previously booked for the night. Hurriedly signing in and managing time for a very quick "wash and brush up", I started off for Valerie's school.

This hotel was situated in quite a wide road with tall three and four-storey houses cum hotels on each side. Imagine my surprise when I had only gone about 100 yards along, when floating down in front of me were one pound notes! I stopped, looked up and down the houses, but could see no windows open anywhere – bearing in mind it was a bleak February day – and there was nobody in the vicinity except for a young man about 17 or 18 coming towards me on the other side of the road. He immediately ran across to me, surprised as I was, and between us we must have picked up about £30 altogether, which in those days was quite a sum of money.

Still no one came to claim the money and after much discussion I asked him where the nearest police station was. He pointed in the opposite direction to where I was going, and as by now I was very late, I asked him to take the money there and I hurried on my way.

Finally arriving breathless at the school I was informed that it would be impossible for me to take Valerie out as measles was rife in the school and all the girls were in quarantine for at least the weekend. Quite stunned by this turn of events but pulling myself together I asked Matron if I could bring my niece in a birthday cake and a few presents so that she could at least celebrate her birthday with her school friends.

On arriving back at the school loaded with all sorts of goodies, I was told I could just say "hello" to Valerie by standing on the door mat and looking up the stairs! The poor girl was in tears and by this time so was I! I was just given enough time to wish her a happy birthday and to say I would be down again when the quarantine was lifted.

Wending my weary way back to the hotel I explained the circumstances, booked myself out and caught the next train back to London, feeling very cold, depressed and by this time very hungry!

It wasn't till I was sitting in the train that I suddenly remembered those floating one pound notes. Where had they come from and had the young man taken them to the police station? I would dearly love to know.'

THE DOWNS PLOUGHED UP

'The Downs were ploughed up for wheat and barley. Country people kept chickens and rabbits for the meat and one pig was allowed per family if meat coupons were surrendered. On the farm at Chiddingly we had off duty policemen, firemen, soldiers, land girls, air force men and even two prisoners of war brought from the camp at Herstmonceux to help us get the harvest in, food was so important at that time.

There was an airfield at the "Gales", Friston from which Spitfires and Hurricanes took off for France. The whole area became a military zone with gun sites and radar. Tanks roared over the Downs, and the Canadians trained in the area for the Dieppe raid for which they sailed from Newhaven. Eastbourne had its share of air raids, with homes and buildings devastated and people killed.'

197

CARRYING ON REGARDLESS

'On 19th September 1939 Alfriston WI held their usual monthly meeting in the Old School Room. It is evident from the minutes of the meeting that members were somewhat subdued. It was decided meetings should take place in the afternoon in the future rather than the evening. In 1940 the army arrived in Alfriston and commandeered the Old School Room so for a while meetings were held at the Star Inn.

Early in the war many children and their mothers were evacuated to Alfriston and the WI gave their support. They met each week in the Scout Room to receive and make clothes for the children and a grant was made from funds to buy knitting wool. The WI also provided a meeting room for the mothers of the evacuees with free lighting and heating, which was much appreciated.

Mrs Edith Barnard, a previous headmistress of the village school, was president during the war years and her responsibilities must have been both challenging and satisfying. She encouraged members to continue with their singing, folk dancing and drama pursuits and concerts were given in the village. Woollen garments were made and sent to the Forces and members organised weekly door-to-door collections of War Savings. In July 1940 Miss Schlesinger offered the use of her kitchen for jam making and fruit bottling. Under a special government scheme sugar was released for this purpose so that locally grown fruit could be preserved and in 1942 Mr Morphew offered the WI the use of a room over his garage at White Lodge as a jam centre. The centre produced 575 lbs of jam and jelly in that year. They also organised a garden produce scheme. A very productive year.

As the war continued more soldiers were stationed in the village, including a contingent of Canadians. The WI were involved in setting up a canteen for them and arranging social evenings. Socks were darned for the men. Whist drives were held in order to raise money for Christmas gifts for the Forces and waste paper salvage weeks were held, the proceeds of which enabled parcels to be sent to prisoners of war. They somehow also found time to fund-raise for the Cancer Campaign and collected newly laid eggs for the Princess Alice Hospital in Eastbourne.

By the end of 1942 the WI were able to hold their meetings once more in the Old School Room with only an occasional interruption when the ARP required the hall for a meeting. As the war continued many new skills were acquired. They made gloves, repaired carpets, made new clothes from old and became expert at making cakes without eggs. The ARP taught them how to operate a stirrup pump.

Members shared sadness when relatives and friends were lost in action and when the home of one member was damaged by a bomb. When reading these wartime minutes, one can only marvel at the energy and enterprise of the members of Alfriston WI. Whilst making their contribution to the war effort they regularly attended "outside" meetings and held music festivals and in 1944 were still urging the government to provide more air raid shelters for the village school. They were also petitioning for more policewomen to be appointed and with the help of their MP, Mr Taylor, secured a bus service to Berwick station. They were in fact, like all Institutes at the time, carrying on regardless.

LIFE IN THE VILLAGES

'The army, mainly Canadians, commandeered all the large houses with grounds in Chailey village, and suddenly it was all action! The tank corps took over Markstates Common and as we walked to school the tanks would be moving out in convoy. These vehicles were fine travelling in a straight line, but on corners they had a mind of their own, veering anywhere and tearing up the kerbstones and paths. We walked sedately along the straight bits of road and ran like mad round the corners – we were petrified of the monsters.

As D-Day approached the build up of troops and vehicles was tremendous, not forgetting the three squadrons of Spitfires, Mk 9s, which left the airfield on the western edge of the village daily. This airfield was known as Chailey ALG (Advanced Landing Ground) 131 Polish Wing. The Polish airmen used to come to the weekly dances in the village, where a team of ladies including my mother served endless rounds of spam sandwiches and sticky buns. The bread and buns were provided by the local baker.

Then they were gone, leaving us with the flying bombs.'

'The first thing I remember about the war was the arrival in Chiddingly of three evacuees from East London, who were frightened of the country and amazed at having to walk two miles to the village school every day. They were fascinated by picking blackberries and getting eggs from the hens' nesting boxes and seeing the milk being brought round in churns, from which our jugs were filled. The eldest, Joanie, became a good friend of mine and for a time we wrote to each other after they returned to London.

Another early memory is of the darkness. When we drove home from, say, Lewes, we could no longer look into people's houses and imagine stories about them. There were no street lamps or signposts and only very reduced headlights on cars, and even torches had a reduced light surface. Indoors, you had to be sure to pull the blackout curtains before turning on the lights.

Over the Downs you could see searchlights beaming high into the sky and, at times, hear the guns in France. On a night when hundreds of German bombers were coming over, which we were watching from the garden, I remember my father saying, "I think I had better put my tin hat on." He was an air raid warden but even so it seemed a typically British reaction to a dangerous situation. We had our share of bombing, machine gun strafing, incendiary bombs (put out with the stirrup pump) and, later V1 and V2 "buzz" bombs, which while you heard them were harmless but when their engines cut out, you just waited.

The WI was there, helping. All kinds of preserves were made including rosehip syrup. Herbs and apple rings were dried and fruit was bottled in Kilner jars and, indeed, one person had a canning machine. The WI set up a jam-making "factory" in someone's garage where village people brought their fruit and it was my job to weigh the fruit, calculate two-thirds of the weight and give them that amount of sugar, especially supplied to the WI on top of ordinary rations. Another job I had was to stick the labels on to the jars – straight or else! I was never asked to cook, which was a very good thing. Every Friday morning vegetable pasties would arrive at our end of the village. I do not know where they were made but the WI organised the scheme. These we set up in the cart shed of a local oast house and sold. They were delicious and a welcome extra to wartime rations, which were quite adequate but boring.

At home we had a samoyed dog, whose long, white, thick hair I combed and saved for a local WI spinner. When spun, she returned some of the yarn to me. I made a pair of gloves with the wool, which made my hands so hot that I have sympathised with dogs in the summer ever since.'

JUST AS DANGEROUS HERE

'When the war started children were evacuated from London to Fairlight, but they only stayed about a fortnight as it was realised that it was just as dangerous here, so close to the French coast, as it had been in London. After them came the soldiers, and we had to empty some of our outbuildings to accommodate them. They set up guns at the top of Commanders Walk. However, the commanding officer decided after a while it was too dangerous for them too, and they withdrew.

We carried on during this time with our smallholding, ploughing up more land to provide food. Later we were sent four German prisoners of war to assist our regular workforce of four women with the heavier work, as all our men were away fighting.'

BEWARE ANIMALS!

'In late 1939 we moved to Shipreed Farm, Ridgewood and I worked on the farm with my father.

In 1943 I used to go to dances at the Yonder Tea Rooms at Ridgewood. They were run by Mr and Mrs Staples and were held three nights a week, entrance fee sixpence. One evening walking home in the blackout, I felt something brush against my leg every so often. I began to get frightened so I walked faster but it still continued. In the end I plucked up courage to put my hand down to feel what it was. It was our collie dog come to meet me!

Another evening, I was returning home with my boyfriend after going to the pictures at Uckfield. In those days, of course, we didn't have cars and we walked everywhere. When we got close to home, we heard noises coming from a cartshed where my father kept his tractor and fuel – very valuable in wartime. The blackout meant that we couldn't see a thing but we stood and listened and heard the noises again. We went indoors and told my father, who decided to creep up and try to catch whoever was stealing his fuel. After a few heartstopping moments, we found it was one of the horses who had got into the shed and was rubbing his leg against an empty drum. The blackout had a lot to answer for!'

IT AFFECTED EVERYONE

'Rationing came in very early in the war and later clothing coupons. The war soon affected everyone and air raids seemed constant, causing much damage and loss of life. Being on the south coast, in Worthing, our raids were mostly of the "hit and run" type. On Saturday evening two bombs fell in our road, killing seven people. We all had extensive damage to our homes and my two boys were very shaken but fortunately not hurt.

The men who were past army age were all engaged in war services such as the Red Cross, the Fire Service or as air raid wardens, and most had allotments or used every possible inch of garden space to grow vegetables to supplement our rations, especially for growing children.

Fortunately our gas masks were not needed and after five long years the war came to an end. Getting back to normal took a very long time but how we appreciated having no blackout and the street lights back on, and later the joy of having more plentiful supplies in the shops – not just food and clothes but also children's toys, household goods and films for our cameras!'

DOING OUR BIT

Whether it was firewatching, working in munitions or factories or nursing, we all did our bit during the war.

TESTING BULLETS

'At the beginning of the war I tested bullets in what was then a bullet factory near the Grenadier pub in Hangleton. They had taken over what was the hardware store at that time. Every bullet was tested separately, and then they were placed in a big vat of oil. I was the fastest one there, but the job only lasted the year. I suppose the process became obsolete.

Then I went to work in Portslade village. There used to be a brewery there but it was taken over by the CVA making component parts for aeroplanes. I was testing the parts as they came off the machines. I stayed there until 1945.'

A WREN IN BRIGHTON

'In 1941 I was a Wren, stationed in *HMS Vernon*, a shore establishment adjacent to the dockyard in Portsmouth. I was a writer, working in the Officers' Pay Section. Air raids in Portsmouth had been so bad that we were all very relieved to hear that the powers that be had decided the section should be evacuated to Brighton.

The ledgers were packed and away we went. For the first few miles we played "Sardines" under the seats of the railway carriage because of "yet another raid"!

My abiding memory of Brighton is of the utter peace and serenity; the ordinary-ness of life. We went to bed – all night; we could work all day (which was something we had rarely been able to do in

Portsmouth). We could go for walks, go dancing in the evening, without the constant interruptions and noise. What bliss!

The Section was at Mowden school, the Droveway, and the personnel were billeted with local people for 25 shillings a week. This, of course, was full board. Most people were welcoming and kind, including Bishop Bell of Chichester, who lived opposite my digs in the Droveway.

The officers were at Roedean school and at regular intervals we went there to deal with queries on pay and allowances. My memory of the premier English girls' school is of prison-like stone stairs and narrow passages. Perhaps we were in the servants' quarters? Oh well, at least I can say "Yes, I was at Roedean!" '

NURSING MEMORIES

'I have vivid memories of being a student nurse in Southlands Hospital (which was then considered as being in East Sussex), and of witnessing some of the atrocities of war.

My first memory is of my mother crouched in a doorway in the brewery passage, in Portslade village, while a sniper did his best to target her. Fortunately to no avail.

Then of the boys that came back from overseas, maimed and blinded, and of those who were brought back from Dieppe, lined up on their stretchers in Shoreham, waiting transport to hospital, when snipers came in and sprayed them with gunfire.

As nurses we were subjected to a period of fear one night when a Molotov cocktail was dropped, hitting the corner of our nurses home and the contents spattering masses of silver, burning debris over the grounds. It lit up the area like a fairground, leading the way for a German raid, but they didn't reckon on the speed of our fire fighters.

There were good times too; the rapport with the soldiers, the dances given by the police and services and also simple pleasures. Southlands was almost self sufficient, growing our own fruit and vegetables. On night duty, during the summer, we took pleasure in creeping down to "the farm" during meal break, with our little torches, where we'd crawl under the netting and filch a few strawberries for our tea.'

A SMALL FACTORY

'The garage at Burwash was built by my husband, his father and brother. It had hand-operated petrol pumps with large glass globes on the top advertising Shell or BP petrol. At the start of the war the

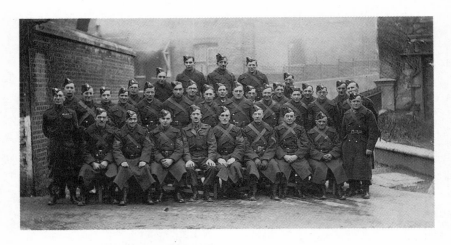

Members of Portslade Home Guard.

garage became a small factory where nuts, bolts and rivets were made for 25-pound field guns and Bofors anti-aircraft guns, and towards the end of the war parts for mine detectors to be used on D-Day. It was mainly girls working ten hour shifts, including myself. I also found time to do 48 hours a month as a telephonist at the Burwash fire station. This brings memories of travelling to Rye, a distance of about 26 miles, on an open fire engine one cold, frosty night with bombers droning overhead. Six of us girls went on that journey to have our gas masks tested by standing in a gas filled shed.'

FIREWATCHING AT THE CINEMA

'I was one of six usherettes aged between 16 and 20 at the Ritz cinema, Seaford in 1939. When the war started in September all the cinemas were closed down. To keep us employed we were split into two groups as firewatchers, and during the time we were on duty we had to scrub every bit of carpet in the entire building – I can smell Scrubs Carpet Soap to this day. Our instructions, as firewatchers, were to run 50 yards along the road to the nearby fire station to let them know if we had been hit by an incendiary bomb! Luckily nothing happened and the cinemas soon reopened.'

'I had just left school when the war started. I joined the Red Cross and did some training at the Bexhill and Hastings hospitals. We had a "Mobile Unit", an old ambulance, based at the Little Folks' Home in Little Common, the children all evacuated of course. When the sirens went I cycled down there at top speed with no lights. The schools in Collington Lane became billets and a canteen for the troops, some of them Canadians, and I helped there too. You had to have a special pass to go through the lane. Later, the whole area was evacuated, and my family shut the house and went to Staffordshire.

I joined the Land Army, and after initial training at Plumpton was sent to a farm at Hartfield. There was a fine herd of Guernseys, all milked by hand, the bottling too, and there was arable as well. Later I transferred into the ATS and spent the rest of the war in the north of England, only getting back occasionally on leave. I can remember lying under a hedge in what is now Birkdale in Little Common while a Battle of Britain dogfight went on above me, very exciting. We didn't get very much bombing, mostly stray jettisoning, and later the odd V1s and V2s which fell short of their targets. We had Marine Commandos billeted on us before D-Day, and we saw the Mulberry Harbours going down the Channel and wondered what on earth they were.'

THE WOMEN'S LAND ARMY

The vital job of food production was entrusted to the Women's Land Army, supplementing the work of those men not yet called up into the services. It was hard work but satisfying, and many friendships were made during those years.

DARKEST SUSSEX!

'Few can imagine what it is like to be suddenly uprooted from a comfortable home and secretarial job in one's teens to become a dairy-maid in the Land Army in darkest Sussex in 1943. I was to become a land girl on a farm at Firle, but some training was first required, and this was to be a four week residential course at Cralle

Place – a large rambling house at Cowbeech reputed to be haunted! The door would open mysteriously at 3.25 each morning in one of the bedrooms, so we were told with ghoulish delight.

At the time I lived in Brighton and had never visited this outback of Sussex, as we had no car or transport in those days, and very rarely went into the surrounding countryside.

On a miserable dark day in November 1943, I reported with my bus-pass with two other recruits (or conscripts as we really were) to the Southdown bus station, and we were put off at Golden Cross, which as far as I was concerned was really the end of the world. We were then picked up by a bumpy Land Rover and transported to Cralle Place, where a dozen or so more land girls were under the supervision of the resident farmer and his wife, with a cowshed full of mixed cows which were reputedly sent by the local farms as being "too difficult to manage", and which were there for us to learn to milk!

We were kitted out in our uniforms of green jumper and breeches with thick socks to the knee, a smart overcoat and hat, but we spent most of our time in dungarees and wellingtons.

The day started at 5 am when we set out in the cold light of dawn, with a large mug of tea and chunk of bread in our stomachs. I soon learnt not to wash my face first thing owing to the cold air. Breakfast came later when the first milking had been completed and cows fed and watered, and the cowsheds scrubbed down. But first the cows had to rounded up in the dark fields amongst scrub and bushes, which was a quite alarming experience for a first time, close confrontation with such a large strange beast.

As we progressed with our training we were instructed in the skills of milking on a rubber cow – affectionately known by all as the "Futility Cow". Water was poured in at the top, and the milker, bucket in hand, milked it out at the other end! We mucked out and learned the art of feeding the cows, grooming with curry combs, and the horrors of artificial insemination described by a local vet. The moment came when for the first time you sat trembling beneath your first real cow, when the beads of perspiration trickled down your face with fear, because sometimes you were kicked out into the gutter, and other times held on by your teeth, while humming nonchalantly to the cow. Another nerve-wracking job we took in turns was going into the cowshed in the dark, because even the cowsheds all had to be blacked out before milking began, and putting the blackout in place right in front of the enormous bull, who snorted horribly only inches away with his ring in his nose.

At the end of the four week period we were allowed home for the first time, and soon after I was given a job as milkmaid on the farm at Firle. My tasks were washing and sterilising the milking equipment twice a day, and organising the milk churns for collection. Mercifully it was machine-milking on this farm. My two colleagues, also land girls, and I used to bring the cows up from the faraway fields across the railway line and we would ring the signalman at Berwick station for permission to open the crossing gates and bring our 69 ladies across the line. Fortunately no disasters occurred, but when I think of it now my hair stands on end.

I was billeted in the village of Glynde just opposite the Trevor Arms, and my Land Army friends were in the row of houses opposite. We cycled the two miles over the hill and two miles along the road to the farm to start work at 7 am where we were checked in by the farmer at the gate. We took a flask of tea and our sandwiches with us, which had to last until five o'clock when we cycled home again. We had an extra twelve ounces of cheese a week as we were "manual workers". One cold frosty morning, I remember skidding on my bicycle on the icy road and ending up in the gutter with my precious thermos flask smashed and my sandwiches scattered. Fortunately the milk lorry came along at that precise moment, picked me up, bicycle on top and delivered me to the farm. There were five farm cats and kittens, and two or three farm dogs gazing at us as we ate, longingly hoping for scraps, but they were not always lucky when we sat round the boiler each morning for our elevenses. Extras were not always forthcoming from the kitchen of the house either.

Other duties were feeding the animals, and specially the newborn calves who had to be taught to drink from a bucket from day one until they went off to market before the end of the week. Another job was filling the trough for the bull twice a day, which took 16 bucketfuls, I clearly remember. I also had the job of fattening up a large pig, of which I became quite fond (not realising that this was to be the family Christmas bacon). One morning I came in to find it with its throat cut and hanging up over a bucket – no mention ever made to me beforehand.

For this 48 hour week we were paid 48 shillings from which my rent had to be found leaving £1 for everything else, including travelling expenses home sometimes. However, I soon got round this by "working my passage" on the milk lorry which called each day, and for my fare I hopped in and out delivering bottles of milk to the various cottages en route to Brighton. This only happened once a month when I was allowed my one day off for the month, the other weeks we had half a day only, because, of course, the cows always had to be milked every day.

I remember celebrating VE Day in the Trevor Arms, Glynde, with other land girls and my landlord, and most of the villagers and lots of visiting soldiers, sailors and airmen who seemed to appear from nowhere.

At the end of the day land girls were not given a medal or "demob pay", and were not even allowed to keep their jumpers or breeches or overcoats, and thinking back it makes one realise how willingly we accepted the hardships and restraints on our lives without so much as a murmur (almost). Nevertheless the experience left me with a deep satisfaction and the introduction to a completely different way of life, and a deep love of rural pursuits!

Many years later, when visiting the Trevor Arms and chatting up two of the locals in the bar, I mentioned that I used to be a land girl in the village and used to cycle two miles along the road to Firle each morning – one turned to the other and said, "Would that be on a penny farthing then, ma'am?" Enough said!'

WE WORKED OUR HOME FARM

'My sister and I both joined the Women's Land Army, and when my eldest brother was called up we worked on our home farm at Herst-monceux. This was unusual, but by this time we had a milk delivery business, and my father's health was deteriorating.

I remember the air raids and the bombs that were often dropped at random when our fighters chased the bombers away from London. When the V1 missiles started coming over us, many cut out before reaching their target and landed in our area. We used to listen to the roar of these machines and wait to hear if the engines stopped – then we had to take cover as one never knew where they would land. I well remember my bedroom window shattering only a few feet away from my bed, and finding myself on the other side of the room!

Needless to say, the war was not all tragedy and there were many amusing things happening at that time. Of course petrol was rationed, and only used for essential journeys. We cycled every-where, to dances held at local village halls, where we found plenty of partners among the soldiers and airmen stationed in the area. In the next village to ours there lived a man who owned a small cattle lorry which he used to convey animals to market or from farm to farm. He also kept a cow to supply his family with fresh milk. This man liked to go out to a pub for a drink in the evening, and in order to use his lorry would take the cow with him. Should he be stopped he had the excuse that he was delivering her to a nearby farm. It was said that the cow got so used to these evening jaunts that the man had only to let down the tail-board of the lorry and the cow would trot in and off they would go!'

I JOINED WITH A FRIEND

'In 1941 I joined the Women's Land Army with a friend. We worked for the East Sussex Agricultural Executive Committee with two other girls in a threshing gang. We came to Hartfield and stayed here throughout the war. In those days there were two butchers, two grocers, a post office and stationer's, a tea shop, a sweet shop, a baker's and a newsagent and shoe shop.

Our wage in 1941 was 28 shillings of which we paid £1 for our lodgings. We did all the jobs around the thresher, as there were few men, and travelled to most farms within a five mile radius of Hartfield. One of us would be on the top of the thresher cutting the bonds on the sheaves, and passing it to the feeder, one or two on the corn stack pitching the sheaves up to the feeder, and one at the back of the machine raking out the chaff, a very dirty job. Sacks of oats weighed 1 cwt, so we helped move those, but wheat was in 2 cwt sacks and too heavy for us.

We had frequent stops for tea, brewed on an open fire usually, and sandwiches, or in the case of old farm workers a hunk of bread, a

Kathleen Field (left) was an enthusiastic member of the Women's Land Army.

By this personal message I wish to express to you

Miss Kathleen I. Field, W.L.A. 94561

my appreciation of your loyal and devoted service
as a member of the Women's Land Army from

13th August, 1942 *to* 28th January, 1949
Your unsparing efforts at a time when the victory
of our cause depended on the utmost use of the
resources of our land have earned for you the
country's gratitude.

Elizabeth R

lump of cheese and a raw onion or turnip, eaten with a pocket knife. Food was rationed but farmers got extra at threshing time and sometimes our sandwiches were supplemented by them. One place we went to was farmed by two brothers, and their mother would always make an enormous blackberry and apple roly-poly about two feet long which she boiled in the copper and it was shared with us. We threshed from August until April going from farm to farm. We worked from 8 am to 5 pm and finished at noon on Saturdays, then we were off till Monday morning. We usually went home and were able to take rabbits, eggs and vegetables to our parents.

In the summer months we worked on various farms hoeing, singling, thistle spudding, haying and harvesting, it was a great life. Once, on Earl de la Warr's farm at Withyham we helped round up some cattle which had been running wild with the deer. It was very difficult despite having two men on horseback as the cattle could run like the deer and even jumped low hedges with them.

During this time the air battles were taking place overhead, and we witnessed many dogfights. Later we were in Doodlebug Alley and a number of V1s were intercepted in this area. On one occasion we were hoeing on a slope and a doodlebug came over the field with pieces falling from it. There was no shelter so we raced up to the top and pushed our heads and shoulders under a haystack. Fortunately the bomb went on for some time before exploring as our lower halves were totally exposed.

I was in the WLA for almost five years and during that time met and married my husband who lived in Hartfield and was serving in the RAF. We were married in 1943, a real war-time wedding – no proper wedding dress, clothes were on coupons. My husband had 48 hours leave and we had one night in Brighton for a honeymoon. No icing for the cake, just a white cardboard cover, and no photographs as we could not get a film.'

DOUBLE SUMMER TIME

'During the war Gate Court at Northiam trained land girls. We had two or three girls boarding with us at a time. They would stay for about four to six weeks and during that time they would be trained in jobs around the farm eg hoeing rows of turnips or mangolds, feeding the animals and helping with the haymaking.

The normal working day would be from 7 am to 12 noon, 1 pm to 5 pm, except during haymaking when they would work until it was dark. When double summer time was introduced work would be from 7 am to 11 pm. This also caused problems with the chickens because each night they had to be rounded up and put into the sheds to prevent foxes getting them. Chickens would only go into the sheds when it got dark so double summer time meant it was very hard work to get them bedded down.'

A CHILD'S WAR

Children, too, did what they could for the war effort, facing the hardships and terrors, the disturbed nights and the shortages.

A BOMB WITH MY NAME ON?

'I can remember a sunny September day in Hastings, sitting on steps outside a friend's house. The french windows were open and a voice on the radio announced that war had been declared. A shiver of fear went through me and I quickly made my way home.

One morning, we were woken up very early by a terrible screaming noise. A stray German plane had dropped a "screaming" bomb. It fell in Bembrook Road, a few seconds flying time from our road, which was Old London Road. After this, we all slept on the floor downstairs.

My father, who was gassed in the First World War, became an air raid warden and he made sure we carried our gas masks everywhere. I also had to carry my identity card and memorise its number, EICB 276 4.

One day I was on the shed roof, which was level with our sitting room window, when I saw a large, low-flying aeroplane dropping about five "things". I called to my sister to come and look. She dragged me into the room and threw me behind some tea chests packed ready for moving. The "things" were bombs. Our mother, who was a bit deaf, was cooking and wondered who was trying to get into the back door when it shook with the blast. The bombs had exploded in Clive Vale – again only seconds flying time from our house.

The schools were evacuated but my father refused to let us go, believing that we should stay together as a family as long as possible. My sister, Joyce, gave me lessons in our bedroom every morning and spelling tests figured high on the curriculum. I hated them! I can still see my blue desk and chair in our sunny room.

One day in 1940 we were given 24 hours to leave Hastings so, carrying my little case and a blanket over my arm (the only luggage we were allowed to take), we made our way to Clive Vale school. At 9 am we boarded coaches which took us to the station. After travelling all day, fed by WVS ladies on the way, we arrived at Swindon. My sister and I were billeted at one end of a street and our parents at the other end. During a thunderstorm the next night, our hosts were rather amazed to see the two of us disappear into a cupboard under their stairs – a pair of shell-shocked evacuees.

Once a year we visited Hastings, and I remember the four of us sitting in a shelter on the seafront eating a two-pound basket of strawberries. Sheer delight! One such holiday, my father carved my initials on a wooden bench seat in Alexandra Park. Why he did it, we did not know, but the next year the seat had gone and a large bomb crater had appeared in its place.

My father always maintained that if a bomb had your name on it, it was meant for you. Had we inadvertently set up a decoy?'

DOING OUR BIT

'I started my teaching career at Hammerwood in September 1940 – the height of the Battle of Britain. There had been an air raid warning at 8.30 am and only six children had arrived by nine o'clock. After the all clear at 9.30, 16 more arrived – 22 out of a possible 32. This was the almost daily pattern for a couple of months. After that other things took over the diary.

The school pump was frequently out of order. This pump drew up water from a well to serve the school, school house and two neighbouring cottages. Until it was repaired all water had to be carried by bucket from the well at another house. Finally at the end of 1945 mains water was connected.

Children grew potatoes in the school garden, enough to supply school dinners until Christmas. One year children picked 60 pounds of blackberries which the school cook made into jam.

A collection of conkers, acorns, beech mast and rose hips helped the war effort. Fifty eight pounds of horse chestnuts were sent to Macleans. One year 116 lbs of rose hips brought 19 shillings and fivepence to the school fund.

One day a parcel arrived at the school from Canada. It contained a bar of chocolate for each child and a large quantity of chocolate powder. There was enough for every child to take home half a pound. The rest was used for school meals.'

'Schoolchildren were as keen as anyone else to help the war effort. Parties of children were sent out from school to single sugar beet, collect acorns, and pick fruit for the Women's Institutes to make jam. To single the beet you started at the end of a very long row and literally singled out a beet plant from each little clump along the row and someone more grown up followed you with a hoe. The Downs were ploughed up for this and the work was hot and dusty.

Apart from these organised trips we all did whatever we were best at to help out. I loved the stage and wrote several plays which I produced, with my best friends in the leading roles, in the Guide hut at Newick. With costumes made from our parents' pre-war splendour and music provided by Mrs Marchant at the piano, we had a wonderful time and all the proceeds went to the Red Cross to buy food parcels for prisoners of war.'

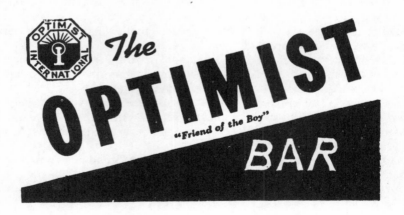
214

The children of Hammerwood school gathered to hear a talk by Major Haddock and Lady Kindersley on National Savings. Gifts from Canada and the USA were very welcome when sweets were rationed.

I WAS LUCKY

'When war was declared on 3rd September 1939 I was on the beach at Paston Place with an older cousin. I was ten years old and it was the first time I'd been allowed to go without my parents. We heard the air raid siren and ran all the way home. That warning was a false alarm.

I had just passed the scholarship to the intermediate school for girls at York Place, later to be renamed the Margaret Hardy School and moved to Patcham.

The boys' school in Pelham Street was hit by incendiary bombs and we couldn't start school until six weeks later and then only on half days as we shared with the boys. They used to leave horrid spiders in our desks. We spent a lot of time in the underground shelters. We played cats cradle and sang.

We had some very young evacuees billeted on us, two girls. They were poorly clothed and had head lice. My mother knitted them vests and jumpers. All our clothes were knitted. Later, when my sister and I were evacuated away from Brighton I realised how unhappy they must have been as it was a terrible experience.

In July 1940 the Odeon cinema in Kemp Town was bombed and suffered a direct hit. A visit to the Saturday afternoon matinee was the highlight of our week. My swimming friend who was sitting next to me was killed. My sister and I were lucky. The noise and blast were horrific. I will never forget it, especially the smell. My parents were so frightened by this and other episodes of being machine gunned in Preston Park whilst having school games that they decided we should go with the school evacuation to Doncaster, and I did not return to Brighton until 1943.'

DISTURBED NIGHTS

'During schooldays at Lewes in wartime, after nights spent in the underground shelter at the bottom of the garden, doing homework by candlelight, I cycled three miles in all weathers to catch the 8.30 am train. When the road was icy, snowy and treacherous, I used to walk the three miles along the lonely wood-lined road, sometimes being passed by long convoys of army lorries on the move. If there was an air raid alert when we arrived at Lewes we were not allowed to walk to school, but had to stay in the station shelters until the all clear, sometimes many hours. Our teachers often asked how many had experienced a disturbed night, no doubt we were bleary eyed, but schooling went on.

I remember spending hours in the concrete air raid shelters at school, continuing lessons and paperwork by candlelight. It seems amazing that we played netball and hockey matches, passed school certificate exams, and that our education went on with dedicated teachers who had spent the nights firewatching on the school roof. We shared the school premises with Tooting Bec boys who were evacuated here. As a girls' school, this caused much interest and we usually managed to pass them in the corridors when classes changed.

Once we were walking in crocodile from the Odeon along Friars Walk having been taken to see *The Young Mr Pitt*, when we saw a plane swooping low over the station. We thought it was a Spitfire, but our feelings quickly changed to horror when we saw the black swastikas. Then the bombs dropped and the whole crocodile dived through the nearest doorways to be welcomed with open arms by the householders, such was the spirit then.

On one occasion our early morning train, crowded with business people and many schoolchildren, was stopped at Isfield station where a porter came along and insisted that we must all lie down on the floor of the carriage. We didn't think we would, but one occupant of our carriage was an authoritative bowler hatted businessman who firmly commanded that we should. Fortunately for the entire trainload, the Dornier that was flying low along the railway line from Lewes turned at the next station, only minutes away at Barcombe Mills, and travelled on to Newick and Chailey, thereby missing a vulnerable target – a near miss.

At home we watched on summer days as the fighter planes fought their battles in the skies above us, seeing the white trails weaving patterns, and sometimes seeing deadly plunges straight to earth. Later we heard the doodlebugs grinding their way across the country, hoping the noise wouldn't stop for then they descended and blew up. Once, when the week's rations had been delivered and set on the tea table, one such came over. It stopped and we all tumbled into the cupboard under the stairs, just as it came down and blew up. Our windows shattered, with glass all over our precious rations, but within minutes neighbours rushed round to help and very quickly another set of rations was allocated, a lucky escape. For years afterwards the twisted remains of the doodlebug rusted away on Piltdown Common.

One morning we viewed with astonishment and disbelief hundreds of Canadian soldiers who had moved so silently and were camped all around us. They were in good spirits, one radio operator over the garden hedge entertained us before breakfast by singing *Night and Day*. One morning at school at about 9.30 we were all called into the assembly hall again to be told the momentous news of the D-Day landings. Then we sang *O God our help in ages past* and as sixth formers we were allowed the privilege of listening to the news as broadcast, missing lessons, an unforgettable morning.'

A LONG TIME IN MY LIFE

'Six years of one's childhood seems a long time when you are between seven and 14 years, though as a child I was unaware of most of the worry, the suffering, the stress and those dark days of war. I lived on the outskirts of Robertsbridge, a small village near Battle, with my parents who were farmers, and life for me continued much as it had done before.

I can remember where I was on 3rd September 1939 when war was declared, as I was enjoying a holiday with my grandparents, but when that announcement came over the radio that was the end of my holiday. I was whisked home that day. One of my memories of those annual holidays on their farm at Bodle Street was the abundance of fruit which was all ripe when I was there in September;

plums, apples and damsons had to be collected from the orchard and I could sample all the different varieties. We had late summer holidays because it was a hop growing area and many families went hop picking every year to supplement their very low incomes.

For the first three years of the war it was school as usual, but we had gas masks issued, fittings practised, and I vaguely remember marching down into underground shelters at school when the siren sounded. Our "dug-out" at home was at the bottom of our garden out in the field, under an oak tree. My father dug out a three foot square hole in the ground, then partly covered it over, and we entered it by three or four steps. I think it was mainly for my mother and sister and myself as we were the only ones I can remember sitting on the little bench on the occasions when the siren had sounded and enemy aircraft were flying over. There were not many bombs dropped in our area as we had no targets, but we were on the route for bombers flying from Germany to London. At night, when my father was on ARP duty in the village we just took cover under the dining table if necessary, and otherwise slept downstairs in the chairs as my mother didn't like being upstairs then, but I don't remember feeling much fear.

In 1942 I changed my school and lived with my other grandparents, Mr and Mrs Cornford at Hellingly during term-time. When I returned home one November for half-term we had had our supper and were just about to retire to bed when we heard planes approaching. There were two explosions in quick succession and a third one very loud, but as if stuck to the floor we just stood there while the window was blown into our living room and the radio standing on a table in front of it crashed across the room. The lights went out and we were in darkness, but of course, candlesticks were close at hand in those days. None of us was hurt, but my father's concern was for his animals. The bomb had landed on a sloping field in line with the back of our house, away from the farm buildings, so fortunately all the animals there were unhurt, but some cows and a horse were in the next field to the crater, and the horse, Madge, must have been killed instantly by a piece of shrapnel slicing through her neck. I believe one or two cows had to be put down. We didn't get much sleep for the rest of that night.

My other close encounter with enemy action was towards the end of the war when we seemed to be in the path of the V1s or doodlebugs as they were called. I had just been to collect my mother's sheets from a neighbour who sent them with her washing to a laundry, when I saw a rocket fast approaching where I was walking up the road. Normally we just watched them go over as they were

218

set for London and there was no fear of them dropping bombs, but one of our Spitfires was determined it should not reach its destination, and successfully shot at it, blowing it up in mid-air just as it had passed over us. I don't know if it was instinct that told me to lay flat on the ground under a tree, or fear, but I got up afterwards unhurt.

Land Army girls were billeted with my grandmother; over a period from 1942 to 1945 I can remember four who stayed with us, three of whom belonged to a threshing gang. Those were the days before combine harvesters, when the corn was harvested in bundles, stacked and then threshed during the winter months round to the following summer. A machine would travel around the Lewes, Ringmer, Ripe, Firle and Arlington area with a gang of about four or five land girls and a foreman in charge. I think my grandmother looked after them very well, and they felt it was like home from home. One whose name was Dolly was a Cockney from Dalston, and had experienced the London bombing in the early years of the war, so I suppose it was an escape to live in Hellingly.'

LIFE IN A GENERAL STORE

'I was born in the village of Catsfield, in October 1935 and my father died in December 1936 leaving my mother with me, my older sister and two brothers. We moved to the shop at Ninfield (the next village) when I was three, shortly before the war broke out, my mother having gone into partnership with her brother.

Our shop was one of two together, next door also being a general store. They did sell a few things different to us but not a lot. There were three girls and a boy in their family and we had some good times with them over the years.

One of my earliest recollections of the shop is seeing all the sweets and chocolate bars laid out and thinking to myself that if I took a small bite from each of the penny bars in the pile nobody would notice. My punishment for this crime was to see my sister and brothers enjoying the damaged bars whilst I had none.

The war, at first, didn't make a lot of difference to the lives of us children, but when rationing was introduced there was of course the additional job of counting coupons. I was too young to be trusted with this job but the others did their fair share. We all had our chores to do as my mother spent a considerable amount of time in the shop; my sister and I had the washing up to do and the potatoes to peel before school, the boys had paraffin to put into cans and deliver on their cart to customers.

All the rationed goods had to be weighed out in their correct amounts, the sugar being split into 2 oz, 4 oz and 8 oz bags. My uncle was an expert at making cones out of thick blue paper in which the different weights were put. The cheese, which came in large rounds, had to be skinned and then cut, quite an art at which my uncle was also expert. The cheese had to finish up in small portions, 2 oz per person per week, and we in the family never actually had a whole piece of cheese but all the slivers that came off in the process of cutting, which was usually had as a tea time treat on toast. The other commodity that had to be weighed out was butter and other fats so there were a lot of fiddly jobs to be done.

When the bombing started we had to sleep in the cellar. We reached this through a trapdoor under the kitchen table. The beds were not very comfortable I remember; my sister and I shared a bed made of wooden boxes with a mattress on them, my mother had a chair-bed and the boys a couple of camp beds. We spent quite a few nights down there, then the very night it was decided it would be safe to sleep back upstairs the bombing started again and we all had to clamber back into the cellar in the middle of the night.

The most frightening experience of the war to me was one day during the Battle of Britain. We were at school that morning when the German planes came over and were machine gunning anything that moved. We had spent most of the morning sitting under our desks and the blackboard (the shelters were not built until later in the war). There was a lull in the activity and our headmaster let the children who lived near go. Well, we had just run down the top path as we called it, where there was no shelter, and reached the part where the bushes grew quite thickly when back they came. We could see the pilots sitting in the cockpits as they went over, shooting all the while. We sat under the bushes and inched our way down the path. Our garden ran to the bottom of this path and it was decided to make a run for it up our garden and into the kitchen. The gate was locked but that did not deter my brother who took a run at it with his shoulder. The gate flew open and he nearly fell on the ground but we all did a dash up the path and into our kitchen, about ten to 15 children. In the meantime my poor mother, who must have been worried out of her mind about us, was coping with a shopful of people who had run straight into the two shops when the bus stopped right outside. Eventually the planes were driven off by our "boys in blue" and we all went back to school for afternoon lessons, the boys picking up empty shells as they went, much to my consternation as I was sure they would be blown up.

The war continued and we had our shop front blown in twice but nobody was hurt and it wasn't until the doodlebugs came that we were offered evacuation, but my mother was of the frame of mind that if we were going to be bombed it was better for us all to be together. I don't know whether her philosophy was right but we all came through unscathed, thank God.'

SIX YEARS OLD

'I was six years old when the war broke out. My memory of those first years is blurred, and I can remember attending the infants class at the church school, now Battle and Langton Primary.

We had five classes at the school, where we stayed until 14 years of age. We were kept to a strict routine each day, having mental arithmetic and spelling tests every morning. Once the war progressed we were encouraged to help in the war effort by digging for victory in the school's own garden, collecting wool from the hedgerows and acorns to feed the pigs, also rose hips to be made into syrup. It became quite a competition to see who could collect the most. We had a jam factory in Battle, Newberrys by name, and we noticed that the factory had deliveries of swede and turnips grown by farmers – they must have been used in the jam making. Lovely fruity smells used to ooze from the factory. Another delicious smell I can remember is when the local grocer, Allworks, ground their own coffee in the cellar. We would stand by the gratings near the shop and inhale the aroma. I think coffee was too expensive for us to buy.

We always had a third of a pint of milk supplied free each mid-morning break at school and were also given a large spoonful of cod liver oil and malt each day. Fruit was in short supply especially citrus fruits and bananas. I remember being horrified when saying our prayers one evening, at my younger brother asking for the war to finish soon so we could have some bananas. I retorted to him, "God will think you are a real little pig."

My father was called up in 1941 to join the Artillery as a gunner. It was a very harrowing, tearful time whenever he had to return after a leave. My mother wrote to him every day and I posted the letter on my way to school. I can still remember his special army number, 1752765, as I always made sure it was correct (my mother insisted this was important). She received letters from him but they were always censored.

I was never evacuated but we had some nasty experiences as children. I was machine gunned by a mad German pilot on our way home from school one day. My young uncle pulled me into a deep ditch by a hedge. Another time I was on my way to school early one morning when a German plane dropped bombs over the High Street;

no siren had sounded beforehand. I ran home as fast as my legs would carry me.

Later in the war years the sinister doodlebugs appeared. We were really terrified of them. As they approached silently across the Channel we were rarely given the air raid alarms, but once overhead they sounded rather like motor bikes with a fiery tail. At school the older boys were trained to be "spotters". If a doodlebug was seen they had to blow a whistle hard. We would dive for cover in a shelter or under our desks. On one occasion one was seen approaching the school but the poor spotter was dumb-struck. However, we soon heard the familiar sound and dived for shelter. Fortunately a Spitfire tipped the "bug" and it veered away and fell in the sewage pit. The school was shattered with glass and plaster but nobody was hurt.

Toys were scarce in the war years, but we found enjoyment with board games, puzzles and books, and radio to listen to. I enjoyed *Children's Hour* with Uncle Mac, *Dick Barton, Special Agent, ITMA* with Tommy Handley, *Music While you Work* and of course Vera Lynn. Our outdoor games were influenced by the war. I remember a gang of boys called "Blackies Army" would play out the war. The girls would act as nurses and would scrounge food from home to feed them.'

A SPECIAL DAY

'I well remember a hot day on 12th May 1944, when we were marched from the village school to the local recreation ground to see Someone Important.

Everything was kept very hush-hush, but in spite of the secrecy a large crowd had gathered. Soldiers and guns were lined up across the field, suddenly a shout went up, "Look, it's Winnie", and there in an open vehicle were Winston Churchill, Field Marshal Smuts from South Africa, Mackenzie King from Canada and Godfrey M. Huggins from Southern Rhodesia, all prime ministers.

They came to Northiam that day to review the troops prior to their departure to Normandy for D-Day. The soldiers had been billeted in large local houses and had been doing manoeuvres in the area for many months. As the prime ministers walked down the field, a salvo of guns went off – and I fainted, so didn't see Winston Churchill close up as he passed me by. I recovered just in time to see him disappearing standing in the vehicle giving the V-sign.

After the war new gates were erected at the entrance to the recreation ground with a plaque to commemorate this historic visit.'

THE STREET PARTY

'When the war ended in 1945 a street party was held for the younger children in our street at Portslade. Tables, chairs and all the food – sandwiches, cake, jelly and lemonade powder – were all provided by the mothers. The older children, including me, were invited to a fancy dress party held in the Rothbury cinema hall, where we played games and had a tea of sandwiches and cake. I enjoyed the afternoon, but many of us felt very shy as it was the first time any of us had been to a social event that was attended by both boys and girls.'

THE EVACUEES

At the very beginning of the war, children from London were sent to East Sussex away from the bombing, but before long it was as dangerous here as the city they had left and our own children began to be evacuated from front line positions. Experiences varied during this unhappy time, but some made friendships that outlasted the war.

MY WAR EFFORT

'I lived in Peacehaven which was then a hotch-potch of dwellings, mainly comprising new bungalows, converted railway carriages and wooden and asbestos chalets.

At the outbreak of hostilities this locality was expecting to receive a mass of evacuees from London's East End, in particular women with children under school age who were to occupy the various empty properties which were at the time advertised for rent.

The village councillors asked all local inhabitants who could possibly spare any kind of furniture, bedding, kitchen utensils etc to donate them for the evacuees and to take them to the village hall for distribution, and volunteers were then required to transport the equipment to the properties concerned.

When I arrived at the hall to help, I was given the task of allocating six chamberpots (some ornately painted, others the worse for wear!) to six different addresses in Peacehaven. These were needed as some of the homes had no indoor sanitation. As I lived in a very scattered community I carried the pots for miles, piled one on another, and at 14 years old I felt terribly embarrassed and carefully avoided meeting my friends whilst engaged on this, my "war effort".'

LEAVING BEXHILL

'It was summer in 1939. We were on holiday with my cousins on a farm in Surrey. Although I did not realise it at the time, the outbreak of war was imminent and, as my father was a teacher, we were recalled to home where preparations were being made to receive evacuees.

It was on the Sunday morning, when we were in church, that war was declared, and within minutes of the announcement the sirens went; the sound that was to become only too familiar in the following years.

Herstmonceux became a reception area, and children from a primary school in Bermondsey soon arrived. My mother took two little girls of eight or nine years of age, who went off happily to bed after a cup of cocoa. It was a pity my mother wasn't told that one girl was not supposed to drink anything after about five o'clock, and one mattress got badly damaged. She stayed with us for quite a while, but the other one was taken home by her parents as soon as they were expected to contribute to her maintenance.

I was twelve years old and attending Bexhill grammar school at this time, and there we had the Roan School billeted in Bexhill and sharing our school buildings with us. We had normal lessons in the mornings and in the afternoons we either had games or classes in local church halls or at our art mistress's studio.

This state of affairs did not last all that long, for, as the Germans advanced into France and the bombing got worse, it was decided to move all our evacuees to various places in Wales, and when the north coast of France fell, the south coast towns became evacuation areas themselves. Herstmonceux itself was not an evacuation area, but Bexhill was, and my school was sent to Letchworth in Hertfordshire.

On the Friday before our departure, we were told that if we wanted to take our bicycles with us we were to get them to school, so we cycled to Bexhill that morning instead of catching the usual bus. On the Sunday morning we had to be at Bexhill station quite early and soon we were on our way. When we reached Letchworth station we were put on to coaches which went round the streets depositing us in ones and twos at the various houses.

Gradually, as things quietened down at home, it became the practice to go home for the holidays, which was of course a ridiculous state of affairs, and finally the school returned home to Bexhill.

By this time, I was in the Lower Sixth and starting on work for what was then called Higher School Certificate, but we were not able to swot up for these exams, or take them in peace because by this time the doodlebugs had started. The whole of this area of Bexhill and Herstmonceux was well in what became known as "doodlebug alley".

The distinctive noise that these machines made became very familiar in the spring and summer of 1944, and we all got used to dashing into the table shelter if at home when we heard one coming, fearful lest the noise should "cut out", signalling its instant descent. When at school, we spent quite a lot of time in the school gymnasium which was considered the safest place, and one afternoon when I was the only one to have an examination, being the only one taking Applied Mathematics, I was put in the Secretary's room next door to the headmistress's room, and given a cup of tea halfway through the three-hour ordeal.

Meanwhile, my mother was becoming quite ill with nervous strain due to these doodlebugs, so as soon as my examinations were over my father privately evacuated my mother and me to my uncle who lived in Bishop Auckland. He took us there by train, and as soon as we got out into the streets of the town the first thing that we all noticed was that all the plate glass windows of the shops were intact and not boarded up. My father returned home alone, and my mother and I stayed with my uncle until it was time for me to go straight to university at the beginning of October. By the October half-term my mother returned home, and I settled down at college.

The war was now in its last phase and VE night came when I was at home, so the final happy ending to my memories of the war took place when the village celebrated its end at a dance for all at Herstmonceux Castle.'

COMING TO NEWICK

'My brother and I were evacuated to Newick soon after the start of the war. Coming from London, it was quite a shock initially, as at that time there was no running water (it had to be drawn from the well), no electricity and the lavatory was halfway down the garden.

We attended the village school, where we occasionally had to practice air raid drill. Several large trenches had been dug in the school playground and we had to crouch in them during the drill.

My most abiding memory of the school is that for the last hour on a Friday afternoon, all the children squeezed into the two main classrooms, which were separated by a sliding partition reaching from floor to ceiling, and we sang folk songs, most of which I remember to this day.

My brother and I lived in Newick for three years and had a very happy time there.'

CHILDREN FROM CAMBERWELL

'A lot of children from Camberwell came to Playden and we shared the school with them. We used it in the mornings and went to the WI hall in the afternoons, then the following week it was the turn of the Camberwell children to have the school in the mornings and the hall in the afternoons.

By then I was in the top class and at eleven years old one of the "big girls" who, when we spent the afternoons in the hall, had to knit khaki socks for the soldiers. How I hated it. Then in the spring of 1940 came Dunkirk, and with it the threat of invasion, and so the Camberwell children were sent to Wales and we had our school back full time. Soon afterwards Rye was evacuated and as I had just won a scholarship to the grammar school I found myself in Bedford for the next four years.'

HIGHDAYS & HOLIDAYS

Lewes bonfire revels—

MAKING OUR OWN ENTERTAINMENT

From whist drives to cricket clubs, every town and village seemed to be able to provide something for its residents, often from local talent. Dancing was a very popular pastime, and ice skating enjoyed an enthusiastic following amongst visitors to Brighton.

SPORTS AND ENTERTAINMENT

'In 1929 a new village hall was built at Laughton, with a pageant involving most of the village organised to raise the money.

Laughton had football, cricket and stoolball teams, and dances and whist drives were very popular. On a Tuesday evening, Rev Chatfield ran a film show in the vicarage stables.'

'I can remember when people would go skating on the field between Gate Court and the river Rother at Northiam. In winter the river sometimes flooded over into the field and then it would freeze over. The ice was just thick enough to enable people to skate but not deep enough to be dangerous. It was very popular as this did not happen very often.

Bathing in the river also took place in the summer time. The river used to be tidal and at high tide it would be salty. This no longer happens, after flood gates were installed further down river.'

'A tennis club was formed at Dallington and the rector at the time said that tennis could be played on a Sunday if the players went to church once that day!'

'Before the village hall at Ashurst Wood was built we used the Institute building at the junction of the A22 and Hammerwood Road. The new hall opened in 1930. There was great excitement. The celebrations ended with a dance and everybody turned out for the occasion. The band consisted of my brother Percy on piano, Jessie Bashford on violin and clarinet, one of the Bradley boys on drums, and a young man who played the ukelele and sang. After that we had a dance every Saturday evening and people came from all the surrounding villages for the "hop". I used to play piano for the first hour, then

The SS Brighton was a meeting place for young people, first for swimming and later for ice skating.

Percy took over and I danced. Long dresses were worn and it was always a grand affair.'

'The Gilbert Institute at East Dean has been in existence for over 100 years and it was used for all sorts of activities, including whist drives and jumble sales. There was a "slate" club and a tontine club, which was based in the Tiger Inn. Members paid a weekly sum of money and drew it out at Christmas. The "big" room at the Tiger was used for all kinds of social occasions, such as weekly dances. There was no village hall in those days. The young men and women walked in to Eastbourne on a Saturday evening.'

THE OLD SS BRIGHTON

'The old SS Brighton (it stood for Sports Stadium) was opened in June 1934. Like many other Brightonairs, I met my future husband there. It was a wonderful place for young people.

Originally swimming baths, the inside was designed like a luxury liner, with the water 15 foot at the deep end. The water, which I believe was sea water, was changed every few hours. After about a year the pool was converted to an ice rink and swimming never returned there.

The first ice hockey team came to Brighton in 1936 and later the

SPORTS STADIUM
BRIGHTON

WEST STREET

TEL.: BRIGHTON 6066

General Manager: D. MITCHELL

Proprietors:
SPORTS STADIUM
BRIGHTON, LTD.

Assistant Manager & Box Office:
R. JACKSON

Directors:
W. HAYWARD (*Chairman*)
F. H. BOWYER
G. W. JACKSON
C. LANGDON (*Managing*)
Secretary: J. M. BAILEY

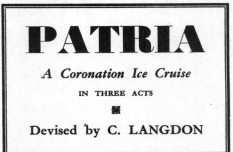

PATRIA

A Coronation Ice Cruise

IN THREE ACTS

Devised by C. LANGDON

COSTUMES designed by URSULA McCONNELL; executed by B. & H. DRURY, Ltd., 23 New Road, Brighton, 1

WAVE BALLET DRESSES by VICAIRE, Paris

LIGHTING EFFECTS by A. EVERETT, of Sports Stadium Studios

SCENERY by DELANEY ET CIE

WATERFALL SCENE by H. BOORE, of Hammersmith Palais de Dance Scenic Studios

ALEC BROWNE AND HIS SWING BAND

Brighton Tigers became internationally famous. The fans adored them and came from miles around to support them.

My husband, Vernon Marchant, was then already very involved with speed skating, stilt skating and ice shows. He was also the Sussex barrel jumping champion! The speed skating boys used to walk along there on Sunday morning to sweep the ice and this gained them free ice time. We skated to the organ played by Douglas Reeve. When we managed to acquire our own skates we treasured them and somehow never felt threatened when we walked down West Street carrying them. West Street was a very undesirable area for "nice girls" in those days!

The old SS Brighton was the heart of the town and many think the place has never been the same since it was demolished so suddenly in 1965.'

COUNTY CRICKET

'During the war county cricket was discontinued. However, we were lucky in the Brighton and Hove area because so many Australian airmen were billeted in the big hotels in Brighton and they played

230

matches at the county ground at Hove. Keith Miller was one of them. In 1946 the Indians came to England to play a test series and a school friend and I watched avidly as they played a three day match against Sussex. Over the years we watched many famous Sussex players, such as John and James Langridge, the Oaks brothers, George Cox, SC Griffiths, Hugh Bartlett and many, many more. Such famous names as Denis Compton, Bill Edrich, Len Hutton, Cyril Washbrook and all their wonderful contemporaries appeared at the county ground to play against Sussex. The summers were long and hot and it never rained! Those were indeed the days.'

MUSIC AND DANCE

'Music has been one of the constant background features of my life, as I'm sure it has, perhaps unconsciously, for lots of people. There have been so many different sources of music – the wireless, church, local town bands such as Hailsham's which I remember having great success with competitions in the late 1940s, a variety of music played at the bandstand at Eastbourne, and dance music.

I was born in the early 1930s and I was lucky to have a mother who had been taught to play the piano as a young girl and who had been given her own piano by her father. So many homes had a piano in those days, a prize possession as it was in our home. It was usual

Dancing was a popular pastime in the 1940s. Dancing teacher Lesley Wheeler and pupil Anne Tupper were photographed at the Winter Gardens, Eastbourne in 1945.

too for several members of a family to learn to play an instrument, the most popular being the piano. Some obviously progressed better than others. My mother was one of these and this led to her being in great demand at any party or gathering but not more so than at Christmas time at home (or any other excuse) when we would all gather round the piano and sing our heads off for as long as she would keep playing. This was of course before television!

In my early days, the wireless really was still a wonder. To hear famous people talking just to us, as it were, was magic. For children, *Children's Hour* was a must and when early in 1942, Mrs Winston Churchill made an appeal on the programme directly to children, we were all ears. She asked us to think of ways of raising yet more money for the war effort, but this time it was specifically for the Russians. Together with two of my friends who lived almost next door, we made little woollen brooches. We then took them to school, Grovelands county junior school as it was in those days, and after the headmistress (Mrs Ivy Rous) had inspected them, we sold them for a halfpenny each. I do not remember how many we made or sold but I do remember many kind folk gave us more than a halfpenny for them! We actually sent off several pounds and we were delighted both to hear our names broadcast and to receive a handwritten letter from Mrs Churchill, thanking us.

Back to the wireless, one heard such a variety of music, popular and otherwise. It is not surprising that even now when you hear certain pieces of music you immediately identify them with those people who played them as their signature tunes, including Max Jaffa and the Palm Court Orchestra (from the Grand Hotel, Eastbourne), Victor Sylvester, Joe Loss, Geraldo and Henry Hall.

My own efforts to learn to play the piano did not produce any talent, I fear. However, Mother eventually suggested that perhaps my feet might better respond to dancing. Now that was something I did enjoy and progressed well. Back in those war years, a school of dancing was held in the rooms above the Grenadier Hotel in Hailsham. Lesley Wheeler was the teacher and she had a devoted following of girls from seven to 15 tapping away. When her pianist fell ill and had to leave, my mother stepped in and remained until Lesley herself left, as she married and moved away. As well as learning the many steps and routines, we performed in shows and cabarets along with many guest artists at such venues as The Winter Gardens, Eastbourne and the Drill Hall in Hailsham. How our mothers made such exquisite costumes from scraps of material and old costumes I'll never know but they always looked super.

Round about the same time, there was a very good Variety Group in Hellingly run by Mrs Tyson Heap and the dancers in that were called the Moonbeams. During the finale each dancer held up a letter which spelled out "Moonbeams", I was the youngest and smallest and so held the dot. This group did many shows for charity at the Hellingly village hall and Hellingly hospital; we always had a splendid supper afterwards at the hospital I remember!'

ROYAL OCCASIONS

Towns and villages all over East Sussex celebrated coronations and jubilees with enthusiasm.

A PRIVATE VISIT

'Tuesday, 5th March 1935 is a day remembered by many people in Alfriston, for that was the day Queen Mary visited the village. King George was convalescing in Eastbourne, and Queen Mary asked especially that the visit to Alfriston be as private as possible. The children in the school were forbidden to go and cheer but Miss Jo Jenner, a former headmistress in the village, recalls that her mother, who ran a small nursery school in her house, took all the toddlers to see the Queen.

The Queen went to the Star for tea, accompanied by Lieutenant-Colonel Gwynne and then visited the church where she was greeted by Rev Rudd. The Queen then travelled sedately in her Rolls round to Lullington church, while Rev Rudd ran over the White Bridge and across the fields, so that he could greet the Queen again in that church.'

SILVER JUBILEE AND CORONATION

'On the Silver Jubilee of George V in 1935 we walked up on to Firle Beacon to join the crowds to celebrate. I remember the dark sky, the unfamiliar look of the dark Downs, the brightness and warmth of the fire. Being near Lewes, there were some fireworks, but we were especially thrilled to see other fires lighting up on Ditchling, Caburn, Crowborough and even further away – an awe inspiring sight. It was a long walk back down to the car!'

233

In Silver Jubilee year, 1935, Eastbourne WIs presented the King with the choicest local produce.

'We celebrated the Silver Jubilee in 1935 and the Coronation of George VI in 1937 at Rye, parading through the streets with banners. All the gold paint came off on our hands! All the children received a mug from the mayor, EF Benson, who was the author of the Mapp and Lucia books.'

'In 1935 there was a celebration on the village green at Nutley, with a dais formed by a draped farm cart. The goings on were overseen by Lady Kent of Chapelwood Manor, and she stood on the home-made stage to present the Jubilee mugs with the lion of England on the handle to the children of the village. There was a great firework display at Oldlands, the home of Sir Bernard Eckstein, to round off the local festivities, and this was talked about for many a year.'

CHANGES

'One of my early memories is of George V's Silver Jubilee. I was already at Newick village school but my brother was still in a tansad (that was a push chair) and it was a lovely sunny day.

The children of the village had a sports day in the cricket field, which is now a housing estate, and then we had a lovely tea. I specially remember the doughnuts which were cut in half and spread with home-made jam. We had a huge bonfire and firework display after it got dark. Newick was and still is famous for its bonfire society and they had built a bonfire as big as a house. The fireworks were wonderful and everybody seemed very happy. We sang *God Save the King* and all the children were given a mug with a picture of King George and Queen Mary on it. I remember being very tired and very happy and probably very dirty too. My father carried me home because I was too tired to walk and John of course rode home in the tansad.

It seemed to me then that it wasn't very long afterwards that my father woke me up one night and carried me downstairs to listen to the wireless and a man saying, "The King's life is drawing peacefully to a close." Daddy whispered in my ear that I would remember this when I was an old, old lady then he carried me back to bed and tucked me in. I do still remember it all these years later and men wearing black ties. I wore a black armband to school. We had a two minute silence in the classroom and were told not to shout when we went out for playtime.

Soon after that the new King Edward VIII came to visit the Chailey Heritage and my mother took us to see him arrive in his big black car. I remember waving a flag and seeing him sitting in the back of

Coronation of Her Majesty
Queen Elizabeth II

2nd June, 1953

Programme of Celebrations

at

Forest Row

Price 3d

the car. I didn't think he looked very happy but he waved at us as the car went by. The next Christmas the big boys and girls used to sing "Hark the Herald Angels sing, Mrs Simpson's stole our King"! Then Princess Elizabeth's father was King George VI and we had another special day off school with sports and a tea and fireworks, only this time I was big enough to walk home and my father couldn't carry anybody any more because his wounds from the Great War meant that he would always have to walk with a stick in future.'

THE SCOUT BONFIRE

'I started a cub pack at Forest Row in 1949 and a Scout troop came into being soon after. During the night prior to Coronation Day in 1953, other Scouters and myself guarded the bonfire that had been built by the District Scout Groups and was to be lit on Coronation evening at the highest point at Wych Cross, at the same time as others all over Sussex. A nightingale sang all night to keep us company. To light the fire, torch bearers ran in relays from East Grinstead to Wych Cross.'

Coronation celebrations at Forest Row in 1953 included sports and an open air service.

237

THE FIRST TELEVISION

'At the time of the Queen's Coronation in 1953, we were one of the first families to have a television set in our street at Rye. Outside there was all the fun of the flags and coloured bunting, and the preparations for the street party, but before that took place everyone who could get in was coming into our house, sitting, standing, curled up on the floor, to see the actual Coronation on television. We were spellbound at the service, the people, the meaning of it all, and not one of us in that packed room uttered a word. Then there was the noise and happiness of the coach taking the Queen back to the palace, and for us the fun of the street party. Wonderful.'

DAYS AT THE SEASIDE

With our wonderful seaside resorts close at hand, holidays were great fun and have left many great memories, some from the days of bathing machines on the beach.

WEEKS OF FREEDOM

'My mother and her two sisters lived with their adored Mama and severe father in Horsham ("a town that is always half asleep", as my mother described it in her journal) and their hopes of holidays away on the coast kept them in a state of longing during the whole of the long, dreary winter, living as they did in a household completely in awe of a dictatorial head of the house.

It fell upon the eldest sister, Ruth, each year to beg Papa to allow Mama to take them away. Ruth was his favourite and if anyone could coax him, it would be her.

Connie, the middle daughter, usually undertook to write to book apartments and in the Easter of 1906 (when they were allowed a holiday because the doctor had insisted on it, as they had all had bouts of flu during the winter) she had extreme difficulty in finding anything at the price Papa was prepared to pay. He had told them, in no uncertain terms, that he would give them £20 and they could stay away as long as it lasted! Eventually, with a shrug of impatience, he had decided to cycle down to Eastbourne and find something for them himself. He managed to procure some apartments in Cavendish Place, not far from the pier, where the landlady was prepared to cook their food but Mama would have to purchase it.

Happy days of anticipation were spent packing the bags and three excited girls set off with Mama to walk to the station, half a mile away, to spend several heavenly weeks of freedom away from the "morgue" they lived in and the "sleepy" town.

Another long walk from the station at Eastbourne to Cavendish Place, the bags getting heavier with every step – no money was to be wasted on cabs – and the apartments were slightly disappointing when they arrived, not bright and sunny like those Connie had found at Littlehampton last year. But nothing could dampen their spirits for this was Eastbourne, the most beautiful town in the world.

"We can see the sea if we go out on to the verandah and it looks so lovely at night," wrote Connie.

They walked up Beachy Head several times and actually climbed to the top once and were "puffed and hot when we reached the top, for we had to pull Aunt Thurza up most of the way as she is rather plump and kept trying to flop down."

"It is lovely and hot and the town is crowded as it is Eastertide. The others have gone for a walk in the park but Ruth and I have been sitting on the beach reading – I have such a ripping book. We have only just come in, although it is quite dusky.

"We went for a row on the sea yesterday morning and drove to Pevensey Castle in the afternoon. It is a lovely old ruin where William the Conqueror once lived. We went by charabanc and the sun was scorching.

"We have been on the pier several times. I have bought a nice table-centre in the town, to be worked – some lovely coloured silks too!"

Later she writes: "Oh, we have had such lovely weeks down here – I've fallen in love with the Minstrels, especially with Ben – he's so nice and so are all the others: Tom, Harry, Fred and Mac. They have their pitch on the beach near the Wish Tower and give about five or six performances a day.

"No home, no school and the Minstrels – oh, I have been in my Seventh Heaven all the week. But tomorrow we go home [the £20 had nearly run out!] and I fear it will break my heart.

"Tom said, as he brought round the collecting box, that it must be ruining us (we have been several times a day, every day!) and Mama laughed and said we would soon be going home.

"Yesterday Essie and I got a lovely seat and could hear and see everything nicely – sometimes you don't get a very good view. Ben

239

sang *My Irish Mollie* much to our delight, and Tom, the 13 year old, Essie's favourite, sang *Come along little girl, come along.* Then it was all over and we watched them pack up the chairs etc while we sat over on a breakwater. Ben saw us and raised his hat and came towards us. I thought my heart would stop! He talked for quite a while – his eyes laughing and crinkling at the corners, in his black, handsome face. We promised we would try and come back in the summer and he assured us they would still be there. Both he and Tom raised their boaters as they left.

"Essie walked down to the water's edge, to shed a tear I expect – but she soon came back and we comforted each other." And so back to Horsham!

The year before, in 1905, they had fallen for the Pierrots, on the green, at Littlehampton, and had stood or sat for hours listening to their comic songs, recitations and monologues and watching their animated pictures. There were eight Pierrots and their wives – the favourite with the girls being Mr Terry, although they were all mesmerized by the "Handcuffed King" who could get out of any type of handcuffs that any of the public might put him into.

But in the year 1906, following the Eastbourne trip at Easter, they were lucky enough to have a second holiday in the summer and this time they went to Herne Bay and all lost their hearts again – this time to "The Gaiety Boys" – especially Mr Douglas, and Ruth, now being 17, felt it might be "the real thing" for her, though Connie secretly stayed loyal to the Minstrels at Eastbourne.

Although all three sisters lived until their mid eighties, they still talked lovingly and excitedly about the Gaiety Boys and Pierrots and especially the Minstrels at Eastbourne, and of the consuming passions they had aroused in the girls' young, Edwardian hearts.'

MACKINTOSH BATHING

'In the 1920s, and maybe earlier, it was forbidden to undress on the beach in Eastbourne before bathing in the sea. I can just remember bathing machines which were drawn out to the shoreline by a horse. You were able to go down the steps straight into the sea without parading in public, but they soon gave way to bathing huts which you paid to use. Our family paid for a site for the season to erect our own tent at the Wish Tower beach. You stored it when not in use in a big store under the Wish Tower slope.

However visitors, especially those staying at hotels on Royal Parade, thought it was unnecessary and they would change in their hotel rooms, put on a bathrobe, cross the road and go for a swim.

This was soon brought to the notice of the authorities and a number of people were arrested for not using the facilities. As a result there was a demonstration of protest when a large number of people from the seafront hotels, all ready for a dip, crossed the road and went for a bathe in defiance. The result of this was a new bye-law on "mackintosh bathing". To wear your bathrobe or mac on the beach you were required to buy a ticket for ninepence. (It was probably a shilling to use a hut.)

At the Redoubt there were two canvas enclosures for girls and boys to undress – twopence to enter.'

'I was born in Eastbourne, the third of four sisters. We lived right by the sea, just east of the pier. Growing up as we did in the 1920s and 1930s with the sea on our doorstep was ideal, as we all loved the water and learned to swim in the sea at a very early age. We would cross the road to the beach with our bathing costumes already on, as dressing and undressing on the beach was not allowed, not in Eastbourne anyway! There were cubicles for hire for that purpose. Along the front of the cubicles were laid lengths of coconut matting and a long length of it was rolled out down to the water's edge for people who were not used to walking on beach stones, to get into the sea without hurting their feet. At the Redoubt bathing beach there was a big, square, open-topped canvas construction, for communal changing, sectioned off for women and girls and men and boys. The visitors staying in hotels on the seafront went "mackintosh bathing".

Some days we would go shrimping. We had a big shrimp net with a bar handle which took two of us to push along the sandy bottom in the shallows. Sometimes as well, when the tide was low, we would venture as far as Holywell, where the cliffs at Beachy Head start, to explore the rock pools there for crabs.

The summers then always seemed so much warmer and longer, and we spent endless days on the beach in the school holidays getting very brown. I remember them as lovely, fun-filled days. Then came 1939 and the war and the threat of invasion and we all went to the seafront to help fill sandbags full of beach stones to form barricades. Great rolls of barbed wire were stretched along the beaches and concrete tank traps were built. Our lovely seashore was no longer ours to enjoy.'

GREAT TREATS

'We rarely had holidays, when I was a child. Great treats, in the 1930s, were visits to Hastings. The ritual was always the same. We

241

travelled by bus from Hurst Green, or by train from Etchingham, and went straight to the beach. Our spot was always the same, just to the east of the pier. I always hoped the tide was out, so I could make sand castles. Often a friend came too and we paddled and, as we got older, bathed, wearing unbecoming black costumes and rubber helmets. Inflatable water wings were part of our gear.

Sandwiches were eaten on the beach, but the great treat was tea at Caves Cafe, just opposite, where there was a lovely smell of ground coffee as you went in and a three piece orchestra played. Tea rarely varied – a pot of tea, bread and butter, no jam, and then, what I couldn't wait for, cream cakes! Once we were extremely daring and had toast, at the suggestion of my friend's cousin.

The pier, with its slot machines, was a great attraction, and I loved the military bands which always played in the bandstand at the shore end. The diver, at the far end of the pier and Biddy the Tubman, who performed high jinks just off the beach at high tide, gave great pleasure.'

BIDDY THE TUBMAN

'As a schoolgirl in the 1930s I, with my parents, would walk the seafront from St Leonards where we lived, to Hastings. There, if the tide was right, we would watch the antics of Biddy Stonham in his tub.

The tub was half a large barrel in which he paddled out to sea, always dressed in navy trousers, a seaman's jersey and a bowler hat. He would spin the barrel round and round at a great pace, then stand on the edge, play the fool, and eventually fall into the sea, making much of climbing back again. It caused much laughter from the crowd gathered on the promenade. A flat cap would go round for pennies. Some lucky children would be given a ride but with only a gentle spin. His barrel and a picture of him are still on display in the Fishermen's Museum at Rock-a-Nore in Hastings.

Another memory of those pre-war days was of the beautiful large pictures drawn on dry sands near the White Rock before the parade extension and underground carpark were built. Pennies were thrown from the promenade to show appreciation. To enter the nearby pier was twopence and the band concert on Sunday afternoons another twopence. The Alexandra Park was also a great attraction and a joy to walk through with well kept, magnificent flower beds floodlit at night all through the summer season.'

AN EXCITING DAY

'As teenagers living in Seaford in 1938, one of our highlights would be a day trip into Brighton. Not earning big wages, we did not bother with the shops but spent our money on the pleasures of the seafront.

We would explore the delights of both Palace and West Piers, gambling on the penny machines and always getting weighed by the man with the jockey scales.

Other entertainments were in the Arches below the Prom by the Fish Market. We didn't notice the smell but in summer it could be rather "high". If we could afford it we'd have a ride on Volks Railway to Blackrock and back, or better still be very adventurous and take a trip on one of the many Skylarks that plied their trade from the water's edge. They were so colourful, all decked out with flags and bunting. We'd tread our way over the shingle to one of the many ramps put down for us to "board ship". If we were lucky there'd be a nice looking young fellow to help us, and lots of girlish giggles if he actually carried us up the ramp so that we didn't get our feet wet. The trip was usually one shilling and sixpence or two shillings and more or less went between the piers or out to a naval vessel if one happened to be on a goodwill visit to Brighton. Weekends there were paddle steamers, the *Waverley* or the *Brighton Belle* going along the coast. They could be boarded from either of the piers and went as far as Eastbourne viewing the Beachy Head lighthouse, or down to Bognor and Littlehampton. They were very lively with music, and of course the bars which were well supported by the day-trippers from London.

If we got hungry during our day out, there were always candy floss and toffee apples to enjoy, or a tasty plate of shellfish from one of the many stalls. Sometimes, we'd go to the Lyons cafe at the corner of St James Street; we could have a feast of egg and chips for one shilling and threepence and a banana split for ninepence. Those were the days.

If we had an older person with us, we were able to stop late enough to see the lights on the front and the piers, or watch the changing colours of the Mazda Fountain in Victoria Gardens.

We'd go home tired but happy, a very exciting day for us small-town girls.'

CELEBRATIONS THROUGH THE YEAR

Flower shows, fairs, donkey derbys, just some of the high days looked forward to every year in the village calendar. Some celebrations of the past have now gone for ever, such as Empire Day on 24th May when all schoolchildren had a half day holiday. And there was always Christmas to look forward to, rounding off the year in traditional style.

BOAT RACE DAY

'Between the wars Boat Race Day was a great occasion and everyone wore favours. You could buy them in all the shops in Eastbourne, and elsewhere – crossed oars with a light or dark blue bow, pale blue or dark blue fluffy monkeys, or rosettes you made yourself. We all had our favourite team.'

MAY DAY

'May Day celebrations were a most joyful occasion at Polegate. The schoolchildren voted for the May Queen from among the senior girls, and the two runners up were her attendants.

On the great day the three were collected in a flower bedecked, horse-drawn waggon and paraded through the village, followed by a procession of local children carrying garlands of wild flowers, to the village green for the crowning ceremony.

After the ceremony the garlands were judged and small prizes given, as well as pretty brooches to the queen and her attendants. Then there were folk songs and country dancing to entertain the onlookers. A tea followed, at the village hall, and in the evening there was a dance for the entire village.'

EMPIRE DAY

'There were Empire Day celebrations on 24th May in all the local schools at Lewes. We girls wore white dresses and most boys white shirts, and we paraded in a field down The Paddock – we would march round singing and after the ceremony had the rest of the day off.'

Portslade Carnival in 1920.

CELERY AND SALES

'Many years ago there were Celery Harvest Suppers at Stream Farm in Dallington every year – for men only – and everyone had to do a turn to entertain the others.

There were also store sheep and bullock sales held in the car park of the Swan Inn in spring and autumn. The animals had to be driven there in those days and the road from Ashburnham to Dallington was crowded with them in the early morning.

On a Good Friday it was the usual thing for two or three girls to get together and walk across the fields to the little river in the wood and paddle. After this they would sit on the bank and eat their hot cross buns. It was also usual to plant the first potatoes on that day.'

VILLAGE DAYS

'Once a year a combined fete and flower show with roundabouts and swings took place in Chiddingly, generally on the August Bank Holiday up to 1940.

The schoolchildren always celebrated May Day with may garlands and maypole dancing. They had a summer treat at the end of term which consisted of a tea and races at a large country mansion in the village. On the first Sunday in August, called Hospital Sunday, an open air service was held in a field, to which all denominations were invited, and the collection went to hospitals in Eastbourne.'

245

COTTAGE CHEESE

'The summer Flower Show at Wilmington was a major event and my mother made as many entries as possible. One hot summer the milk, delivered at the doorstep and measured into a jug, went sour – as it frequently did. There was a class for cottage cheese in the show catalogue, so the sour milk was tied in a piece of muslin and suspended from the clothes line. When anyone passed going or returning from the garden, the rule was that hands, clean or grubby, were to give the bag a friendly squeeze to remove the whey. The muslin gradually took on a dirty grey hue. Too short to reach the swinging bag, I contented myself by waving a stick at the many flies showing an interest in the drying cheese. Cottage gardens were a mecca for blow-flies, bearing in mind all that was buried, not always too thoroughly when the earth was hard.

The day before the show the cheese was scraped off the muslin and my mother added chopped chives, standing in the tiny kitchen by the copper with the Valor cooker making happy glugging noises as it gave off a strong smell of paraffin.

Finished! – the cheese was taken proudly to the village hall. And in these days of so many hygiene regulations, with all rules and regulations broken the cheese would have been cast away in the dustbin. But ... guess what ... in Wilmington in 1931, Mrs Ivy Giles's cottage cheese took first prize!'

BATTLE FAIRS

'Battle fair day, held in November, was a day to be remembered. Our school had a holiday because the teacher considered it not safe when the roads were filled with cattle being driven into Battle. There was a fair on the Abbey Green and the cheapjacks plying their trade in the High Street. Local bakers made special red and brown lollipops which were enjoyed by the children. This tradition has long gone, as has the cattle market. Luckily the Bonfire Night tradition and Good Friday Marbles have survived.'

'I remember the excitement of the Battle Pageant when coachloads of people came from near and far to see the re-enactment of Battle's history, with lots of local people dressed up to take part. Special steam trains were laid on from London. Then there was the animal fair when there were stalls in the street and horses and cattle were sold, and sometimes the men would have too much to drink and have fights. The only time I played truant from school was on fair day, I was fascinated by it all. In those days attendance officers would call

246

William the Conqueror (Edward Laughan) makes an appearance at the Battle Pageant in the 1930s.

on your parents if you missed school but somehow I was not reported and my parents did not get to hear about it until years after.'

DONKEY DERBY

'The first Donkey Derby in Britain was at Wivelsfield in October 1951.

The next year 20,000 people headed for Wivelsfield on Whit Monday to watch the donkeys racing around the village green. Chaos ensued on all the local roads and people getting off the trains at Wivelsfield station (on the outskirts of Burgess Hill) had to walk nearly four miles to get to the village. The local farmer Colin White opened his fields opposite for parking at ten shillings a car. There were no toilets for the public and villagers nearby had to help out.

The races were great fun and even the donkeys weren't sure where they were supposed to go. Bookies had come to take the bets and Jim Dinnage who had organised the event would be able to repeat the event for several years. A poster for these Donkey Derbys was even to be found in Lloyd's underwriting room in London. This would probably have been put there by Peter Bowring who lived in Cuckfield and helped with charitable events.

Famous showbusiness people sponsored the donkeys. Arthur Askey's was called Playmate, and even Muffin the Mule was a member of the Donkey Club.

247

The donkeys were rescued animals and subsequently were housed in a sanctuary on land where in 1972 building started on the St Peter & St James Holiday Home (now Hospice and Home) built by Mrs Dinnage in memory of her husband Jim and son Peter, who had died at the age of 14 from Hodgkins Disease.'

LEWES FUN

'I was born in Lewes in 1902 and have lived there all my life. I recall those early days and how we enjoyed a much more leisurely life. Lewes being the county town was always busy. Shops were owned by private people, who gave each customer good service. The Cliffe High Street was the main shopping centre and at weekends crowds of shoppers filled the narrow streets. Monday was market day, when herds of cattle were driven through the streets to be auctioned to local farmers and butchers. How frightened I was if I met a herd of bullocks on my way to school.

Once a year a sheep fair was held at the foot of the Race Hill. Large flocks of sheep and lambs were driven by shepherds dressed in their best smocks. The sheepdogs knew every command and gently drove them through the town to the Race Hill.

Each year on 24th May, Empire Day was celebrated in the Dripping Pan field, once part of the Cluniac priory. All the schoolchildren gathered there to sing national songs and play games, finishing the happy day with a wonderful tea. I can remember how the women all wore long skirts which swept the ground, large hats held in place with very large hatpins. Most elderly ladies wore bonnets and shawls and dainty lace mob caps indoors; they all wore buttoned boots, including the children.

The 5th November was celebrated by the bonfire societies and large crowds of people came to the town.

During the summer flat racing season, horse racing was held on the racecourse and once a year Edward VII attended, always walking to the railway station to take the train to London. We had few motor cars, only horses and carriages. Two or three times a week a stage coach travelled from London to Lewes, stopping at the White Hart Hotel to change the four horses, and passengers refreshed themselves in the hotel before starting off again. It was a lovely sight to see them, complete with the bugler blowing the coach trumpet.'

'I remember in summer, I believe in August, being got out of bed very early in the morning and taken to the front gate of our house in

248

Beddingham, to watch the circus animals walk past on their way from Newhaven to Lewes. There were camels, dromedaries, elephants and horses, and caged animals in carts. The whole procession took a very long time to pass and to us it was very exciting. We were later taken to Lewes, walking to the carnival and back in the dark, my father picking up glow worms and putting them round the brim of his trilby hat.'

'A great event in the county calendar was the Lewes Bonfire Night celebrations, still held today but now much quieter and the burning of the effigy of the Pope has been discontinued. My grandmother remembered shops being boarded up and tar barrels being rolled down School Hill into the river Ouse at the bottom. She recited this ditty to us as children:

Remember, remember, the fifth of November,
Gunpowder, treason and plot,
I see no reason why gunpowder treason
Should ever be forgot.
A farthing loaf to feed old Pope
And a faggot of wood to burn him.
We'll burn his body from his head
And then we'll holler "Old Pope is dead!"
Cheer, boys, cheer!'

A MARVELLOUS SPREAD

'Every year prior to Christmas, the WI ladies at Polegate would prepare a marvellous spread of goodies for the whole village. The tables were beautifully decorated.

Having enjoyed the tea, everyone capable of moving cleared the tables to leave room for dancing and games, and so began an evening of real family fun. Games and dancing were interspersed with humorous sketches and musical items. Each year the village family would patiently listen to, and applaud, the delightful old-fashioned solo songs or duets performed by the senior guests, which would bring a glow of happiness to the well worn complexions of the singers and gladden the hearts of their families. The evening ended late but always too soon.'

'Christmas decorations were prepared by the children with coloured paper and home-made glue of flour and water. Only a few families in Nutley would have Christmas trees, and some of these would be

249

only a bushy branch taken from the Forest, but they were decorated with baubles made by clever and excited fingers. There were always good meals at Christmas time, plenty of bacon and delicious beef puddings, a great favourite. Presents were few, perhaps an orange, an apple and an item of clothing in the stocking – and the clothing was not for everyone each year, they took it in turns.

Lady Castle Stewart gave the most wonderful and memorable Boxing Day parties for the schoolchildren in the old Memorial Hall. They all got a present worth two shillings and sixpence, a lot of money in the 1930s, and a most sumptuous tea was served and consumed. My word, those cream cakes were an absolute treat.'

THE LOST GEESE

'One of my lasting memories of the time when the children were young concerns some geese. We had seven children, and times were far from easy. My husband and I always raised something during the year that we could sell around Christmas time to ensure that the family had a good Christmas. In about 1928 my husband, who was a gypsum miner, went to market about six months before Christmas and bought six small goslings, which we kept in a large old stable at our home in Whatlington and fattened up for Christmas.

Three weeks before Christmas my husband had arranged to sell all the geese to other miners, and had collected the money, which we had already spent on presents for the children, and Christmas was happily organised.

Just two weeks before the geese were due to be collected, we had a really dreadful December day, very cold with a thick mist. How it happened I do not know, but the stable door must have been left open, and the geese all flew away. In the thick mist no one saw them go, or had any idea which direction they had taken. In a panic I rushed round to my neighbour. We had no money to replace the geese, or refund the miners, and I was desperate. My level-headed neighbour said, "Get a bucket of corn, we'll find them."

We set off, peering through the mist, and listening hard. Down the road to the village hall, and then we turned off along the river bank, thinking that might be the most likely place. Picking our way carefully and slowly, straining our eyes and ears, and getting more and more worried. Eventually we came to the bridge leading to Sedlescombe and there, much to our relief, were the geese all huddled together.

Geese, like sheep, can be herded, and my neighbour got behind them with a twiggy stick and I walked in front with the bucket of corn, sprinkling small handfuls as I went. Slowly, very slowly, we managed to drive and lead them back through the mist along the bank to the village hall, and up the road to the cottage. Not being able to see very well, and with the uneven ground, we were on edge all the time in case we lost one, but eventually we got them back to the shed, and I can still feel the sense of relief and thankfulness as I closed the shed door.

Our Christmas was safe, the miners' Christmas dinners were safe, and it was six months before my husband knew anything about it.'

NEVER A STAR SO BRIGHT

'Every year at Willingdon we enacted a Nativity play in the church, which of course needed many rehearsals, when possible held in the church itself.

The three shepherds had to walk up the aisle to the chancel (to reach the stable) talking of this wonderful thing that had happened. Francis had to say, "What is that star that shines so brightly? Never before has a star shone so bright as that." His voice was dull and all on one note, with no elation or happiness in it. "No Francis, no," I said. "Be surprised, be amazed, be joyful," but no, he remained wooden.

Then Mr Kirby Wood had a bright idea. The beam in the chancel had no rood figures on it in those days. He made a large silver star and a pulley of cords and he fixed it over the beam, then hid himself in the pulpit, pulling the cords, and the star moved slowly across the beam.

Francis and the other shepherds came up the aisle. "Say, what's that star that shines so brightly?" Awe and wonder shone in his face as he saw the star move. "Never before 'as a star shone like that," then in an awe-struck aside he looked at me in wonder and whispered, "It did move, didn't it?" and entered the stable to worship the Babe of Bethlehem.'

Index

List of Contributing Institutes

Entries have been received from the following East Sussex Women's Institutes:

Alfriston, Anderida, Ashdown, Ashurstwood, Barcombe, Battle, Beckley, Bells Yew Green, Bishopstone, Bodle Street Green, Brambletye, Brede, Brook Valley, Burwash, Burwash Weald, Butts Brow, Buxted, Catsfield, Chailey Evening, Chiddingly, Chyngton, Coleman's Hatch, Cross in Hand, Crowborough Morning, Crowborough St John's, Crowborough Vale, Dallington, Danehill & Chelwood Gate, Denton & Mount Pleasant, Ditchling, Eastbourne Cornfield, Eastbourne Upperton, East Dean & Friston, East Hoathly & Halland, Etchingham, Fairlight, Fairwarp, Firle & Beddingham, Five Ash Down, Five Ashes, Fletching, Forest Row, Fourways, Framfield & Blackboys, Frant, Glyne, Groombridge, Hailsham Afternoon, Hailsham Evening, Hammerwood & Holtye, Hartfield/Medway, Hastings Croft, Hastings Old Town, Heathfield Tower, Hellingly, Herstmonceux, High Hurst Wood, Hooe, Horam, Hove, Hurst Green, Icklesham, Iden, Iford & Swanborough, Isfield, Jevington & Filching, Kemp Town, Kingston, Landgate, Langney, Laughton, Lewes Neville, Lewes Westgate, Little Common Afternoon, Little Common Evening, Magham Down, Manor Barn, Manor Park, Maresfield, Mark Cross, Mayfield, Mayfield Evening, Meads, Meeching, Meridian, Micheldene, Mile Oak, Netherfield, Newick, Newick Green, Northiam, Nutley, Old Heathfield, Ore & Baldslow, Ovingdean, Patcham, Patcham Evening, Patcham Morning, Peacehaven, Peasmarsh, Pett, Playden, Plumpton, Preston Village, Ringmer, Ringmer Evening, Ripe & Chalvington, Robertsbridge, Rodmell & Southease, Rotherfield, Rotherfield Evening, Rottingdean, Rushlake Green, Rye, Rye Harbour, St Helens, St Leonard's, Saltdean, Saltdean Oval, Saxonwood, Seaford, Seaford Blatchington, Seaford Martello, Sedlescombe, Sedlescombe Green, Sidley, Southdown Evening, South Heighton, Southover, Staplecross & Ewhurst Green, Stonegate, Telscombe Cliffs, Three Oaks, Ticehurst, Uckfield, Wadhurst, Waldron, Wannock Glen, Warbleton, Warren Woodingdean, Wartling, Westdene, Westfield, Westham & Hankham, Westham Evening, Whatlington, Wilbury Hove, Willingdon, Winchelsea Beach, Windmill Rottingdean, Withyham, Wivelsfield, Woodingdean, Woodsgate Park.